Choral Voices

Choral Voices

Ethnographic Imaginations of Sound and Sacrality

Sebanti Chatterjee

BLOOMSBURY ACADEMIC
NEW YORK • LONDON • OXFORD • NEW DELHI • SYDNEY

BLOOMSBURY ACADEMIC
Bloomsbury Publishing Inc
1385 Broadway, New York, NY 10018, USA
50 Bedford Square, London, WC1B 3DP, UK
29 Earlsfort Terrace, Dublin 2, Ireland

BLOOMSBURY, BLOOMSBURY ACADEMIC and the Diana logo are trademarks of
Bloomsbury Publishing Plc

First published in the United States of America 2023
Paperback edition published 2024

For legal purposes the Acknowledgments on p. 161 constitute an extension of
this copyright page.

Cover design: Louise Dugdale
Cover Illustration: Map of Imagination for Sebanti Chatterjee's Field of Study in Goa by
Raisa Janice Vaz

Bloomsbury Publishing Inc does not have any control over, or responsibility for, any third-
party websites referred to or in this book. All internet addresses given in this book were
correct at the time of going to press. The author and publisher regret any inconvenience
caused if addresses have changed or sites have ceased to exist, but can accept no
responsibility for any such changes.

Whilst every effort has been made to locate copyright holders the publishers would be
grateful to hear from any person(s) not here acknowledged.

A catalog record for this book is available from the Library of Congress.

ISBN: HB: 978-1-5013-7983-3
PB: 978-1-5013-7987-1
ePDF: 978-1-5013-7985-7
eBook: 978-1-5013-7984-0

Typeset by Deanta Global Publishing Services, Chennai, India

To find out more about our authors and books visit www.bloomsbury.com and
sign up for our newsletters.

Contents

Figures

Prologue: Warming Up

Sanctus Sanctus Sanctus Dominus/Holy Holy Holy Lord
Sanctus Sanctus Sanctus Dominus/Holy Holy Holy Lord
Deus Sabaoth/God of Power and Might
Deus Sabaoth/God of Power and Might
Deus Sabaoth/God of Power and Might
Deus Sabaoth/God of Power and Might
Pleni Sunt Coeli Et Terra/Heaven and Earth
Et Terra Gloria/And Earth Are Full of Your Glory
Pleni Sunt Coeli Et Terra/Heaven and Earth
Et Terra Gloria/And Earth Are Full of Your Glory
Pleni Sunt Coeli Et Terra/Heaven and Earth
Et Terra Gloria/And Earth Are Full of Your Glory
Pleni Sunt Coeli Et Terra/Heaven and Earth
Gloria Tua/Your Glory

> From the Armed Man: (A Mass for Peace) Sanctus by Karl Jenkins

You are such a Christian te, Sebanti. That's what I feel when I see your intensity in researching the choral music scene in Shillong. You remind me of Antara, another Bengali girl who sings in our choir.

It is heartwarming to see a Bengali Brahmin girl researching choirs in Goa.

These two vignettes from my field-sites always fascinated me about the shifting nature of the situatedness of faith. I realized at once how I was accepted and emplaced through my own formal sacred identity and an attributed sacred identity throughout my immersion in the choral soundscape of Goa and Shillong. My ascribed identity which includes growing up in a Hindu, Brahmin, middle-class home and my adopted identity showcasing a Christian cultural-musical belonging helped me arrive with an emic notion of sacred during the course of my ethnography.

I remember the first instance was on a day that I had joined the Aroha Choir for a Sunday church service where Aunty Pauline had also given a speech during the worship session. The Aroha Choir, as I discuss in detail in my third chapter, is an entertainment choir which comprise people from different ethnic and

Christian denominations. They also had a Bengali, Hindu girl who sang in the soprano section. She was happy not only that someone from another region and faith had interest in a musical genre associated with Christian worship tradition but also that my markers of identity also resonated with one of her own choristers.

The second instance was when I had been invited to give a lecture at the Art Chamber in Goa. My sister was visiting me at that time. Father Loiola Pereira, secretary to the Goa Archbishop, had come to attend the talk. I discuss at length about his intersectional allegiance to music and faith in my fourth chapter. He was pleased to finally meet someone from my family and was rather thrilled that someone with completely dissimilar identity labels was invested in a culture and tradition different from hers.

As a part of my initial ethnography, I spent four months in Goa, from November 2013 to February 2014. In Goa, notational and stylistic competence in Western classical music stems from the 451 years of Portuguese rule, the spread of Christianity, and the presence of parish schools or parochial schools.[1] The latter, especially, played a significant role in creation of a generation of choir masters and priests immersed in Western musical traditions rooted in Catholicism with a sensitized musical aptitude. Seminaries like Rachol and Pilar continued this tradition of theological and musical training. The legacy continues. The fourth chapter of this book looks at the lives of the Seminarians and Goan Sacred Music as a genre.

> On the Mount Festival we will present a beautiful program that develops two ancient Gregorian chants; the Ubi Caritas Deus ibis est and the Da Pacem Domine, introit. Both are very old introits[2] of the Western vocal tradition dated before the tenth century. We will combine them with some psalms and sacred motets from different composers about the idea of peace.

This was the email sent to all the singers of the Goa University Choir by the choir conductor and course instructor Professor Santiago Luserdi Girelli, Goa University, Anthony Gonsalves Chair.

---

[1] As discussed by Pia de Menezes Rodriguez, Bradley Shope, Gregory Booth alongside others who have written on music in Goa (1997, 2014, 2008). Parochial schools, founded in Goa in 1545 admitting solely male students became central to the process of evangelization as well as a system of education focused on reading, writing, and arithmetic. There was also music education that included training in solfejo (solfas), singing and learning an instrument, mostly, violin. (Sardo and Simões, 1989).

[2] Introits refer to entrances which are part of liturgical services.

How this email landed in my inbox will be my first point of departure to talk about my experience. My research urged me to look into the activities of the thriving choirs in Goa: both sacred as well as professional and institutional. Goa University Choir turned out to be one of the newly formed choirs that made its mark for the first time in 2013 when they performed at the Santa Cruz Church. It was a regular day for me, observing the protocols of rehearsal of the Goa University Choir. I encountered many new faces and discovered that not all were part of the university. Some had experience with church choirs or vocal training and some had come after seeing the university's advertisement for auditions. In fact, a few were simply blessed with good ear and voice; they could not read music. I was taking cello lessons at the Kala Academy during that month, hoping that being part of a string ensemble family will bring me closer to observe choral traditions. One of my friends, a violist, encouraged me to take part in the auditions. We both auditioned and got chosen for the soprano section. I discontinued my cello lessons shortly afterward and focused on training my voice.

Thus began a six-week rigorous rehearsal schedule. The conductor made sure that we met thrice a week for at least two hours. We had to work on intonation and pronunciations of the vowels as per the composer's and the conductor's ruse. We had to do the do-re-mi-fa-so-la-ti from lower to higher octave and vice-versa as a thumb rule. We were taught how to support our voice, producing the sound from the abdomen and stomach. We had to concentrate on the head voice and finally release a melodious sound with the help of rounded notes appropriately shaded. We learned about dynamics, particularly to produce barely audible sounds as the church acoustics would play havoc otherwise. There were passages where we had to emit louder sounds, making sure that our voices did not sound shrill. That was where we learned the method of altering the shape of the vowels to get the perfect sound without distorting the word.

In the piece "The Lord is my Shepherd" by John Rutter, for instance, there were special instructions to stress "tra" and make it sound like "Thra" when it came to belting out the word "trouble." According to the conductor, he wanted a Russian sound for Ts. The last piece we learned was *"Di Es Irae"* by Benjamin Britten, based on war which required a staccato rendition with a perfect blend of animation and release of breath. It was the most difficult yet the most enjoyable experience for the choir. "Ground" by Ola Gjeilo had a few passages that demanded straining our vocal chords as some of the notes were really high. There arose similar difficulties with "The Lord is my Shepherd." The conductor divided the soprano section where a few of us followed the Alto line just for certain sections with extremely high notes, while the rest continued with the melody line. I discovered the mezzo-soprano category that day. For "*Esurientes*" and "The Lord is my Shepherd," both by Rutter, we had soloists. This required attention to concentrate on where exactly to come in and fade out. Especially, there was a part where the tenors and the sopranos needed to come one after the other, and a little distraction could make or break the sound. After rigorous rehearsals and versatile voice and body exercises, we did come up with a well-balanced sound. The discipline and the need to gauge the overall rhythm and harmony introduced me to the actual practice of making music.

Use of an orchestra comprising two violins, one viola, and a cello along with a double bass, cajon, sitar, and tabla were part of the ornamentation as well as the conductor's interpretation of the chosen compositions. The Indian instruments were specially introduced for the Karl Jenkins pieces. The solo violin brought about an unanticipated lilt to the solo songs. The bold cello strokes effortlessly produced the preparatory stages for war during "*Dies Irae*."

Meanwhile, we had a Western music course running at the university, which lasted for eighteen hours. It was called Western music and Its Dialogue with Fine Arts: History, Philosophy, and Politics. In a nutshell, the course turned out to be exactly what Professor Lusardi Girelli imagined it to be during our personal interview—*the course is about Western music and all the other Western arts, the basic things about Western music tradition and all those things without going too deep into the theories.*

We were exposed to Gregorian chants and the beauty of singing in unison. We were taught how to identify the different voices and sort out the lines for the different instruments. We were in a way taught to interpret a score. We were also exposed to different philosophical schools and their approaches to Western music. We particularly worked on the ideas of John Cage and his concept of new sounds. Our final assignment expected each one of us to come up with our own "music manifesto" attuned to the contemporary events in the world.

The voice training and the music course were not a package. Both were university initiatives that were not restricted to the students alone, and each enterprise had its specific goal sets. They have performed widely across and beyond Goa. They performed at NCPA, Mumbai (November 2018), and the Ketevan World Sacred Music Festival in Goa (February 2019). The Western Music Education course has also had further modules thereafter. I have performed with the Goa University Choir thrice, twice during the Monte Festival and once during the Ketevan World Music Festival in 2014 and 2016.

My own pedagogic experience allowed me to distinguish between a rehearsal voice, a recital voice, and microphone voice. In the context of live music,[3] Thomas Turino (2007) talks about participatory music performance (where there is no distinction between the artists and the audience) and presentational music performance (where artists plan and prepare a program for the audience). For participatory music performance to appeal to a wide range of people, it should have many roles that induce different difficulties and degrees of specialization. This is an extension of Csikszentmihalyi[4] (1996) flow theory, where an adequate balance between the inherent challenges and the skill sets of the actor is taken into consideration. For example, roles may include simple activities like clapping the basic beat and singing a chorus melody and other specialized activities may include playing a core instrumental or performing a solo vocal section, and activities that involve further expertise also feature in this format. The value in a participatory performance is distinctive as it is indicated by the extent and the intensity of participation rather than the overall musical sound quality. Regardless of the quality brought forth by individual performers, preference is toward encouraging the participation of others and the sociality around it. Unlike participatory music performance, presentational music performance requires members of an ensemble to possess similar musical and performance abilities. The parity allows a greater control and predictability during presentations. Here, the performers do not have to think about the comfort level of everyone, which enables a greater degree of artistic freedom to use creative contrasts of any type (Turino, 2008: 26–75). The rehearsal voice encourages a participatory music performance where everyone adjusts to a vocal register conditioned by vocalic possibilities and its underlying social nurturing. The recital voice advocates presentational music performance where there is a degree of performativity allocated as per the overall creative parameter as well as the distribution of voices to produce a desired sound.

My own experience of singing at the Ketevan Music Festival in 2016 exposed me to the tricks of developing a microphone voice. It was the first time that the Ketevan Music Festival took place and one of the venues was the ruins of Old

---

[3]   Thomas Turino, *Music as Social Life: Politics of Participation* (Chicago: University of Chicago Press, 2008).

[4]   Mihaly Csikszentmihalyi, *Creativity: Flow and the Psychology of Discovery and Invention* (New York: Harper Collins, 1996).

Goa. Our vocal training opened up the muscles that were necessary to sing. This was perfect for singing in church acoustics, but open-air singing required microphones. On the day that we sung at the St. Augustine ruins, we had to organize ourselves around a set of microphones. Without prior familiarity with dealing with microphones as a group, we sounded flat in certain places. We had only one song to perform that day: "I Offer You Peace" by Jenkins. The event made me realize how voice takes on different dimensions, depending on the acoustic setting. During the same festival, on another day while we sang "Sanctus" from *Armed Man: Mass for Peace* by Karl Jenkins inside the church, we had the Bombay Chamber Orchestra and a few instrumentalists from Seville University accompanying us. Inside the church, we sang with our recital voice and not microphone voice. We had to bring in full power in our articulation, maintaining a parallel soundscape with the instrumental ensemble. The general feel portrayed by us was a mediation between a mellow and solemn sound. The bold cello strokes, precise tones of the flute, clarinet, oboe, and the horn alongside consistent bows of the violin and viola helped create a consistent soundscape mirroring the expressivity of the choir. Inside the church, microphones were not completely absent but strategically placed depending on the solo voice or instrumental moments. We were a large choral group and thus a lot of emphasis was given to standing arrangement of the choir and the seating plan of the orchestra.

Anna E Nekola,[5] in her introductory essay on "Worship Media as Media Form and Mediated practice" (2015), writes about how microphone is more than an amplification device. It inhabits a larger negotiation around the meaning and process of worship. At the onset, microphones resolve issues related to volume and balance. In a worship scenario, this device portrays a hierarchical and aesthetic singer-audience relationship and also reflects on the size of the worshiping community. When placed in front of a singer, she or he acquires a position of musical and institutional authority. Thus, microphone encourages and legitimizes specific voices over others (Nekola, 2015: 5, 16). Placement of the microphone is of utmost importance in creating a sound and altering the degree of intensity according to the conductor's imagination and interpretation of the music.

---

[5] Anna Nekola, "Introduction: Worship Media as Media Form and Mediated Practice: Theorizing the Intersections of Media, Music and Lived Religion," in *Congregational Music-Making and Community in a Mediated Age*, ed. Anna Nekola and Tom Wagner, 1–24, 1st ed. (London: Routledge, 2015). https://doi.org/10.4324/9781315573434

Beyond the rehearsal, recital, and the microphone voice, I constantly struggled to delineate a sacred voice for myself. Going back to the very first vignettes I began with, I always asked myself what was the voice that I portrayed? As a part of my ethnography, I have traveled with various choir groups to events that they have participated in, cheered for them as a member in the audience, hummed all along a car ride to that one song that they will perform, sang in a quiet voice, in a corner of a rehearsal space, and of course sang along in formal festivals when I myself identified as a choral voice. As a mezzo-soprano choral voice of the Goa University Choir, I have mostly followed the baton of my conductor alongside his bodily gestures. It included widening or squinting of the eyes to show his agreement or displeasure with a certain sound, placement of his index fingers on lips indicating *sotto voce* (silent, fading voice), pointing his index and second fingers toward his own pupil and directing it back to the singer with a long serious look to demonstrate that he has identified a drop in the sound quality. His baton and gestures always moved in synchrony. Mediating between watching his directions and waiting for the instrumental cues like a distinct trombone, an urgent cry of the principal violin or the occasional rustle of the clarinets, we had to turn our pages so that we do not forget the consistency and surprise of the musical patterns that were dotted on the musical register we embodied. This is the sacred voice that the performance demanded, and I inhabited it each time I stood on the stage as a chorister. It didn't matter then that I was not committed to the language of faith advocated by various Christian denominations or that choral music had its origin rooted in sacral imaginations. Between my formal sacred identity (born into a Hindu Brahmin family) and attributed sacred identity (Christian cultural-musical belonging), I discovered the sacred in maintaining the sanctity of the performance rituals and cadences. When I saw myself as an element of a musical production, it became rather important to incorporate this sacred voice amid my negotiations with the rehearsal, recital, and the microphone voice. Thus, the sacred, for me, emerged as an expression of performance rather than that of faith. While there remained an absolute skeletal of a performance and a musical presentation, each time, the myriad points of musical references elaborated on an idea of the sacred inherent to the performativity and to the genre in itself.

Here what Lefebvre tells about rhythm becomes one way to posit the sacred. In the field of rhythm, broad spectrums also take on a specificity. Rhythm cannot exist without repetition in time and space, without reprises, without returns, thus taken together, it cannot occur without a measure. He also says

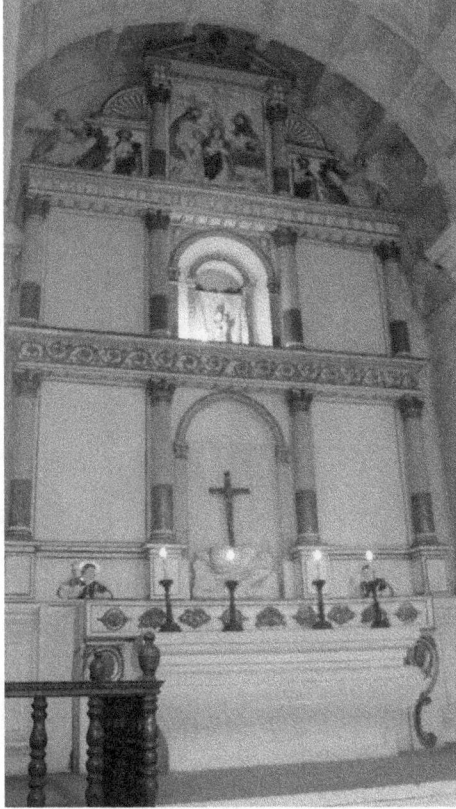

Figure P.1 Inside the chapel of Mount. Photo credit Sebanti Chatterjee.

that an element of difference intrudes the repetitive everyday festivals, rites, and the rituals. Novelty presents itself negating the possibility of an identical absolute repetition (Levebvre, 1992: 6).[6] The sacred like rhythm exists in reprises and in returns. The rehearsals and training prepare one to understand that each part of the body, like the throat, chest, abdomen, larynx, and head, produces different aspects of sounds and together they enable the formation of a range, style, and visualization. The importance of speech, text, and throw of the intonations also become central to the overall sonic membrane. The art and expression of vocalization as an embodied creative process comes full circle when the collective is in sync and the audience instinctively responds to the performance. The liveness of choral music stands out as a crucial marker due to its audio-visual structure. The musicking comes through the interiority and the

[6] Henri Lefebre, *The Production of Space* (USA: Wiley-Blackwell, 1992).

Figure P.2 Goa University Choir. Photo credit Old Goa Music Society.

singularity captured in the collective. Following Christopher Small, "Musicking is part of that iconic, gestural process of giving and receiving information about relationships which unites the living world, and it is in fact a ritual by means of which the participants not only learn about, but directly experience, their concepts of how they relate, and how they ought to relate, to other human beings and to the rest of the world." (p. 9).[7] This interiority and the singularity animate the sacred quality of choral music. My sacred voice helped me organize, navigate, and observe how the ritualistic and performative attributes bring to life a Christian musical tradition. It interrogates the cultural process that is informed by religious, colonial, vernacular, and immediate life-worlds. The meanings and expectations of faith may vary from one person to the other who are involved in a Christian vocalic tradition like choral music but the essence of faith remains the soul of the practice and rendition of the craft.

---

[7] Christopher Small, *Musicking the Meanings of Performing and Listening* (USA: Wesleyan University Press, 1998).

Introduction

Choral Beginnings: Inside the Chapel and a Home Studio

Sometime toward the end of 2015, I got a call from Maestro Santiago Lusardi Girelli,[1] conductor of the Goa University Choir, about joining the Old Goa Music Society team to organize the first Ketevan Sacred Music Festival in February 2016. Goa that was under Portuguese government sovereignty until 1961, is located on the western coast of India and is one of the smallest states in the country.

The festival aimed at holding performances, offering workshops at orphanages, and conducting a lecture series discussing musical syncretism along with music traditions across the West and the East. It was being planned across the Capella da Nossa Senhora do Monte and St. Augustine ruins in Old Goa. I was still a PhD student and thus wasn't sure if I wanted to extend my fieldwork at that point in time. The involvement meant spending at least six weeks in Goa. I had just decided to organize my main chapter on Goa around the seminaries, and the idea of gaining more insight as a traveling choir member got me excited. While doing participant observation, I had thoroughly enjoyed singing with them during the 2014 Monte Festival at Old Goa. As an amateur singer with no formal training, the prospect of singing with a set of musicians who had been practicing and performing consistently sounded quite challenging to me.

You all will have a costume for this festival and everyone must arrange an appointment with the tailor. For details, you have to coordinate with A.

---

[1] We lost Maestro Santiago Lusardi Girelli to Covid-19 in May 2021. Ever since he came to Goa in 2013 as a visiting professor, Anthony Gonsalves Chair, he contributed immensely to the pedagogy, research, and performance of Western Classical music, Choral music, and interesting collaborations with Indian classical music.

I squealed with joy. I had goosebumps. We all had to pay for our costumes, and it wasn't easy finding the designer's workshop at Dona Paula. I took a bus from Panjim that dropped me near Raj Bhavan. I had to follow the instructions given by my group members about whether to turn left or right within the numerous alleys, lest I got lost. Halfway through the walk, I was glad to find P. We finally made it together. They had taken our measurements at the university the previous week and today was the trial. We had to go in person so that the tailors could make alterations if necessary.

The gown designed by Syne Coutinho was in a lighter shade of brown and quite lovely. The white cloak that we had to don over it gave the impression that the entire attire was pristine white. That day, I felt like I belonged there. Despite being a Calcutta-born Bengali with no connection to Christianity or training in Western musical traditions, there I was, standing among my research interlocutors who by now had become friends. Why was it necessary to have a costume that looked angelic and royal at the same time? The idea was to conjure an image of the sixteenth-century Georgian queen, Ketevan. Owing to a tragic turn of events, after she died, Queen Ketevan's bones were smuggled out of the country and placed in a tomb at the St. Augustinian Convent in Goa by one of the Augustinian brothers she had befriended. This fact made the choice for the festival location even more appropriate. It was only after taking due permission from the Archaeological Survey of Goa that for the first time, an event was organized at the Augustine ruins. The inaugural day had performances in the open air at the ruins. Along with a Canadian Kathak dancer who enacted an almost improvisatory performance of Queen Ketevan, there were Indian ragas on piano, Indian classical flute, Indian classical on slide guitar, flamenco, and music from the Sephardic traditions. On that day, the Goa University Choir sang only one song, Karl Jenkins's "I Offer You Peace," based on Gandhi's words, part of the Welsh composer's album titled *The Peacemakers*.

Our program was around the corner. The moment I received my costume for the choir was when I felt that somewhere I too was connected to this beautiful landscape. I recall the day that we were all dressed up to perform along with the Bombay Chamber Orchestra and the Seville Choir inside the chapel of the Monte. I felt queasy looking at the large audience seated right in front of me. This wasn't my first time inside the chapel as an audience or as a performer, yet I found myself lost in the details of the murals and searching for the choir loft thinking of the perfect view of the stage. I was suddenly very aware of the fact that I was performing someone else's music. The ominous bows of the strings, the loud, gloomy sounds from the woodwind section, the percussion effects, and militancy in the vocalic expressions came through our rendition of Karl Jenkins's "Sanctus" from *Armed Man*. Santiago made sure that throughout the performance, we reflected upon the grit, pain, and woes of war. Standing on the stage, I felt that even though this sacred music was not part of the religion that I was born into, I was now part of a collective that voiced a part of their identity through repertoires of sacrality.

It was similar to a moment Michelle Bigenho[2] describes in the opening chapter of her book *Intimate Distance—Andean Music in Japan*. Bigenho talks about how her cropped hair upset any possibility of wearing fake blonde braids, a traditional folklore costume for Bolivian music. She was already uneasy about playing someone else's music as a *gringa* or *gaijin* anthropologist, alongside the Japanese and the Mestizos (nonindigenous Bolivians) playing Bolivian indigenous music. The intimacies shared by the Bolivians and the Japanese were held together by performing an indigeneity built on a shared imagined ancestry, while keeping their respective nationalisms and colonial experiences intact. This was further motivated by the *symbolic economy* of global Andean music.

The book grapples with the broad theme of looking at voice and genre as social objects. In this endeavor, it traverses through the central notions of indigeneity, piety, schizophonia, nostalgia, and finally affinity that makes the locations interact with each other while still embarking on their respective paths.

In April 2014, I made my first trip to Shillong, Meghalaya, located in the East Khasi hills of Northeast India. I got ready for the first appointment with the world-renowned Shillong Chamber Choir. They gave me directions to reach Whispering Pines once I had reached the Children's Hospital at Pohkseh. D and K made me comfortable and I was thrilled to find myself at the home studio of the famous choristers. After the initial ice-breaking session, I asked them if they were in the middle of a rehearsal.

"We practice our vocal exercises every day during a scheduled time. We have to understand the strength of each of our individual voices. We have to work on the shape of our vocalic renditions. We also need to bring out our controlled pitch and perfect it little by little each day. Based on our voice quality, we decide on the parts that would work for us individually and as a choir. In fact, we have scheduled hours for different aspects of the performance. We assign considerable time for movement training. We focus on light, catchy moves for the soloists

[2] Michelle Bigenho, *Intimate Distance: Andean Music in Japan* (Durham: Duke University Press, 2012).

and more homogenized, breezy gestures for the choir as a whole. These become essential markers of live performances."

As evidenced through the aforementioned ethnographic encounter, the importance of the visual vis-à-vis the aural became a prominent thread in locating choral traditions once I started to find my way into the landscape of Shillong. Here, my engagement was more in the capacity of a keen observer and a participant at community gatherings rather than the actual events. The site was no longer a chapel.

To gauge the sound map of Shillong, I particularly traced the performing cultures of three choirs. They presented religious-classical music in Broadway formats, gospel-jazz-tinged light entertainment, and spiritual-popular renditions. One common marker for all these choirs was that Medley itself emerged as a genre that spanned across the classical, popular, religious, and commercial.

It is important to understand the purposes of documenting an artistic or musical tradition and how regional specificity enhances the local motif. Roma Chatterji (2009) in her work on tracing sociohistorical documentation of "patuas"[3] talks about framing an archive based on discontinuous events, but one that renders specific forms to its overall structure. While discussing discrete events central to shaping the folkloric archive in Bengal, Chatterji emphasizes how the definition of a region is so much more than just a geographical site. She says that region is self-consciously constructed and carries a distinctive signature. The meanings that are conferred upon it are derivatives of economic, cultural, and kinship ties and knowledge systems. It is rather organized by a style of doing and saying things that inform about location and locality. This becomes telling in mapping the choralscape of Goa and Shillong as the signature of the Catholic Goan lifeworld, and a Khasi lifeworld comes alive in the rituals, rehearsals, social interactions, and performance cultures of the choral voices. While the seminary immersion introduces us to the patterning of a catholic theological and liturgical system, experimental choirs from Shillong add a regional flavor to a mainstream musical imagination through attire, repertoire, and performativity.

Piety is a central motif to understand the evolution and ethnically peculiar rootedness of sacred music as a thriving genre among the Catholic Goans. Piety

---

[3] Roma Chatterji, *Speaking with Pictures: Folk Art and Narrative Traditions in India* (New Delhi: Routledge, 2012). The adoption of "Chitrakar" as a title went hand-in-hand with the recognition of *patuas* as "folk artists," rather than "folk performers" for whom displaying scrolls and singing was a form of begging. Most writers privilege painting and picture display as the two primary occupations of the chitrakars: p9.

experienced as a form of symbolic activism while adhering to a religious code, and piety showcasing closeness to God by denouncing material luxury, opens up varying perspectives to define it. Essentially piety relies on a moral compass to spearhead compassion and devotion. Choral music in Goa and Shillong are often considered as essential signposts of sacrality and piety. Saba Mahmood (2005) analyzes how Islamic women embody the veil to embrace piety, while for secularists, the veil does not really make a case for modesty. Through multiple concepts such as Lila Abu-Lughod's "feminist consciousness," Judith Butler's "performativity," and Michel Foucault's "technology of the self," Mahmood questions the modalities Islamic women embody to seek assertions over social norms. This feminist embodiment of the veil and Islamic scriptures to access male-centric religious spaces in Egypt's mosque movement becomes important in locating how two strands of Christianity, with imperialistic associations, complicate the indigenous responses. This becomes particularly useful in tracing how the seminarians in Goa play out their sacred selves through different pedagogic instructions; be it in terms of learning the Gregorian chants, conducting masses in Konkani, mastering different instruments to aid the seminary choir, or composing motets and hymns, while also immersing themselves in vocalic practices to be able to sing along during the service. It is, of course, ironic as the seminary, like the mosque, is a male space and the nunneries in Goa follow a completely different routine. This is especially interesting as women become part of the choirs only during annual festivities. Outside the formal setups which are designed to produce gendered bodies of priests and nuns, there is a quest to persuade pious bodies to inhabit musical motifs beyond their gendered selves toward vocalizing piety. These pious bodies freely inhabit sites such as churches or chapels as well as auditoriums outside the domain of sacred institutions.

In Christianity, worship is led by men either as priests or pastors, depending on the denomination of Christianity. There are various fellowship events like the Youth service, Men's division program, and other dedicated worship and liturgical occasions. Many days are observed to pay homage to particular saints. Women do not hold a primary position in facilitating these events. Choral voices are an inevitable part of the rituals. On the one hand, the four voices require feminine and masculine manifestations; on the other hand, choral singing, which is an integral feature of sacred rituals in Christianity, only allows feminine agencies to fully express themselves as a collaborative enterprise even in their enactment of piety. This takes another interesting turn when one looks at the gestural innovations weaved into the structural conditioning of a choir when placed in nonsacred sites. The latter is mainly observed when following the Aroha Choir and Shillong Chamber Choir. However, the conductors of both these choirs come from the Presbyterian denomination, which has historical ties with the Welsh Calvinist missionaries. Thus, gestures and bodily movements are an embedded code of their representation of sacred music. The gestural comportment is analyzed in conjunction with experimentations with the genre. Overall, similar to an enactment of feminine modesty, an enactment of Christianity in the Roman Catholic tradition imbued with local language as a part of vernacularization becomes one way to engage with its normative presence. The underlying sentiment of piety is central to capturing the sacrality and musicality pinned to the tradition of Christianity as evinced by seminaries like the Rachol and Pilar.

Piety is a core concept in understanding religious traditions and sacral intent. *Jesus in Our Wombs: Embodying Modernity in a Mexican Convent* (2005) proved extremely helpful in structuring how diverse practices impact the seminarians in Goa. The author, Rebecca J. Lester, writes about a congregation in Sierva, Mexico. Lester explores how the women establish an intimate connection with God. Through a long and arduous process, women take upon vows that embody a certain kind of femininity to practice complete detachment from material objects. The other integral component of sacred music apart from piety is creation of distinct sounds. Creation of a specific sound world requires engagement and detachment from a particular musical style. To enable a clear, consistent, novel sound, borrowing, rearranging, and interspersing dissonant elements helps. Medley is not simply a pastiche of sounds but rather a creative imagination of a genre by highlighting specific sounds to be hierarchical in certain representations. In this context, Steven Feld devises the notion of acoustemology to manufacture varying ways of sounding the world. The sound world of the first has the ability to introduce one to dwell in quietude. Colin Turnbull (1961, 1965) reflects on how the Mbuti songs and forest ecology look toward restoring the stillness or the quiet (*ekimi*) sprinkled with joy (*mota*) in their endeavor to let the forest continue to talk. This also helps to counter the noise and silence alongside their most sinister form, the death. "The Mbuti say 'su bongisa ndura, ndura pisu ekimi'—we rejoice the forest, the forest gives us quiet" (p. 290). Feld uses this trope of stillness and ambient spaces to express how musicians across different landscapes, eras, and genres get tied due to the muddled copyright practices in music industries. Drawing examples from various musical replication that originated with *hindewhu*, an onomatopoeic imitation by the Central African Pygmies, produced by alternating voice with that of a single-pitch papaya stem whistle, Feld goes on to explain the meaning of "schizophonic mimesis." "Schizophonic mimesis" concerns itself with aural replications, resonances, lingering strains, and simulations across historical, political, and cultural possibilities. In the context of the choir, on the hand, "Schizophonic Mimesis" finds itself imperative to the creative processes that showcase Medley as a genre. The latter is noticeable in a particular manner among choirs from Shillong that I interacted with. In Goa, a singular genre set the tone for their ritual and creative processes. However, selection of the sacred hymns by the sacred music commission and reimagination of sacred tunes outside the church space did engage with multiple sonic possibilities, both in terms of rhythm and genres.

While "mimesis scizophonia" destabilizes a singular pattern of sound, belongingness to a region solidifies peculiarities associated with a place. This contention of articulating a moderation between what is global and what is indigenous has its own complexity.

The definition of a region with its specific signature style influenced by certain cultural, socioeconomic, and interpersonal relations becomes central in understanding how a sense of community develops among worshippers, choristers, and seminarians. Genres also speak of style. The two sites reveal very different sonic impressions even when it comes to choral music. There is a denominational approach which is contingent upon religious decrees and advisory boards entrusted with decision-making regarding sacrality, representation, melody, and lyrics. There is also an element of performativity which surpasses the religious trope, instead, adopting an entertaining approach. The entertaining approach is focused on the intentionality of the creative piece, the audience, and the larger soundscape as well as the situatedness of the musicians and their lifeworld. This regionality animates concerns that overlap local, indigenous, colonial, and global discourses. It is built around sacred sounds and its manifestations across stylistic mediums such as Medley, branded resonances incorporating hymns and gospels, and folkloric spins.

A Biography of Community: Delineating the Sacred and the Heritage

Biographical sketches became a mode to capture the vocalic traditions in distinct landscapes. Choirs which are indicative of a collective sentiment in terms of both adding to a religious spirit and providing a community fellowship. Within this collective union, individual choices and values thrive as well. To understand this phenomenon, I use Muriel Swijghuisen's notion of "communal individuality." Muriel Swijghuisen talks about a one-of-a-kind indigenous Australian and Hopevalian sense of self. The local kinship networks informed a different material and physical conception of self. The Hopevalian sense of self was more aligned to a larger communal identity. At the same time, there was also a deep sense of personal autonomy and value embedded in the Hopevalian community members. Personal idiosyncrasies, ill-humor, and disturbed mental well-being were accepted as personality attributes. Individuality was accepted, respected, and also accommodated at a communal level. The author distinguished this as "communal individuality." This largely translated to the fact that individual responsibilities for community and kinship well-being were assigned as per age, gender, ethnicity, spirituality, and personal strengths and weaknesses (Swijghuisen 2008: 105–7). The notion of "communal individuality" becomes prominent in the context of Goa and Shillong as well. Not all members of a sacred choir, especially entertainment choirs, were seeking God or piety through their musical commitments, and those who were demonstrated different degrees of intentionality, commitment, and participation.

Further, the author also noted how two distinct timbres were recognized and maintained by the Hopevalian community choir. As a choir facilitator, the author's vocal timbre was seen as Western, classical, and that which conveys vibrato, whereas the Hopevalian vocal timbre was associated with a nasal timbre, interspersed with the use of aboriginal English tonal varieties and diphthongs typical of a Hopevalian musical identity (Swijghuisen, 2008: 122, 126, 137). This is very telling in the context of choral conductors who bring with them their own sound world, peculiar acuities, and structures of intonation and voicing. This precisely explains why the Goa University Choir, Stuti Chorale Ensemble, Aradhon, the Goa Institute of Management Choir, Aroha Choir, Shillong Chamber Choir, Serenity Choir, and Mawkhar Presbyterian Choir, to mention a few, had their own unique signature style, feel, and approach. On the one hand, the priorities and the intent of each choir varied to a large extent, while on the other hand, the conductors entrusted with their training and growth also earmarked a sense of branding that they embossed upon the choir. These together resulted in scripting biographies of choral groups, seminaries, and festivals, and also discuss contributions of select choral conductors, choristers, and seminarians. While biographies help us understand the lifeworld of communities, heritage tells us about how we choose to document certain cultural artifacts.

Heritage refers to the past but is not automatically and directly inherited from the past. It is the outcome of a selection of certain cultural forms which are—more or less persuasively—canonized. Once brought into the framework of heritage, cultural forms are made to assume additional or even new value. The powerful effects of such framing become clear once it is realized that even ordinary everyday objects, coded as heritage, may be elevated to the level of the extraordinary and achieve a new sublime or sacred quality (Meyer and Witte, 2013: 276).

I am interested in how Birgit Meyer establishes a connection between the heritage and the religion through different sites across Brazil, Laos, Ghana, South Africa, and Mauritius. The two processes involved are the heritagization of the sacred and sacralization of heritage. While the former looks at how religious traditions are portrayed and sanctioned within the ambit of heritage, the latter concerns itself with how sacrality informs heritage in a manner that the impressions emitted by heritage seem authoritative, authentic, and irrefutable.

In the context of Goa, sacralization of heritage gains currency through sacred music festivals such as Monte Music Festival and Ketevan World Music Festival. Both festivals give primacy to the Goan-Catholic liturgical and Western classical repertoires. However, rather than restricting the other forms of music to Indian classical music alone, one finds herein folk and traditional repertoires of various countries, particularly India, Portugal, Spain, and Brazil. Further, the architectural layout ranging from the precincts of the churches, courtyard, and ruins around the church helps animate the implication of the sacred. Modifications of vocal timbres become useful in understanding the sacred and nonsacred nexus, when choral imaginations are not limited to worship services. Choirs are also taking on different forms such as the folk repertoire offered by the Cotta Family Choir in Goa, a nonsacred collective put forth by Omar Loiola De Pereira, and the entertainment and corporate framings offered by the Aroha Choir and the Shillong Chamber Choir. Here, overlap between the indigenous, classical, and the cosmopolitan shapes the vocalic textures. The Hopevalian sense of "communal individuality" becomes co-opted toward understanding the nostalgia-tinged construction of the Goan sacred music repertoire. There is a conscious selection whereby the attributes and genesis of specific genres are accepted and accommodated to fully capture the threshold of Goan vocalic traditions.

One central way to understand the place of sacred and heritage in the Christian musical communities across the landscapes is to observe how the "musical character" finds voice in their larger sacred and nonsacred repertoires. For Goa, nostalgia in liminal spaces makes its way into the cracks and pauses that shape the category of sacred. Catholic sentiments, rituals, and sociality further add to the stronghold of the category. For nonsacred collectives and experimentation, too, a "Catholicity" engulfs them. For Shillong, playing their exoticism, aka indigeneity as per the pulse of the audience, always balances itself out alongside an ingrained sense of piety that they have promised as soon as they have committed themselves to Christianity. The cultural arcs are maintained to claim their legitimate space within the sameness/difference trope, and religiosity helps structure their cultural expression through the aperture of faith. Thus nostalgia in the case of Goa and novelty in the case of Shillong sacralize heritage get notated through the biographical presence of various institutions and personalities.

Establishing a Musical Cadence

Practitioners in the field have produced novelty by devising specialized creative processes. There isn't a single category of choral tradition or Western classical music in India. Indigenization has taken diverse roots and formed singular notions of connect, bringing out the flavor of a particular culture and region. Appropriation of Western classical music has taken on many forms and has of course become embedded in different places. The genres that have come together to generate a repertoire is indicative of the processes. Choral tradition is just one of the forms of Western classical music whereby voice and the vocalization technique find prominence. Through musical borrowings, there is an innovative range of cultural confluences located in different regions. One cannot deny the traces of colonial intervention in either Goa or Shillong, but the proficient adaptation and constant experimentation in musical styles speak of a certain kind of artistry that surpasses the imitative quality associated with an interpretation of a musical tradition born out of fractured lineages. It is pertinent to understand how music found its purpose in the sociopolitical world order. There are larger questions ordered around sociohistorical claim-making that cut across ethnicity, class, caste, tribe, and gender. The understanding and manufacturing of genres in this context alongside accommodating a cosmopolitan desire of sound is invested in gauging how assemblages of patronage patterns, political orders, recording studios, and production companies converge.

In *Noise: Political Economy of Music*, Jacques Attali (1977) primarily argues that music prioritized giving legitimacy to the existing social order, in order to counter "noise" and any dissent from the margins. Attali spoke of four types of music: "sacrifice," "representation," "repetition," and "composing." During the early period, music existed as an ancillary toward sacrifice so as to dismiss violence. During early Renaissance Europe, there were wandering musicians like troubadours who functioned under the capitalist economy, producing music as "representation" focused on the written text and performance as per the demands of the nobility. With the emergence of the broadcasting trend and recording culture, music as a mass-produced commodity emerged and soon took upon the format of repetition. In the last stage, Attali speaks about composition. Composition is an activity "in which the musician plays primarily for himself, outside any operationality, spectacle, or accumulation of value; when music, extricating itself from the codes of sacrifice, representation, and repetition, emerges as an activity that is an end in itself, that creates its own code at the same time as the work" (Attali, 1977: 135). The status quo of the established social order was always determining the nature and flow of music, yet other musical styles and rebellions coexisted. Even the four types of music never completely disappeared due to the advent of another music type. However, he conceived of music prior to the digital era. In *Music Genres and Corporate Cultures*, Keith Negus (1999) discusses the creation of "genre cultures" that he extends from Steve Neale's sociological reflections which foray into industry, text, and subject. Negus's own work studies how recording industries impact the creation and consumption of musical categories and forms of entertainment. Political economy facilitates the involvement of corporate ownership into the process. On the one hand, culture creates industries that allow people to form meaningful worlds where sounds, words, and images in popular music find coherence. On the other hand, industry generates conditions within which specific genres and creative techniques come together. Overall, he points to a genre culture with its complex interactions across commercial organizational structures, promotional labels (he even talks about territorialization and re-territorialization while creating international genres where the regional artist lets go of his/her cultural nuances), appreciation among fans, listeners, and audiences, network of musicians alongside larger histories that comment on the broader social formations. In *The Anthropology of Texts, Persons and Publics—Oral and Written Culture in Africa and Beyond*, Karin Barber (2007) looks at how genres act as tools or templates for giving specific forms to utterance. It facilitates an interaction between the speakers and writers, and listeners and readers to derive meanings from the utterance. She goes on to talk about macro approaches, for instance, the Marxist Sociology of Literature outlines texts or literary works within the framing of an epoch, a social class, or inter-related classes to enable a social formation (Barber, 2007: 39). Micro approaches focus on the local, non-Western, oral genres and spread outwards from a specific case. They use an emic, contextual concept of genre that concerns itself with how a local culture defines and differentiates between various speech forms and how they are ingrained in the lived experiences. Macro approaches rely on a morphological concept of genre that can be applied across cultures. Louise Meintjes (2003) talks about production of sound in a recording studio. "Modumo wa Afrika! Afrika!"—translated as "sound of Africa"—is the highest form of compliment that a white sound recorder earned for cracking the code to achieve a peculiar warmer version of a well-rounded raspy synth riff with its deep, coarse repeated sixteenths, not just on the tonic and dominant but repeated throughout the song. The synth bass typifies an African feel due to an intense pulse and vibration. The sound should capture every guitar line, every vocal line and have that drive ultimately. It should eventually induce a "jumping effect" which occurs due to a heavy bass sound that pushes the parallel record grooves to fuse into one another. The Black aesthetic identifiable by a heavy dancing beat with a percussive clicky attack is molded by the technological jump one hears when listening to the record (Meintjes, 2003: 121).

In my work, I have used the concept of "micro genre," as explained by Karin Barber, to see how the choral repertoires across the regions represent their musicalities and identities. Keith Negus's "genre culture" has helped me identify the elements that become important in formulating a particular repertoire. My study looks at the processes of making music and situating it within a cultural terrain. It does not delve into the dynamics of political economy associated with the market and industry, and how Attali is interested in exploring the perpetuation of certain class structures through the transformative stages of music. The liveness that is discussed in producing an African aesthetic becomes useful in the context of understanding the performativity code required in choral music in India.

Western classical music as a genre or particular aspects of the genre, such as Christian sacred music, has been part of Southeast Asian countries. Structured around political events, it has infused a new spirit among the practitioners of these musical traditions. Further, vocalic traditions have a distinct mode of pedagogy that focuses on individual and collective modes of producing and polishing sounds. Sheila Melvin and Jindong Cai (2004) discuss the trajectory of Western classical music in China through a few personalities and certain events—the May 4th Movement, the Second World War, the Communist victory, the setting up of the People's Republic of China, and the Cultural Revolution followed by its consequences. Until the Cultural Revolution, the Communist Party had never ceased to use the arts as a political tool. Their control declined in the wake of modernization and a favorable disposition toward the musicians in terms of artistic choices. *Singing the Seoul: An Ethnography of Voice and Voicing in Christian South Korea* discusses how a European-style singing voice becomes a distinct feature of Korean Christianity, highlighting affluence and social transformation (Harkness, 2013). *A Different Voice, A Different Song* deals with tracing the Natural Voice movement that is ordered around the principle that "everyone can sing." It borrows heavily from the oral singing traditions of various communities across the world to adopt a more inclusive approach (Bithell, 2014). *Singing the Classical, Voicing the Modern* brings to the fore politics of voice in twentieth-century South India and the notion of the authentic voice and instrumental imitation, while establishing Karnatic classical music as a genre (Weidman, 2006). Charles Edward Mcguire, in the chapter "Christianity, Civilization and Music: Nineteenth Century British Missionaries and the Control of the Malagasy Hymnology" (2016), provides a compelling argument about the initiation of pedagogical technology through British sight singing notation of Tonic Sol-Fa among the nonmusical, noncongregational group of slaves. He looks at London Missionary Society's attempt of introducing British musical sensibilities to the Protestants in Madagascar (1862–95) and their use of various modes of persuasion, including force, to write in what the British referred to as the civilizing process within the evangelical order of thought.

The book shows that the public life of Western classical music in India is not just a mere mimicking of performance and studying the art form. Choral traditions in Goa and Shillong promise regional and cultural distinctiveness alongside the aural archives punctuated by colonial exchanges. The careful crafting of voices lends itself to the formal aspects of a musical genre. The performativity weaves in both devotional and conventional elements rooted in Western classical music. Indigenization in this case is informed by sonic innovation that factors in the constraints of a musical structure, an embedded foreignness associated with colonial ritual and performative aspects. Furthermore, there is an internal othering that operates within the framework of a more visible, celebrated, majoritarian cultural repository.

Recent works on Western classical music in India undertaken during similar timelines include that of Hannah Marsden, who focused on how Western classical musicking in Mumbai differed from local values and ideologies that held the city together. Thus, through an archival and ethnographic approach, she looked at how as a transnational music with historical roots in European high art traditions, it coexists alongside local values in a postcolonial site. She found in the course of her fieldwork that considering Western classical music to have a universal language and an independent art form was something that was essentialized by a few pro-Western classical local discourses in Mumbai. This highlighted the tensions and debates that structured musicking in the city. Through the works of Green, Yoshihara, Feld, Taylor, and Appadurai, Hannah also brings in the question of familiar musical values, particularistic, ethnic responses through a lens of othering and differences, so as to maintain one's own sense of identity and culture (Marsden, 2018: 11, 25, 29, 32). Joanna Heath has researched on the compositions by the Mizo Christian community in Mizoram, Northeast India. Her dissertation has focused on the *Khawar zai*, the repertoire of hymns composed during 1919 and 1930. It examines the importance of this repertoire of funeral singing, centered on the notions of hope and nostalgia in the realm of eschatology and evangelicalism. The author demonstrates how the revivals led to many original manners of Christian worship, including drumming in church, dancing together in a circle, and ultimately the practice of *lêngkhâwm zai* as it presents itself today. Khawar zai (bereavement songs) is part of lêngkhâwm zai (singing together) which include songs for praising God, charismatic events, Christmas, and Easter. The bereavement songs, owing to a particular vocal style, tune, and use of drums, render an atmosphere that makes these hymns equivalent to voices of hope. For the funeral songs, *lunglênna* (the Mizo term for nostalgia) is usually articulated in the song. Much of Mizoram's musical heritage can be traced to Myanmar, located close to the river Tiau. Khawar zai, which originated in Khawbung, a village close to the border, helps in lending an expression of a much older Mizo identity contrary to what the recent history suggests (Heath, 2013: 16, 17, 22, 39, 42). Rupert Avis, through an ethnographic engagement, assesses that the position of higher music education in India is complex. He looks at KM Music Conservatory, a private higher music education institution based in Chennai, India. KM's accreditation by Middlesex University makes it a potent market for student recruitment. KM's student body is indicative of an expansion in the interest of internationally recognized music qualifications among India's affluent middle classes. The founder, A. R. Rahman, well trained in Western musical styles, *qawwali*, Hindustani classical music, and a range of other musical practices, has established himself as an influential figure in the Indian film industry. This has contributed toward sustaining KM Music Conservatory as an institution of repute. The situation of Western classical music remains abstruse whereby many students simultaneously challenge and reiterate different ideologies, discourses, and inequalities such as colonial legacies and Hindu nationalism. The stereotype of considering music education as a predominantly feminine career pursuit also exists (Avis, 2020: 230, 231, 233, 244). All these works point toward the urgency of addressing how the character of musical genre or a vocalic tradition needs to be located within the cusp of ethnic and global paradigms. These are further impacted by particular colonial, social, and cultural encounters. This book also seeks to exemplify the role of indigeneity and newer meanings of sacred and community.

Framing Choral Music within Christian Landscapes

This book looks at how the sacred derives many lives through an integral component of Christian worship—choral voices. Existing scholarship has focused on establishing and nurturing specific musical genres, placemaking across various landscapes. Prior studies have also explored the creative forces and imaginations and how sacred spaces transform musical experiences. This work focuses on how many meanings of faith and many meanings of genres come together to build indigenously evocative musical imaginations.

All the themes, namely indigeneity, piety, schizophonia, nostalgia, and affinity, are shaped around the notions of the authentic, traditional, sacrosanct, and the transformations and expansions that carve out a dialog. In light of the foregoing discussion, it's natural for one to wonder what exactly is authentic. Given that the choral repertoires preserved in the hymn books traveled to these landscapes courtesy of colonial motivations and ingenuity, how is it that they acquire an indigenous framework? What makes the local and folk musical traditions different? How does one factor in the negotiations that translate the musical and extra musical aspects of a vocalic tradition? How much of the choral renditions submit solely to the domain of sacred? How much of it is about pedagogical reflections of vocal training? Does choral music as a genre possess the ability to shine on its own sans the cloak of faith? What about the practitioners? How does this particular mode of singing add to the intent of the chorister?

Is it really necessary to make way for an indigenous repertoire? Which are the specific sounds and voices that explain the repertoire? Accommodating colonial encounters and artworlds by lending it to the regional-ethnic feelingfulness and sounds leads to the kind of indigeneity that my fieldwork exposed me to. Indigeneity here is very different from what we usually understand. This is not about starting a movement to claim particular territories, humanitarian rights, or assertion of identities. Indigeneity in this book is about making space for a splintered faith understood through vernacularized experiences. The process involves political and cultural immersions and a cultivated vocalization that buttresses harmonic, spiritual, and commercial thresholds.

Whenever we start any work on art forms, the first query is always around the origin and the qualifiers that are indicative of its authentic footprints. Therefore, even with choral music, we start with exploring the characteristics that highlight its authenticity. Within a church scape, choirs are to religious sermons what illustrations are to texts in a picture-book. What I mean is, the sacral tone will always accompany the shrill tone, the raspy tone, the husky tone, the barrel tone, the showman tone, the vibrating tone, or the fading tone. The glimmer of faith shows itself in the voices when the activity of singing is being demonstrated as a part of a mass or a worship ritual. Thus, an authentic way to look at choral voices is to presume that it is a part of a religious ritual associated with Christianity. Choir, as a formal organization, is steeped into a pious mold which then extends to the extramusical world of a sense of community, an informal space of vocal pedagogic training, and explorations that impinge on the sacred, social, and regional. What happens to the authenticity of the same setting of a choir with soprano, alto, tenor, and bass when located in a nonsacred space? The spiritual veil is lifted; the presence resembles one of protagonist collective rather than an accompanist collective. The community feeling is heightened; yet individual skill is nurtured because it then becomes an embodiment of the creative process.

How do the choral repertoires acquire an indigenous framework? Logically, given the rules of Vatican II in the Catholic Church and the desire of the Presbyterian and other Protestant sects to be more intrinsically located within the cultural fabric of society, vernacularization and the quest for indigeneity became a sacred qualifier. These were in keeping with the Christian infrastructural arrangements. A pertinent moment follows this. How do the locals make sense of keeping their traditions alive amid colonial encounters and evangelical pursuits? Conversion due to various circumstances leaves one conflicted about what comprises one's culture. While mapping culture, how does one think through the tropes of language, custom, faith, rituals, sociopolitical rules and predicaments, relationships, and finally professional and leisurely happenings? Then again, there is the looming force of globalization which is geared toward interlocking subcultures into a grand meta-culture. Categories like authentic, folk, local, indigenous, hybrid, and global thus complicate any unified way of defining culture. It is always evolving and constantly aware of the compositional limitations that certain historical, political, and social circumstances prepare them for. Coming back to the original inquiry—the indigenous becomes a life force that attempts to define a particular society with its unique geographical, historical, and political givens and exchanges. In the case of choral repertoires, melodies, tunes, instruments, rhythms, and various techniques of vocalizations take on an indigenous flavor. It is through a conscious choice of what resonates with the formal characteristics of a choir as well as its artistic possibilities. It also makes one aware of how the definitions of authentic, imported, hybrid, and local have shifting meanings.

What makes the local and folk musical traditions different? Looking at Goa and Shillong, one observes how specific instruments become symbolic motifs to represent their folk customs. For Goa, it is the *ghumott* which along with violin makes for the instrumental component of their widely popular folk musical tradition, *mando*. A few of my interlocutors suggested that mando as a musical form originated in the villages of Loutolim and Curtorim. These villages were known to have converted who were originally Saraswat Brahmans. This makes the upper-caste signpost a part of the musical practice. Goan musical genres have a close connection with its Portuguese past. Susana Sardo writes about how "Portuguese Asians" create a luso-sonic world. The ACPA (Association of Portuguese Communities in Asias) based out of Malacca (Malaysia) that has members living in different Asian territories organized their first conference in the year 2016. These people, associations, and/or communities, attribute it to a Portuguese ancestry, thereby claiming a uniqueness within a nation that categorises them differently.

Mandó, dulpod and even deckni in Goa (Sardo 2011), are musical genres that describe what the Goans who nurture and perform them, want to safeguard and expose simultaneously. These repertoires are locally generated ethnographic archives, sung in Konkani, in the case of Goa but covered in acoustics incorporating a Western flavor, due to the functional harmony found both in the choir singing as well as in the instrumental accompaniments of guitar, piano, violin or mandolin. Lusosonia songs accommodates the notion of liberation despite originating from a point of oppression. "Their holders established with it a double relationship of belongingness: they feel that the repertoire belongs to them and, at the same time, that they belong to the world represented by the repertoire."[4] The violin is easily indicative of the Iberian classical music expression. Mando ultimately is a light dance form where two partners—one male and one female—are involved. Fados are sonic expressions *of Saudade* through which the Portuguese embodied pain, loss, crime, politics, as well as mobility. Since the lyrics of mandos reflect political satire, suffering, and romance, the analogy comes up. The makers of ghumott are associated with a lower-caste village, and even though it is used in classical music accompaniments alongside the widely acclaimed mando, ghumott has never been part of a church service or a Christian sacred performance. In Meghalaya, Khasis consider *Ka ksing* and *duitara* to be the most common folk instruments. Ka Bom, (Big drum). *Ksing Shynrang* (male drum) and *Ka KSing Kynthei* (female drum) are largely associated with the Nongkhrem Festival, which is part of Ka Niam Khasi tradition. It is a harvest festival where women at the onset of their puberty take part in the traditional dance. Duitara is part of Khasi folk songs. They also have other instruments like the *tangmuri, ka besli* (Khasi bamboo flute).[5] Of all these instruments, I have only seen the duitara as a part of special services on Sundays at Presbyterian churches. Along with *pnar* and *bhoi*, Khasi too was originally part of an oral culture, and in the process, they have a lot of folktales and myths. As a part of their folk musical traditions, they also use particular instruments to narrate those tales. The locally produced instruments signify materiality, labor, place, climate, and its social associations. Thus, the local or the folk instruments may not belong to the sacred or classical cannon owing to the politics of faith, class, caste, and ethnicity. Also, since folk music documents the struggles and intimacies of communities, they like setting aside specific instruments to reinforce their significance.

This automatically takes us to the next question as to how to negotiate the musical and extramusical attributes of a vocalic tradition. As we have been discussing throughout the chapter, vocalic traditions are rooted in larger structures that focus on training, nurturing creativity, and visibly shining through rituals and performances. In the case of choral voices, there are these sacred spaces namely the church, seminary, Sunday school, and the nonsacred spaces like the school or public auditoriums, recording studios, or music schools.

---

[4] Sardo (2022: 185).
[5] https://pari.education/articles/the-khasi-drums-are-rolling/ accessed on June 3, 2022.

The negotiations involve oscillating between aural attentiveness, mellifluous tones, and the costume, styling, and movements. Choral music requires a group synergy, a collective sense of warmth, and a balanced sound to convey its purpose and performativity, be it in a sacred space or in a space of entertainment. The intent of the creative process helps to align the voices and the genres that come together to push ritualistic and artistic boundaries. A lot of it is also to do with how one moves across ranges and finds the comfort to stay within a particular range while accepting all the expectations and myths associated with a particular vocal range. This also highlights the urge to perhaps learn an instrument to enhance one's vocalizing skills. In Shillong, there is a natural affinity toward learning the piano. In some cases, people chose to learn the guitar. In Goa, it is dominantly the violin, piano, or guitar. This is followed by the viola, cello, or double bass. It is a good idea to understand why the preferences vary across the two sites. Goa has many string ensembles and orchestras apart from choirs. In many instances, one finds people who inhabit both the orchestral spectrum and the choral spectrum. The sacral tinge associated with the engagements is quite optimum as well. In Shillong, the voices float around much more convincingly than the instruments. There are no orchestras or accompaniment collectives to keep the motivation going.

It is a good idea to take the next set of questions together. How much of the choral renditions submit solely to the domain of sacred? How much of it is about pedagogical reflections of vocal training? Does choral music as a genre shine on its own without the cloak of faith? What about the practitioners? How does this particular mode of singing add to the intent of the chorister? Is it really necessary to make way for an indigenous repertoire? What sounds and voices explain the repertoire? We have actually been navigating these interrogations so far. There is also a definite interconnection between these questions. While I try to unpack these sitting at a café with "Hark! The Herald Angels Sing" playing in the background, I am reminded of a bus journey with the Stuti Chorale Ensemble back in 2014. We were returning after the choir's performance at the Holy Church of Margao. I was just an attendant and a researcher for that occasion. My friend E accompanied the choir on viola. We all started singing that particular song, taking parts and harmonizing as we sought our comfort within the melody and the rhythm. It is a Christmas carol by Felix Mendelssohn and differs from hymns. But on the question of intent, here, for instance, we were just looking for a song to infuse a cheerful spirit and that was in sync with the mood of Christmas. Coming back to choral music as a genre, it is embedded in sacred content and intent. However, there are possibilities of imagining a public life of choral music that extends beyond the sacred blanket as we discuss in this book. Regarding indigeneity that appears as the main motif to understand the Christian ethic vis-à-vis the ethnic-feeling-fullness, it is about what captures the momentum and flow of musical and extramusical features. To make sense of the curated and cultivated choral repertoire, one has to dig deep into what goes into the making of a repertoire. It is clearly organized through rigorous training, rules, word of God, discovery of a sensory harmony within the precinct of the ensemble, specific sounds, texts, and vocalizations. It promises musical situatedness, innovation, and possibilities.

Aural Intentions: Summary of Chapters

The second chapter explores the definitional possibilities of the indigenous in the context of choral musical imaginations in Goa and Shillong. Choral traditions that comprise an essential component of worship rituals interact with the local worldviews and sounding patterns to formulate sacred repertoires. This interaction is labeled as sonic interculturality, which incorporates, eliminates, and negotiates colonial associations. Ultimately, it extrapolates localized understanding of the soulful expressed through indigeneity.

The third chapter sees how "Medley" emerges as a genre in Shillong. Steeped into the reality TV show expectations and rigorous vocal training opportunities, choral singing leaves the premises of church and presents itself as an entertainment form that interjects a singular notion of "classical." This shifting characteristic makes this genre not only difficult to pin down but also fragmentary and strategic in approach. It tries to address issues like: For whom is this performance intended? How is the music molded to make way for specific stylistic demands? The chapter contrasts the experiences of the Shillong Chamber Choir with the Aroha Choir. Gilles Deleuze's notion of "territorialisation" (1987) helps in situating eclectic sounds within the framework of a particular genre. The novelty that is inscribed in the repertoire is enabled by intertextuality and synchronicity.

The fourth chapter grounds itself into the seminary tradition while looking at the lives of select seminarians in order to understand the emergence of a niche sacred music repertoire in Goa, the likely choral singing tradition. It attempts to understand how piety and worship protocols not only stem from imperialistic histories but are also informed by cultural processes. One of the central question that emerges is: What is Goan folk music and what is considered as Goan sacred music? To map the process, Hirschkind's concept of ethical listening (2006) that instills *inshirah* (opening of the heart in a manner of being closer to God) helps understand how routine activities in the seminary attune the students to sacral matters and achieve oneness with God. Sarbadhikari's study on embodying Vrindavan by singing *kirtans*, practiced among the Bengal Vaishnavaites (2015), situates how the knowledge gathered at the seminary helps in articulating the contours of the form and content of sacred music. The selection of the repertoire is indicative of "restorative nostalgia" (2001), as explained by Svetlana Boym.

The fifth chapter explores voice in the choral singing tradition. It delves into the hierarchy ascribed to soprano or the melody line and extramusical elements associated with voice. It looks at how geographical locations impact one's perception of voice. What is the voice of performance? What is the voice of the congregation? The hierarchization is explored through a Deleuzian understanding of an assemblage—in this case, a choral assemblage. Through the contrapuntal narratives that inform the musical choices of my respondents, a sense of place is constituted as a sociality around voice. Chatterji's concept of "mirroring" (2016) brings forth the human and the cosmic time in the scroll paintings created by the *chitrakars* of Bengal. Two motifs, namely nostalgia and novelty, help enframe the repertoires of Goa and Shillong.

The final chapter emphasizes that choral voices in Goa and Shillong have a sacred intent. Although religion and culture embrace a conscious colonial and indigenous interplay, the soulfulness retains creative and nostalgic hues.

2

Making of the Indigenous

Interrogating the Indigenous

The occasional strumming of the duitara,[1] melodies arranged in the formats of mandos[2] and *dulpods,*[3] and hymns sung in Khasi or Konkani are a few noticeable symbols of indigeneity in choral traditions. It is interesting to observe how Christianity has organically structured itself in both Goa and Shillong. This is a result of the emphasis on vernacularization, localization, and innovation across Catholic and Presbyterian denominations.

How do we arrive at the definitional possibilities of the term "indigenous"? At the outset, it is about certain essential features that are rooted in the community. In this case, it refers to the ones who are immersed in the creative process that lies at the intersection of faith and music. It involves responding to the grammar of an overarching idea of a culturally informed and socially conditioned set of norms, rituals, and sonic associations. Specific intonations, liturgical references, musical accompaniments, and maneuvering the spatial and the architectural realms assume a certain degree of significance in the imagination of the choral. People who are part of this endeavor organize their notions of intimacy, productivity, authenticity, and artistry to make sense of the indigenous.

---

[1] A four-stringed instrument used in Khasi folk songs in Syiem Lapynshai; see *The Evolution of Khasi Music: A Study of the Classical Content* (New Delhi: Regency Publications, 2005), 41.
[2] Mando is a slow verse and refrain song dwelling primarily on sad and nostalgic love lyrics. https://folkways.si.edu/mando-of-goa/india-world/music/album/smithsonian (accessed February 26, 2022).
[3] Dulpods comprise of everyday musings of the Goan Catholics. They are dance music having quick rhythm of two-line verses that are sung in Konkani. https://folkways.si.edu/mando-of-goa/india-world/music/album/smithsonian (accessed February 26, 2022).

Indigenous sounds are driven by conscious choices. Here it becomes pertinent to question why it is not common to witness a *besli*,[4] *tangmuri*,[5] or *KSing Kynthei*[6] be part of the special Sunday service at a Presbyterian church at Riatsamthiah, for instance. These local instruments are very much a part of the fabric of the Khasi sonic-scape but do not immediately align with the gospel or congregational framework of Shillong. In Goa, one does not witness any folk instrument during Catholic liturgical services. Ghumott[7] is popular both in terms of visual and rhythmic representation in the case of mando performances, one of the folk musical traditions from Goa. Even though the latter musical style is approved by the Diocesan of Sacred Music, the instrument finds no resonance, at least in the format of worship. In both cases, language arguably emerges as a vehicle for inserting the ethnic footprint. Along with the sung text, the tones, breaks, pauses, and the lilt shine through. The words are thus organized in a manner suitable to the intent and the form of the musical genre. Ethnic footprint refers to the larger cultural reference that speaks to the geographies being discussed. Language too has diverse connotations. While Khasi—which once was an oral tradition before accepting the Welsh alphabets and discarding the Bengali alphabets—takes on a unique dialect, Konkani finds different expressivity across the Catholic and Hindu communities. Moreover, the church plays an important role in preserving the use of Konkani in daily activities, which otherwise experiences a marginalized presence amid English and Marathi. In the context of this research, indigenous is therefore informed by colonial, local, traditional, and aspirational elements. It traverses the terrains of visual, sonic, as well as tactile mediums, especially because it is centered on communities and their participation in aesthetic and spiritual exchanges. Mapping the indigenous therefore does not insist on the continuity of certain local artistic practices but rather on how one goes back to their roots every once in a while.

---

[4]   Ka Besli (flute) usually acts as an accompaniment of folk music but it also is used for solo renditions or in conjunction with other musical instruments in Syiem Lapynshai. *The Evolution of Khasi Music: A Study of the Classical Content* (New Delhi: Regency Publications, 2005), 108.

[5]   Tangmuri is a Khasi windpipe that is also played like a flageolet in Syiem Lapynshai. *The Evolution of Khasi Music: A Study of the Classical Content* (New Delhi: Regency Publications, 2005), 50.

[6]   Ka KSing Kynthei (a female drum) and Ka Padiah (small drum) are folk instruments that can also be used in ritualistic music in in Syiem Lapynshai. *The Evolution of Khasi Music: A Study of the Classical Content* (New Delhi: Regency Publications, 2005), 35.

[7]   Ghumott is a membrane instrument popular in Goa, Andhra Pradesh, and villages of Karnataka. It is also an essential part of both religious and folk traditions among both Hindus and Christians in Goa. https://www.thehindu.com/entertainment/music/ancient-instrument-with-cultural-link/article24103373.ece (accessed February 26, 2022).

The "indigenous" in the repertoire of the sacred in Goa incorporates the Gregorian chants and motets holding on to the Roman and Portuguese religious traditions. As mentioned earlier, in the case of local folk traditions, mando easily finds synergy within the theological framework. If one looks closely, the elite association cannot be obliterated and here it becomes evident how the musical patterns are structured by specific languages. These languages, both in the guise of conversation and music, are pointing toward people from specific social locations, upper class/upper caste, depending on the geography associated with them. This also brings to the fore how systemic hierarchies continue in sacred spaces.

On Easter, the cathedral at Laitumukhrah, Shillong, ends its celebration with a brass band procession. This has been part of the Khasi liturgical tradition owing to the growing influence and teachings of the Society of the Divine Saviours, the Salvatorians who arrived in Shillong in February 1890. They were the first Catholic Missions to arrive in Shillong. The brass bands have active participation in the public life of Khasi sacred music twice a year. A formidable fact about this brass band is that its continuity to date is practiced through family lineages. My conversation with the band leader in 2016 laid bare some of the insecurities about the way forward.

Emplacing the Indigenous

Monique Ingalls talks about sacred travels in relation to North American evangelical conferences and how participants experience a spiritually directed musical moment. The author mentions an "eschatological discourse" where the congregational singing of the student conferences at the cities of North America—Urbana and Passion—connects the community in heaven, the abode of God. Drawing on Wegner's notion of "narrative utopias" in formulating imaginary communities that combine material, pedagogical, and political impacts, Ingalls sees how the participants in the interdenominational evangelical conferences create their idyllic world that connects heaven and earth through carefully chosen musical styles and specific social organization (Ingalls, 2011: 262–8).[8]

---

[8] Monique Ingalls, "Singing Heaven Down to Earth: Spiritual Journeys, Eschatological Sounds, and Community Formation in Evangelical Worship," *Ethnomusicology* 55, no. 2 (2011): 255–79. https://doi.org/10.5406/ethnomusicology.55.2.0255.

This becomes helpful in emplacing certain instruments, intonations, and folk traditions. These build on the idea of the "indigenous" in the case of Goa and Shillong. Here, "imaginary community" gets shaped by particular sounds and styles of music in engaging with the everyday. This is carefully designed keeping in mind the materiality of the instrument that is conducive to the vocalizations and musical form. Also, the popular folk traditions or rhythmic movements are more easily accommodated in the process.

The assertion of indigeneity also bears a political significance. The fact that Christianity, especially in these regions, has been a Western import, situating it within the subcontinental framework becomes a necessity. Furthermore, being a minority group, the continuity and the discontinuity of the religion and the culture is an ongoing dialog. While Meghalaya maintains a distinct separation between the two axes, the Catholic Goans seem to have overlapping features that are sacrosanct. Lila Ellen Gray in her book *Fado Resounding* (2013) talks of the "soulful" in fado. On the one hand, there are the very acts of listening, performing, and accessing the different musical styles, guided by the cultural code of shared history, and on the other hand, these styles are ensconced in sensual particularities that inform the "socio-musical world of the soulful." Fado, a sung poetic genre that was formulated in the early 1800s in Lisbon, had links with criminality, prostitution, Portuguese colonial ambitions, and Moorish musical features, among other characteristics. It was subjected to rituals of sanitization by the upper class in Lisbon in 1800 and since November 2011 has been declared by UNESCO as "an intangible cultural heritage of humanity." The public life of "the soulful" in fado thus offers a transcultural perspective about the communities that participate in creating it—both collectively on a global/transnational scale and individually on a local level—by processing and transforming the historical, aesthetic, cultural, and social meanings of the genre. The indigenous in the choral traditions of Goa and Shillong, too, grapple with the continuum of global and local Christianity. Further, whereas, faith is contingent on music in Goa; in Shillong, faith and music seem to operate as independent arcs.

Understanding Indigeneity, Inculturality, and Decoloniality

Traditional indigenous knowledge systems encompass a network of knowledge, belief, and traditions that are exchanged both formally and informally between kin groups and communities in the manner of the indigenous processes, rituals, oral narratives, insights about harvesting, protocols of hunting and gathering, detailed approaches to understanding local ecosystems, and also through the creation of specialized tools and technologies. Traditional ecological knowledge is adept at organizing site-specific and culture-specific instructions that add to the localized understanding of the landscapes and emphasizes particular skill sets. Oral traditions incorporate elements of narrative and performance (Bruchac, 2014: 3815–19).[9]

Indigenous beliefs were treated as religious superstitions in comparison to imperialist ideologies and bigger organized religious movements. In North and South America, Australia, and New Zealand, traditional communities found it hard to continue living harmoniously as they were devoid of political power. The Maoris, for instance, were left with little control of their land and future (Smith, 2012: 175).[10] Indigenous knowledge is embedded in the sensory and human experience of complex relationships established between multiple organisms in particular ecosystems (Apffel-Marglin, 2011[11]; Augustine, 1997[12]; Smith, 2012[13]). International environmental law ensures the protection of indigenous rights in the form of cultural resource management and access to traditional landscapes (Ellen et al., 2000[14]; Menzies, 2006[15]; von Lewinski, 2004[16]). Oral traditions, folklore, ecological knowledge, indigenous languages, and traditional names are now a part of intellectual property (Gnecco and Ayala, 2011[17]).

In *Decolonizing Methodologies: Research and Indigenous People*, Linda Tuhiwai Smith (2012)[18] mentions how Western theories and academic research concern

---

9   Margaret Bruchac, "Indigenous Knowledge and Traditional Knowledge," in *Encyclopedia of Global Archaeology*, ed. Claire Smith (New York: Springer, 2014), 3814–24.

10   Linda Tuhiwai Smith, *Decolonizing Methodologies: Research and Indigenous People* (London and New York: Zed Books Ltd, 1999).

11   Apffel-Marglin Frederique, *Subversive Spiritualities: How Rituals Enact the World* (New York: Oxford University Press, 2011).

12   Stephen J. Augustine, *Traditional Aboriginal Knowledge and Science versus Occidental Science* (Canada, 1997). Paper prepared for the Biodiversity Convention Office of Environment, Canada. Available at: http://www.nativemaps.org/?q¼node/1399, (accessed on April 4, 2021).

13   Claire Smith and H. Martin Wobst, eds., *Indigenous Archaeologies: Decolonizing Theory and Practice* (London: Routledge, 2005).

14   Alan Bicker, Roy Ellen and Peter Parkes, eds., *Indigenous Environmental Knowledge and its Transformations: Critical Anthropological Perspectives* (Amsterdam: Harwood Academic, 2000).

15   Charles R. Menzies, *Traditional Ecological Knowledge and Natural Resource Management* (Lincoln: University of Nebraska Press, 2006).

16   Von Lewinski, ed., *Indigenous Heritage and Intellectual Property: Genetic Resources, Traditional Knowledge, and Folklore* (The Hague and New York: Kluwer Law International, 2004).

17   Cristóbal Gnecco and Patricia Ayala, *Indigenous Peoples and Archaeology in Latin America* (Walnut Creek: Left Coast Press, 2011).

18   Linda Smith, *Decolonizing Methodologies: Research and Indigenous Peoples*, 2nd edn. (London: Zed Books, 2012).

themselves with findings ordered around discovery, followed by depiction and definition of a cultural death of the indigenous people. The latter may have their lands and resources altered by the state that furthers their marginalized status, determined by the contours of economic and social policies. This concern with the "indigenous problem" was framed around militarism and "policing" that was aimed at silencing the rebellions. Research continues in a manner whereby the issues are frequently found to be organically linked to the "indigenous individual or community," ignoring the systemic fallacies ordered around social, economic, and policy matters (Smith, 2012: 91–3). She also introduces Kaupapa Maori, a new epistemological way of conducting Maori indigenous research. In *On Decoloniality: Concepts, Analytics, Praxis*, Walter e. Mignolo and Catherine E. Walsh (2018)[19] talk about how, during the late 1980s and early 1990s and as reaction to the neoliberalism in the region, both the Indigenous Regional Council of Cauca, Colombia (Cric), and the Confederation of Indigenous Nationalities of Ecuador (Conaie) looked upon interculturality as an organizing principle that interlaced the political and the epistemic narratives of struggle. Interculturality is not just a dialog between different cultures but rather transformations across structures, economy, society, polity, and culture, creating fundamentally contrasting societies. On the other hand, multiculturalism thrived on inclusivity aligned to the interests of the dominant order, which also emerged during the late 1980s and continued through the 1990s to contain resistance as per neoliberal logic. In the politics and policies of the World Bank, however, interculturality was accommodated as a language of the World Bank, especially after the uprising of the 1990 in Ecuador directed toward the indigenous people. In the first decade of the twenty-first century, interculturality was the principal premise of Ecuador's indigenous movement's historical project as well as their plea for a plurinationalist state. For conaie too, interculturality implied participation of the indigenous people in decision-making and access to political power in a new democracy or a plurinational state.

Drawing from these historical and sociopolitically contingent modes of looking at decoloniality, I am interrogating the emic categories of indigeneity that form an integral component of the university spaces in terms of music curriculum and education as well as specific compositional tropes that dominate the spectrum of performance.

---

[19] Walter Mignolo and Catherine Walsh, *On Decoloniality: Concepts, Analytics, Praxis* (Durham and London: Duke University Press, 2018).

Music and Decoloniality

This section will document indigenous musical traditions across the globe. It will explore vocalic and aural traditions in sacred and secular spaces. It will then focus on similarities and differences with South Asia.

Jorge Martínez Ulloa[20] writes about how the 1930s witnessed a migratory shift of the Mapuche from their original homeland in rural, Southern Chile to Santiago and other urban centers. During music making, the indigeneity is recalled in the process of observing urban *palin*, where the "blue force" or the ancestral power of the Mapuche community comes alive. The individual and the collective experience "mapucheness." Palin refers to a duel between two groups of players who by using sticks of curved end (*weñu*) aim to push a small leather ball (*pali*) to the rival team's territory (*tripalwe*). The team that manages to do it consistently for four times emerges as the winner (2016).

In 1885, musicology found itself focusing on two different approaches. On the one hand was the historical musicology that concerned itself with European music and on the other hand, there was the systematic musicology that tried to map musical elements varying across cultures. The aim was to postulate universal laws about musical elements as well as a schema for the classification of instruments. This led to the scholars working on Southeast Asia systematically taking on a synchronic mode, relying on phonograph recordings of music performed by Javanese, Siamese, and other troupes performing at trade fairs, such as the Exposition Universelle in Paris during 1889. A few of the systematic musicologists presented factual details about Southeast Asian tunings, scales, tone systems, and even the making of certain instruments. Indonesian scholarship took shape after the First World War. Their focus was on court art forms that were available in Java and Bali. A few noncourt art forms across Nias, Flores, and Sulawesi had also been recorded. The aftermath of the Second World War saw revisions or translations of works by earlier scholars such as Kunst, McPhee, and Holt. The 1980s saw a large number of Southeast Asian-born scholars coming back home from overseas to undertake research organized around Southeast Asian arts. In the context of Malaysia, Tan Sooi Beng writes about how at the start of the 1980s, research on performing arts was mainly about pre-Muslim theaters and music, but later a dialog between

[20] Jorge Martínez Ulloa, "Indigenous Music and Identity: Musical Spaces of Urban Mapuche Communities," in *A Latin American Music Reader: Views from the South*, ed. Javier F. León and Helena Simonett (Urbana, Chicago, and Springfield: Illinois University Press, 2016), 356–78.

performing arts and Islamic religious practices emerged. The other themes concentrated on Chinese-Malaysian arts, radical theater, and music that was constantly repressed by the Malay government. During the 1990s, Indonesian ethnomusicologists established their own scholarly association and issued a journal. Their focus was on decolonizing the scholarship, and the shift of the discourses saw the analyses framed around socioeconomic and political realms rather than discussions on particular music, dance, or drama items or repertoires. The post-structuralist approach to look at popular music, dance, and theater is to take into consideration the always-evolving technology with its compositional and consumption patterns. Other interrelated realms such as fashion, hairstyle, clothing, and filming also acquire significance (Kartomi, 1995).[21]

As a choral music educator, Deborah Bradley talks about introducing global songs to propagate an anti-racial pedagogy that encourages multicultural human subjectivity. She draws examples from Stephen Hatfield's repertoires and points toward the empathy enframed in the manner in which the composer arranges the song and his detailing of the event that triggered its creation (Bradley, 2009).[22] The author categorizes global songs in a manner that includes indigenous music, classical, or art music of European and European-derived traditionally marginalized folk practices such as Balkan or Celtic music. Given that the choir and music written for choral groups are a definitive Western construct, incorporating different singing patterns may be looked upon as popular multiculturalism and otherwise be indicative of ever-present colonialism in both the popular and official and multicultural domains. The author uses an anti-apartheid song called "Siyahamba" as an example to demonstrate how its original musical and sociohistorical context will be guarded, only when sung unaccompanied. However, different arranged versions along with piano and band are available due to its catchy melody and rhythm. The author himself retains the unaccompanied version for the treble choir but the rhythms are a tad different from Nyberg's earliest North American publication, the collection *Freedom Is coming! Songs of Praise and Protest from South Africa*. The publishing industry's tilt toward popular multiculturalism depoliticizes the music.

[21] Margaret J. Kartomi, "'Traditional Music Weeps' and Other Themes in the Discourse on Music, Dance and Theatre of Indonesia, Malaysia and Thailand," *Journal of Southeast Asian Studies* 26, no. 2 (1995): 366–400, http://www.jstor.org/stable/20071722.
[22] Deborah Gail Bradley, "Global Song, Global Citizens? The World Constructed in World Music Choral Publications," in *Exploring Social Justice: How Music Education Might Matter*, ed. Gould and Countryman (Canadian Music Educators' Association, 2009), 105–20.

In *The Indigenization of Tamil Christian Music: Musical Style and Liberation Theology, the World of Music*, Zoe Sherinian (2005)[23] discusses the importance of broadening cultural exchanges between Western missionaries and local Tamil communities so as to include the voices of both elite and lower-caste/class groups. This encourages diverse indigenous perspectives. The author accords importance to language, musical style, and theology in indigenizing Christian music as well as the principles of worship. In the sixteenth century, the Italian and Portuguese Catholic missionaries introduced Christianity to Tamil Nadu; the German Lutherans appeared in the eighteenth century, followed by the British and American Protestants in the nineteenth century. The contemporary Christian folk music project rejects both the cultural tropes atypical to the colonial period and the seemingly benevolent earlier indigenous modes like Sanskritized Carnatic music. Reverend James Theophilus Appavoo came up with spiritually transitory liturgy relevant to the society, especially the exploited groups who form the majority in the Tamil Christian community, borrowed? from Adi Samayam (original religion), a religion for the Dalits, markedly different from Brahminical Hinduism alongside folk music and cultural indicators of resistance. The Tamil Protestant Christian community responds to disrespect toward the lower-caste culture in two ways: by reintroducing village folk culture and aping elite cultures. From the 1980s onward, Appavoo included village metaphors and languages with local intonation into the folk music repertoire used in liturgy. There was an emulation of British and German lifestyle and education. This led to the influence of the English or German hymnody and Carnatic music tradition. From the 1950s onwards, light classical or popular music (films, etc.) has been used (Sherinian, 2005).

In *Ochtoechos of the Syrian Orthodox Churches in South India*, Joseph J. Palackal (2004)[24] talks about chants that are an integral part of Syrian Orthodox churches. Christian music repertoire in South India has Syriac chants, which originated in the Middle East. Syriac is a version of Aramaic that Jesus and his disciples spoke. The liturgies of the early Christians in Antioch (Antakya, in southern Turkey) and Persia (present-day Iran and Iraq) became part of the liturgies of the St. Thomas Christians. The Syrian Orthodox churches celebrated the liturgy in Syriac till the 1960s. Vernacularization was initiated in the early

---

[23] Zoe Sherinian, "The Indigenization of Tamil Christian Music: Musical Style and Liberation Theology," *The World of Music* 47, no. 1 (2005): 125–65, http://www.jstor.org/stable/41699625.

[24] Joseph Palackal, "Oktoēchos of the Syrian Orthodox Churches in South India," *Ethnomusicology* 48, no. 2 (2004): 229–50, http://www.jstor.org/stable/30046265.

1960s. The mass was translated first into Malayalam, the language of Kerala and home for most Syrian Orthodox Christians. In 1965, the Tamil translation of the Mass and prayers was printed for Tamil Nadu. A Kannada edition of the mass for the residents in Karnataka was published in 1980. In recent times, mass and offices are rendered in Syriac and Malayalam in the seminaries of Kerala (Palackal, 2004).

Exploring the Relationship between Indigeneity and Sacrality

Why does the indigenous feature in its own distinct manner across different sites? This is owing to the cultural foibles that interact with the overall milieu. Sacrality too has its own specific roots and paths. When indigeneity and sacrality are juxtaposed, their meanings lend a consciously formulated outcome.

Indigeneity both in local and global disposition follows a religious protocol, making it an ingrained process. NREL—Indigenous religion(s): Local Grounds, Global Networks, the editors, and some of the contributors to the volume titled *Handbook of Indigenous Religions* were part of a multi-sited production that aimed at creating a comparative framework to understand the networks of indigenous religions with varying degrees (Johnson and Ellen Kraft, 2017, 3).[25]

While defining what indigenous religion-making entails, four categories emerged. Translations look at how different groups manage to articulate global indigeneity and its inherent limitations and contradictions. Performance in varying art forms, including music, interposes itself between the cultural-religious activity and the discourse of global indigeneity. Contemporary media introduces new instruments which are often contrary to the features of indigeneity yet become part of it so as to articulate the changing forms of global indigeneity. The question of sovereignty becomes the final category, allowing the indigenous community to exercise political control or an agency suitable in the wider settler societies (Johnson and Ellen Kraft, 2017, 6–7).[26]

In the article "The Developing Field of Congregational Music Studies" (2014, 148–58),[27] Mark Porter tries to address the marginality and the challenges associated with congregational music studies. He reflects on how the entire

---

[25] Greg Johnson and Siv Kraft, "Introduction," in *Handbook of Indigenous Religion*, ed. Greg Johnson and Siv Ellen Kraft (Leiden: Brill, 2017).

[26] ibid.

[27] Mark Porter, "The Developing Field of Christian Congregational Music Studies," *Ecclesial Practices* 1, no. 2 (2014): 149–66.

approach of music scholarship is tied to the professional services of choirs and composers that represent elite institutions. Church music becomes a concern for musicologists, historians, and ethnomusicologists to understand its musical quality, ethicality around style, and cultural negotiations. Scholars working on congregational music insist on formulating a "multi-voiced dialogue" that intertwines methodological approaches, disciplinary perspectives, and the standpoint of scholars in view of the communities that they represent. He speaks about ethnodoxolology, a specialization in missionary studies that emphasizes on locally responsive Christian music that seeks inspiration from ethnomusicology. It is more fitting as applied research as it diverges from the secular component of the ethnographic community. This debate becomes crucial when conceptualizing and discussing the evolution of music that lies on the interstices of the sacred and a localized understanding of indigenous music as noticeable in the case of Goa and Shillong.

Congregationalism suggests the local Christian congregations to be independent and practice self-governance. The "Congregational polity" differs from "Episcopal Polity" that is commonly associated with the Roman Catholic Church, the Orthodox Churches, and the Church of England. In an Episcopal setting, the bishop governs the church. They appoint priests and all the bishops come together to chart out the beliefs and practices of the church. Congregationalism, one of the liberal branches of Protestantism, has a stronghold in the United States of America but its origins can be traced to late-sixteenth-century England (Robert S. Ellwood, Gregory D. Alles, 2008: 101).[28] In my book, congregational instances acquire importance particularly in charting out the sacred sonic sphere of Shillong.

In "Are Adivasis Indigenous?" Gregory Alles (2017)[29] aims at presenting how global indigeneity seeps into local contexts by alluding to his work at Chhotaudepur Taluka in the eastern part of Gujarat. Through certain vignettes, he insists how his field people are aware of the UN Declaration on the Rights of Indigenous People or how a few of them celebrate the Indigenous People's Day. Through the works of various scholars, he also explains how Scheduled Tribes have come to be typified through revisions of various committees. He has explored how the meaning of Adivasi is perceived across different geographies

---

[28] Robert S. Ellwood and Gregory D. Alles, *The Encyclopedia of World Religions* (Chelsea: Infobase Publishing, 2008), 101.

[29] Gregory Alles, "Are Adivasis Indigenous?" in *Handbook of Indigenous Religion*, ed. Greg Johnson and Siv Ellen Kraft (Leiden: Brill, 2017).

of India and the many possibilities of indigeneity. Richard Lee (2006 quoted in Alles, 2017: 256) points toward differential political experiences. Following Karlsson (2009 quoted in Alles, 2017: 256), the author speaks about the extremes associated with indigeneity, one being that caste Hindus are the authentic Indian Indigenes and thus justifying a Hindu nation (Hindutva) and the other being the stance of the Government of India's refusal to consider anyone from India to be indigenous. Xaxa (1999 quoted in Alles, 2017: 256) explains how being Adivasi does not have a limiting connotation such as the original inhabitants of India but rather how in comparison to dominant communities such as Bengalis in West Bengal and Gujaratis in Gujarat, they have no control over the land, forest, river, and resources in the lands that they live in. Alan Barnard (2006 quoted in Alles, 2017: 257) states indigeneity refers to nondominance and self-ascription. Peter Berger (2014 quoted in Alles, 2017: 257) interprets how the notion of indigeneity acquires a presence among the Gadaba in Odisha. "Indigenous indigeneity" looks at how local customs and rituals are organized around specific groups of people, coming from certain villages. "Ascribed indigeneity" is indigeneity allocated by teachers, government officials, and the tourism industry. "Claimed indigeneity" hints at how people make claims about their indigenous selves in public and political realms. Indigeneity thus has a complicated genealogy and inserts itself through various positions. The category "indigenous indigeneity" finds resonance in charting out the meaning of indigenous music in Goa and Shillong.

Indigeneity is also an evolving category, which incorporates the shadows of the past as well as interrogates newer negotiations. In *Ethnographies Returned: The Mobilisation of Ethnographies and the Politicisation of Indigeneity in Ifugao, the Philippines* (2017: 300–6),[30] Jon Henrik Ziegler Remme talks about how the Ifugaos' indigenous religion has moved through various transformations across time and space, through ethnographic imaginations and representations. The government-aided National Commission of Indigenous People (NCIP) was born out of the American colonizers' Bureau of Non-Christian Tribes and it was involved in a particular mode of operation in 1997. Due to extreme vigilance on the part of the government, the UN Permanent Forum on Indigenous Issues in 2014, a joint statement of a variety of Filipino and Cordilleran human and women's rights organizations accused the NCIP for not opposing the militarization of the

---

[30] Jon Henrik Ziegler Remme, "Ethnographies Returned: The Mobilisation of Ethnographies and the Politicisation of Indigeneity in Ifugao, the Philippines," in *Handbook of Indigenous Religion*, ed. Greg Johnson and Siv Ellen Kraft (Leiden: Brill, 2017).

indigenous communities and a series of human rights violations. By immersing into the cosmology of the different worlds like the SkyWorld, the Underworld, the Earth, the Upstream, and the Downstream regions, different processes were orally documented and observed, and even though at a later stage, it felt threatened due to the ushering in of the Pentecostal faith, the communication between the old and young Mumba'i continued. The author has observed how these Ifugao assemblages have made the voices of the past anthropologists an embedded patchwork, making room for newer negotiations and conversations, which he refers to as the "manifest absence." This process of arriving at an understanding of indigeneity in Ifugao helps to ascertain the fractured assemblages of identitarian and indigenous pursuits across Goa and Shillong.

In "Sounds Indigenous: Negotiating Identity in an Era of World Music" (Hackett,2017),[31] Karl Neuenfeldt writes about *didjeridu*, its traditional roots in Northern Australia about a thousand years ago and its uses in contemporary music scene as a symbol of aboriginality with all the technological mediation, ensuring a sonic representation of the indigenous community. In one of the later works, he scrutinizes the work of a successful producer of Australian Indigenous recordings, Nigel Pegrum. The recording studio transforms into an industrial, musical, aesthetic, and cultural space where the musicians introduce their own cultural inferences. When recalling the tourists from the United States and Japan who wish to carry back the earth-connected ancient sounds of didjeridu, Pegrum discusses the challenge of tackling the diverse markets.

> Those kinds of people wouldn't want to [buy something too traditional] although we did do something very traditionally sounding albums . . . which would be bought by the slightly more serious eco-tourist(s) who only wanted, as far as we could tell, the purer form of the didj. But that in itself is a totally other argument because who knows what the didj sounded like five hundred years ago. (Neuenfeldt, 2005: 95)[32]

Neuenfeldt is concerned with the addition of the synthetic sounds to the real sounds of didjeridu in sync with sentiments associated with deserts; while the latter is not a real fact. The entire aural spectrum needs to balance the didjeridu

---

[31] Rosalind Hackett, "Sounds Indigenous: Negotiating Identity in an Era of World Music," in *Handbook of Indigenous Religion*, ed. Greg Johnson and Siv Ellen Kraft (Leiden: Brill, 2017).

[32] Karl Neuenfeldt, "Nigel Pegrum, 'Didjeridu-Friendly Sections,' and What Constitutes an 'Indigenous' CD: An Australian Case Study of Producing 'World Music' Recordings," in *Wired for Sound: Engineering Sounds Indigenous 119 and Technology in Sonic Cultures*, ed. P.D. Greene and T. Porcello (Hanover, CT: Wesleyan University Press and the University Press of New England, 2005), 84–102.

sound with the other vocal and instrumental sounds. However, Pegrum feels that it is difficult to ascertain the "indigenous" owing to the complexity of the indigenous and nonindigenous performers, sounds, and markets.

Indigenous Possibilities in Curricula and Performance: Field Narratives

Music quite naturally featured in the undergraduate colleges of Shillong. I had the opportunity to speak to a few of the teachers at St. Anthony's who informed me about the Indian classical, Western classical, and regional departments of music. There was equal parts emphasis on the mode and the manner of instruction as well as the performativity that emerged from these classroom learnings. This pattern became clearer when I spoke to the head of the Fine Arts Department of Martin Luther Christian University (MLCU). She said that the students from the department perform a designed program toward the spring and autumn semesters. They also have something called the "Music by the Lake," which happens every alternate Saturday. For the project, the students perform at music cafes, namely, Cafe Shillong and Mellow Moods. The students also get invited to perform across universities and outside the university. On every second and third Friday, two student groups organize their rehearsal day. The students choose the items that they wish to perform. They are marked on the basis of their performance. For the cafes, there is also an audience feedback form for group and solo performance. Through this experiential learning, it becomes an extended program to showcase the students to potential employers. She recalls that one of the students was invited to be a regular performer. In this manner, the students get a chance to explore more in the field of music. Not only do they get a chance to develop their creativity and artistry in music, they also entertain others at the same time. Indigenous music is being popularized now. A collaboration with All Saints Cathedral Youth Fellowship and National Service Scheme, *Carols under the Christmas Tree*, accommodated indigenous music. The Master's batch of 2015–17 took part in this project. The board of studies modifies the course once in two years. This is as per the choice-based credit system as notified by the UGC. The students have to take minors and they can choose from nutrition, English, event management. Social work promotes Khasi culture and music. Subjects like guitar, piano, duitara, KSing Kynthei, and voice are open to other departments in MLCU. This is similar to an open course or interdisciplinarity. The Fine Arts Department is a young department that was inaugurated in 2007. For the purposes of evaluation of bi-annual concert recitals, externals are held accountable and for the performances by the lake, the mantle is upon the teachers. Usually, performances include one indigenous music and one Western music and there is a combination too as students sometimes like to go for experimental music. They have the Bachelors of Music and Masters of Music, and the department is looking to expand in order to include PhD as well. Of all the seven faculty members associated with the Music and Fine Arts Department, MLCU, six are ex-students and only one of them is not from MLCU. For the purpose of performances outside of the university, students went to Tura in 2012–13 and Delhi in 2015. They participated in Octave 2008 (a program of the Sangeet Natak Academy in Kerala) and the North Eastern Service, Tripura, in the same year. They also participated in the Traditional Music Festival by the Arts and Culture Department, Mizoram, in 2009 (Personal Interview, March 2018). During my fieldwork, I remember attending an event where the students from MLCU were pulling off one of their public concerts, and I still remember their use of the familiar intonation, strumming of duitara, and appropriate local drumming to frame an idea of new music embossed with indigenous strokes.

Shillong Chamber Choir, founded in 2001 by Neil Nongkynrih, has always used language to break the structure of the Western notion of the choir. Using "Medley as a genre" (this will be explored in detail in Chapter 4), the choir managed to fuse together elements of the sacred and secular. Using the recurrent trope of Bollywood music, the choir left a lasting impression on the Indian subcontinent. To challenge colonial expectations, they incorporated and experimented with many regional languages of India, including their own, Khasi. This quest continues till date and their recent album *Come Home Christmas* (2020) has Christmas songs sung in Hebrew, Aramaic, Urdu, Parsi, Khasi, and English. In all their interviews across news channels and newspaper articles, the choir confirmed how the year in lockdown had actually helped them take a break from continuous touring and focus on producing an album. How is an excursion into multiple languages a symbol of exercising indigeneity? Rather, the approach to enable vernacular and usually marginalized dialects to share a space to articulate a global Christianity is what sets this project apart. Indigeneity becomes a motif to reclaim Christmas which by happenstance appears as a predominantly Western/Europeanized festival and ritual.[33]

---

[33] Anurag Tagat, "Hear Shillong Chamber Choir's Multilingual Holiday Album 'Come Home Christmas," *RollingStoneIndia*, December 18, 2020, https://rollingstoneindia.com/shillong-chamber -choir-holiday-album-come-home-christmas/.

Aradhon, a contemporary choir in Goa founded by Omar De Loiola Pereira, specializes in improvising traditional Konkani hymns and uses the classical guitar and keyboard as accompaniments. During the 2018 Monte Festival, they presented a range of sacred hymns that were sung in Konkani, Latin, and English. He runs a YouTube Channel called Sounds from Goa, whereby he records choral renditions with his group Aaradhon and contemporary folk songs with another group Entre Nos. One of the featured videos is the Konkani hymn "Mari Matek Ballok Zala," written by Manohar Rai Sardesai and set to music by Micael Martins. Arranged by Omar, it speaks about how mother nature partakes in celebrating Mary's motherhood. This was one of the sacred hymns that formed a part of their 2018 repertoire. Aaradhon Choir, in their 2021 Monte Festival repertoire of Goan folk songs in the choral arrangement, had used gumott as an accompanying instrument, something that I had not witnessed during my fieldwork years from 2013 to 2018. I decided to follow up on the choice of their repertoire for that year's festival. Despite the harrowing second wave of the pandemic almost numbing our senses in India, Omar was kind enough to indulge me in a telephonic conversation. I discovered that he now focuses on three groups. I mentioned two of the groups already but he spoke of a new group called the Invox, which concerns itself with nonsacred music from Goa. He mentioned that most likely, the members of Invox and Aaradhon will be the same. Omar had initially wanted to perform under the banner of Invox for the 2021 Monte Festival as their presentation was geared toward making Goan folklore more representational by expanding its scope beyond mando. They were performing along with the renowned Goan Fadista, Sonia Shirshat. They still performed as Aradhon as the registration was underway. However, because it was nonsacred music, their venue was naturally the courtyard of the chapel rather than the inside of the chapel. The songs chosen included a Goan lullaby, a deknni Medley,[34] a mando, and a polyphonic fado. Gumott had been a cognizant choice since it was part of Goan folk music. Mando, a sophisticated folk musical tradition, looked to the guitar, violin, and keyboard for melody but the rhythm was set by the gumott. While distinguishing between mando and deknni, there were some definitive differences that Omar pointed out. "While mando is a couple's dance and is closer to form and feel to the waltz and tango, acquiring a regal label. Although dekni is not a couple's dance, it is danced in numbers. Thus, it's not individualistic in nature. Deknni, performed by women, showcases

---

[34] Deknni repertoire can be traced back to the devdasi or kolvont tradition of temple dancers https://folkways.si.edu/mando-of-goa/india-world/music/album/smithsonian.

a much more rustic background and is individualistic in nature." At this point, it becomes pertinent to reach out to schools and universities to at least pass on the playability of the gumott. However, gumott is always learned through informal channels and a consistent mode of improving on the playing styles finds fruition during mando competitions, which is discussed in Chapter 4. Here, it is also important to understand the principle of curation adopted by Omar.

> I like to pick stuff that have an emotional connect or beautiful pieces that have gone unnoticed. Then there are those songs that I haven't heard in a long time and the nostalgia assumes center stage. I try to connect my trio or choir in a manner that the priority is accorded to the emotional and the nostalgic content. For instance, Dol Mhojea Bai,[35] the Goan lullaby that we did, loosely translated as rock my girl child, is a song from a Konkani film *Nirmonn* that became popular in the late 1960s and 1970s. Take the song Sobit Amchem Goem[36] (our Goa is beautiful), which is a poem set to music, [and] has various versions. I remember performing this twenty years ago and today, with this bigger platform, I wanted to take it further, taking a slightly different approach. It sets out as a mando ad lib where the soloist takes on unrestricted singing and the guitar and the chords follow the voice. The instruments need to be very attentive in this case for the two verses as the rhythm follows the voice. We also have an *alaap* in the middle of the mando. (Zoom Interview with O on May 7, 2021)

This is equivalent to spinning a new perspective on a traditional template, either by inducing a recall value wired around nostalgia or by contributing toward the curation of a repository of Goan traditional sounds. The emotional and nostalgic binder also pushes toward preserving the Latin vibe incorporating Spanish, Brazilian, and Portuguese alongside the Konkani folk. The definition of indigenous finds a rapture through mixed lineages and geographies in Goa. Thus, what emanates is a complicated notion of indigeneity where native and European folk contribute to a soulful stitching of emotion and belongingness. During the recent interview, he confessed that being the conductor, founder, and the working sound engineer for the three groups, creating music as a group without a common template such as a backing vocal, the sounds will never be the same as making real-time music. Audio production is still something he is exploring and so far, his crash course in Australia and timely inputs from his friends help him sail through difficult moments.

---

[35] Words by C. Alvares and music by Franz Fernand.
[36] Poem by Manohar Rai Sardesai.

I also spoke to a percussionist, Carlos Gonsalves. At the age of six or seven, he started out with making sounds using pots and pans to be able to imitate the sounds that he heard at the Tiatr performance his uncle took him to. He explored bass drums and drill drums during school and college. He later became the drummer for Royal Challenge Bangalore team. He even played for FC Goa. However, what he really wants to pursue is to make gumott a symbol of Goa. He has traveled to China and Malaysia with the Bauls of Bengal under the banner of Banglanatak dot.com. Gumott was used by Adivasis before and he took it to the Ministry of Art and Culture. Gumott started to be used in traditional feasts in villages like Sangolda and Saligao. For performing songs with traditional music, each one had to get coconut shells or gumot (earthen pots). Usually, monitor lizard skin used to be heated to get the tone but the Ministry of Environment banned it. Nowadays, goat skin is being used. Older musicians still have the collection with monitor lizard skin. These gumots are hung in the kitchen. The instruments need to be kept warm. Fire is used on the side, which helps to stretch or tighten the tone. The earthen pot is tied with coconut fibers or strings to hold it together. It is essential to understand how muds are mixed. This is an exchange that passes down from family to family. It must be baked at a certain temperature. The potter has a wheel and makes sure that there is a small vent downward for sound. This art of mixing mud is a special skill and unfortunately, few are left and the art is dying. Gumott is used in traditional weddings and Ganesh festivals. There are different patterns associated with gumott when playing for temples or during *zagor*. He created his own patterns/sound by playing solo and making a big band sound. It is ultimately the rhythm that captures the audience. There is a class or hierarchy associated with the sound of the gumott. He wants to change it. It should not only belong to kitchens but hallrooms as well. (Zoom interview with Carlos on May 7, 2021)

> I use my own ideas to get different sounds. Like the Djembe sound, there should be a spontaneous sound. I rattle the skin, use it as a ghatam. By making sounds like dum-dum, evoking creativity on glass bottles. I scat on the mouth. The rhythm should be as smooth as raining or talking, a scooter passing by or birds chirping. The gumott originated in the coastal belts amongst the Kunbis in the interiors of Goa at Cancona. Most of the players were fisherfolks, paddy tappers or temple workers. I want to put gumott on international maps. I have also started teaching at Blind school and at Nirmalla. I do shows as well as teach. Now women are also playing, earlier it used to be male instrument. Music starts from folk or tradition and that is why Gumott becomes central to Goa's culture. Without roots, trees cannot stand.

The Goa University Choir,[37] led by Santiago Luserdi Girelli, had the first Ketevan World Music Festival in 2016. I was part of an organizing team of that festival. There were musical performances and a symposium series. The lectures explored various syncretic traditions in the domain of sacred music and also looked at Western art music and folk music traditions in different cultures. When it came to the repertoire for the week-long festival, there was colonial sacred music from Cathedrals in Mexico, Guatemala, Bolivia, and Peru. "Lux Aeterna" by the 1943-born American composer Morten Lauridsen introduced Gregorian chants. This apart, there was an integration of Medieval, Renaissance, and contemporary sounds. There were Bach's select arias and choruses of cantatas and passions. There were also a few pieces from Requiem and Armed Man by the 1944 Welsh composer Karl Jenkins. We also experienced Jewish and Sephardic music, flamenco and Indian classical music. Canadian kathak dancer Joanna De Souza surprised the audience by enacting the life and journey of the sixteenth-century Georgian queen Ketevan at the St. Augustine ruins to mark the beginning of the festival. As a participant along with many trained musicians from the Goa University Choir, Bombay Chamber Orchestra, and the Seville Choir, it literally taught me how difficult vocalizations can be unless one is closely following the conductor's instructions like "sotto voce," "bel canto," and punctuated gestures. I particularly recall the piece "Sanctus," where certain moments of coming together and fading out brought out the essence of the phrasings written by Jenkins. The song "I Offer You Peace" by the same composer required an appeal toward harmony which demonstrated not only strength but also a certain touch of softness in the message. Some of the songs also used percussion instruments from different cultures along with the strings and woodwind sections of the orchestra.

All of these specifically organic developments chart out the emic categories that contribute to the making of the indigenous. The experiential learning phenomena within the ambit of the UGC-approved music curriculum, a multilingual immersion using snippets of widely known classical and carol compositions, and the use of pointedly "folk" instruments or instruments prominent to other musical traditions speak of a certain essence of interculturality and decoloniality that surpasses the initial missionary forays into vernacularization as per denominational prerequisites.

---

[37] Sebanti Chatterjee, "Youngest Festival in Goa: Ketevan World Sacred Music Festival," *Serenade Magazine*, March 29, 2016, https://serenademagazine.com/reviews/youngest-festival-goa-ketevan-world-sacred-music-festival/ (accessed May 31, 2021).

Toward Sonic Interculturality

The aforementioned works attest to the fact that indigeneity is arguably one of the primary features to understand sacred singularities. Despite the presence of an uncomfortable veil of coloniality and repeated discussions about how the independent nation-states structure their devotional principles stemming from the colonial, interculturality allows newer patterns to ensue. British rule during the mid-nineteenth century in West Africa brought about transformations in Christian, commercial, educational, political, and cultural realms (Collins and Richards, 1982 quoted in Newell, 2011: 340). In situating the particular and the universal in global cultural flows, being cosmopolitan equates to being homeless, free from nationalism and local cultural references (Hannerz, 1990 quoted in Newell, 2011: 337). To understand new social relationships in West Africa, a para-colonial framework that accounts for the local cultural productivity across generations, together with and in addition to the British influence, becomes valuable (Newell, 2011).[38] Decoloniality does not obliterate colonialism. Rather, as a praxis, decoloniality motivates a multiplicity of discernment arrived at, through a colonial wound impacting everyone, uniquely and unequally. Delving into the historical contexts of Ecuador and Bolivia, Mignolo advocates for indigenous-led struggles to establish a plurinational democracy, drawing upon decolonial interculturality (Mignolo and Walsh, 2018).[39] Thinking through the ideas of "para-colonial," "decoloniality," and "decolonial interculturality," I want to introduce the concept of sonic interculturality which negotiates various meanings of colonial as well as indigenous imprints by foregrounding sonic materiality. The sonic materiality is not restricted to the trajectories of the universal and particular but rather builds on an aural dialog that accommodates and expands indigeneity and cosmopolitanism.

To understand this, I return to the concept of the "soulful of the fado." Lila Ellen Gray writes:

> for most fadistas and listeners, an idea of learning had nothing to do with fado. For many, the concept of learning was anathema to fado, canceled it out; either one is born with fado na alma (fado in the soul) or one is not. Ser fadista não se ensina, não se aprende, nasce logo quando nasce uma pessoa (One is not taught, nor does one learn to be a fadista; one is born a fadista) . . . . To admit

---

[38] Stephenie Newell, "Para Colonial Networks: Some Speculations on Local Readerships," *Colonial West Africa, Interventions: International Journal of Postcolonial Studies* 3, no. 3 (2001): 336–54.

[39] Mignolo and Walsh, *On Decoloniality* (Durham: Duke University Press, 2018).

to learning might be to reveal an essential lack, to não ser fadista (to not be fadista), as singing with sentimento (feeling) is widely understood as something that cannot be learned. (Gray, 2013: 28)[40]

This notion of being born into the world of fado is complicated because of the multiple origins that it stems from and the sentimental world it offers through its vocalization and instrumentation. Even listening is an act of feeling. Fados are characterized by feeling-filled silences that are driven by the affective aura of the fadista's vocalization. In a way, it calls for a collective intimacy which teaches the audience to interiorize the sentimentality expressed by the singer. Fado's distinctive attribute of not constituting a point of learning came to be challenged during 2000–10 soon after the institutionalization of fado increased. This was partly due to UNESCO's label of being an intangible heritage in 2011 along with the refashioning of the Fado Museum in Alfama, Lisbon, in 2008. The origin of the fado goes back to Mouraria, which is the "fabled home" of not only the nineteenth-century prostitute Fadista Maria Severa but also many other well-known fadistas. Bairro Alto, with its carefree, lowly airs, and Alfama, the dockside neighborhood displaying racial hybridity due to the presence of Africans and Portuguese, figure prominently as imageries of fado's inception as well as spaces, recognizably touristy. The author uses the term "sentimentalize" to refer to the poetic and musical signification of nostalgia which becomes the trope to understand the placename fados. The nostalgia is built around an improbable beauty or an ambiguous longing for the past, and sometimes both. Fados also have an association with criminality and marginalization as expressed through fados titled *Meia Laranja*. Fado, as a musical genre with its impulsive mannerism to plot syncretic recurrences, organizes topographies of affect and public feeling that intersperse placemaking and lived experiences of the communities who belong to these places. Fados also have an association with social protest put forth by left-leaning anti-fascist groups, yet the genre also flourished during Salazar's era of *estado novo*, marked with extreme religious conservatism and dictatorship from 1932 onward. Much like the famous fadista Amalia, whose vocalizations do not promise a fidelity to either of the two ideologies, the genre has a fractured sense of belonging. Furthermore, the nineteenth-century figure of Maria Severa, who according to legends brought fado to the aristocracy by sleeping with a count in the early 1800s and died in her early twenties in 1846,

---

[40] Lila Ellen Gray, *Fado Resounding: Affective Politics and Urban Life* (Durham: Duke University Press, 2013).

features as a bohemian trope in stories, lyrics, and visualizations of fado. Some lyrics even mark her early death to usher in a deep sadness, which underlies the affect of the fado. The genre is depicted as an anthropomorphic version of an abandoned child (Gray, 2013: 28, 63, 114, 116, 130, 135, 163).

The idea of sonic interculturality is noticeable in the ethnographic accounts of Goa and Shillong. Indigeneity stands out as a connecting thread between the identities that the communities belonging to these regions fall back upon to navigate through their multiple stories of origin. Catholicism and Protestantism have their individual religious trajectories. The religious denominations deal with how they engaged with local communities as a part of their empire-building strategy in the garb of civilizational tropes. Choral traditions which are an integral part of these worship rituals interacted with the local worldviews to generate sacred repertoires interlaced with indigenous sound patterns. This interaction is labeled as sonic interculturality which transcends and transforms colonial associations but also retains the sentiments that have been passed down. A certain kind of nostalgia comes through in the process of envisaging choral voices and folkloric sonic traditions as observed in the vignettes from Goa. Gumott, a folkloric instrument which has its origin among lower-caste groups, somehow becomes part of the sanitized and elitist folk traditions of Goa, namely the mandos, and enters the nonsacred choral collective. The voices are arranged in a four-part structure akin to that of a choir, which hints at innovations not only within the sacred fold but also within the folkloric frameworks. This sonic interculturality incorporates the Portuguese cultural stains which have now been reinterpreted as an indigenous innovation. Where does loyalty belong? How do voice and genre sentimentalize indigeneity? How does one locate the soulful in the making of the indigenous? In Goa, the sacred and the folk maintain different markers but engage in aural dialogs across genres. The indigeneity builds on the sonic interculturality by specific placemaking in the form of home rehearsal spaces and sound studios and festival sites. The Music Department of Martin Luther Christian University in Shillong demonstrates an educational curriculum that maintains separate choices and engagements for the sacred, the regional, and the Western classical genres. Khasi music through specific intonations, duitara, and the KSing go back to the myths related to Ri Hynniewtrep (the land of the seven huts). When it comes to the sacred choral renditions, duitara is common during special services on Sunday. These instruments are synonymous with local culture amid those who speak Khasi, Garo, and Pnar. The placemaking when it comes to the East Khasi Hills in Meghalaya refers to recreational parks, state-managed and public

Figure 2.1 Choir rehearsal at the Mawkhar Presbyterian Church, January 2015. Photo credit Sebanti Chatterjee.

Figure 2.2 Goa University Choir performing at the Monte Chapel during Monte Festival 2014. Photo Credit: Old Goa Music Society.

auditoriums, exam halls, and churches. The language in which one chooses to render their vocalizations becomes an important assertion of one's identity as explained through the recent album of the Shillong Chamber Choir. One of their key ethics woven into the performance narratives is to bring languages that are not mainstream to the Western opera, carols, and Christianity at the center stage.

Figure 2.3 Laitumukhrah Cathedral Shillong during Eucharist procession in November 2014. Photo Sebanti Chatterjee.

The sonic materiality comes through with the vocalization patterns, specific choral arrangements, and the use of particular instruments, intonations, and languages that speak of these fractured belonging, which is also indicative of the soulful expressed through indigeneity. The following chapter will explore in depth how the choirs in Shillong generate repertoire across different spectrums (see Figures 2.1–2.3).

3

From Loft to the Recording Studio

Shillong Diaries

What Brings You to Shillong? Introduction[1]

Shillong, the capital of Meghalaya that became an independent state of India in 1970, originally piqued my interest as a field-site after I read about an opera singer from Meghalaya making headlines in the year 2012 at the Season 4 of India's Got Talent. I started reading more about Toshanbor Singh Nongbet and discovered about the Aroha Choir. This was during a time when I was looking to finalize my PhD proposal and was hoping to expand my field-site beyond familiar landscapes. Even before finalizing my PhD idea, I started a conversation over email with the founder of Aroha Choir, Pauline Warjri. We had planned a phone conversation which didn't materialize at that point. Much later, when I visited Shillong in 2014 and acquainted myself with the winners of the Season 1 of India's Got Talent, Shillong Chamber Choir, I was again directed to Aroha Choir. Neil Nongkynreih, founder of the Shillong Chamber Choir, and Pauline Warjri were siblings. Fondly known as Aunty Pauline, I felt welcome the very first time we met. On learning about my project and methodology, she offered her home as an option for accommodation. On conversing further, I was thrilled to discover that she remembered our email exchanges from a year ago. *She jokingly told me so you heard about us before the Shillong Chamber Choir? In a way, you came in our pursuit.* That indeed became a pursuit of a sort, joining them from one rehearsal to the other, following them to schools, Christmas concerts,

---

[1] Parts of this chapter have been published in the following journals-
Chatterjee, S. (2020). Performing Bollywood Broadway: Shillong Chamber Choir as Bollywood's Other. Society and Culture in South Asia, 6(2), 304–327. https://doi.org/10.1177/2393861720923812; https://cafedissensus.com/2020/03/21/promisesof-thekwai-discoveringvoices-thatsing/

recording studios, and even securing an audience invite at the Rashtrapati Bhavan in Delhi. One of the members gave me a nickname "choir-hunter" and they soon got used to my endless scribblings in my field diary, to documentation over mobile cameras, occasionally on a DLSR camera, and frequent socialization with members outside fieldwork parameters.

My engagement with the founder and the members of the [2]Shillong Chamber Choir was completely different from Aroha Choir. I reached out to the manager of the choir, K, through the help of a journalist-musician-interlocutor and a Shillong Chamber Choir fan from Goa, N. They were set apart as a celebrity choir after their magnificent win in the Season 1 of India's Got Talent in 2010. I had even sent them my PhD proposal as I had intended to do an in-depth ethnography on them. Upon my arrival, I was informed by K that they all had a meeting regarding my proposal and were willing to participate in my research. Everyone was warm and welcoming and quickly told me about their daily recording rehearsals as I witnessed two members trying out vocalizing, each time incorporating inputs from the other members on how to make the sound rounder and find comfort in the chosen register. I was given a tour of their apartment *Whispering Pines*, where all the members live. I also had my first and only interview with Padmashri Neil Nongkynreih, face to face. They had given me a list of choirs that I should explore in Shillong which included Aroha Choir and Serenity Choir. They told me to explore all the other choirs and then return to them. A friend from my university had passed me a contact of someone who sang with the Serenity Choir. Further into the fieldwork, I discovered that at least, when it came to these three choirs, there was some overlap or familiarity among the members. Eventually, my association with the Shillong Chamber Choir took the form of "green-room" ethnography where I saw them live and interacted with the members during their performances in Shillong, Guwahati, Calcutta, and Delhi. Memories from ethnography sometimes remind us of missed opportunities. One such moment was when I had reached too late and ended up not being a part of a personal concert organized by the Shillong Chamber Choir.

This chapter discusses the repertoire of the choir. It explores how sophisticated, religious, and kitschy sounds blend together in a Medley. The latter becomes a modality arrived at through novelty and theatrics as well as a musical genre in itself. The stylistic representations and the Bollywood trope are

---

[2] Padma Shri Neil Nongkynreih passed away on January 6, 2022, due to perforated ulcer. With the founding of the choir, he introduced choral music in an interesting popular genre format and put highlighted Northeast India, particularly Meghalaya on the global map.

explained through Deleuze's *territorialisation* and Feld's *Schizophonic Mimesis.* At the outset, Welsh Calvinist influence in the Khasi and Lushai Hills helps map the religious and musical trajectories. Then it looks at the motivation and possibilities in curation of music. Shillong Chamber Choir gave legitimacy to the procedure of Bollywoodization of a choir. Choral music specifically reinvents itself through the reality TV show and the vocalist as an icon parameter. Thus, there is always a popular spin to the look and feel of the final Medley. One finds a bit of Western classical, solemn sacred, nostalgic Bollywood melody, 1950's jazz, indigenous intonations all tied together by beautiful, coordinated harmonization. This helps in understanding their artistic choices and creative processes. The piano and orchestral accompaniments are mere ornamentations as vocal icons emerge as soloists and as a collective. The theatricality shows itself through the stylish outfits and well-organized dance and gestures. The last section looks at how Aroha Choir does it differently while embracing and embodying Medley. Medley remains the connecting node as is evident in the way both choirs introduce themselves as a "multi-genre" and a "masala" choir. Rehearsals, performances, and recordings encounter a sociality structured by cultural locations, cosmopolitan outlines, and identitarian outlook. Sacrality finds an aperture through entertainment. It demonstrates a different tone and intensity as its melds into realms that are not sacred. This leaves us wondering if sacred music can also have a fan following outside religious pursuits and how musical intentions can be embellished and crafted through innovative artistic interpretations. Thus, a choir whose original role is to aid in Christian worship takes on a different perspective outside its usual gospel reincarnations.

Cusp of Sacrality, New Technologies, and Creative Processes

A significant moment to consider here is how the Shillong landscape pins down an otherwise sacred genre to a popular-music category by embracing Medley as a trope. Drawing from Gramsci's relative autonomy of sociocultural epicycles and varying inertia, Richard Middleton addresses moments of radical situational change through "bourgeois revolution" of the eighteenth century driven by market forces, to the "mass culture" phase dictated by internationalization, followed by "pop culture" moment after the Second World War with the aid of various forms of technologies (Middleton, 1990: 10–13 quoted in Manuel, 1992). Peter Manuel refers to Middleton's second "radical situational change" to emphasize how film culture such as Bollywood represents a "culture of mechanical reproduction" and how for a bulk of population from South Asia and beyond, Indian films provide a window to fantasy, fashion, moral values, and discourses and in a similar manner film-music culture figures prominently in the domain of production. It is quite common to find South Asians remodeling film melodies in localized flavors incorporating fresh lyrics, songs, and dances throughout live presentations. The problem lies with the fact that in India, mainstream Bollywood cinema tends to be dominated by a homogenous song style, in Hindi, focused on romantic love and is usually brought together by a clique of producers and sound-alike singers (Manuel, 1993: 60, 62).[3] In a later section, I discuss more about the sound and tone of Bollywood music but suffice to say that reorganization of old film-music melodies is something that existing production and consumption patterns are well attuned to. What makes Shillong Chamber Choir particularly innovative in this regard is their ability to blend sacred music, an excluded geography (Meghalaya forming the Northeast part of India), and a mainstream popular-music genre, Bollywood, dictated by a new technological impulse in the format of a reality TV show. Through the process, Medley emerges as a genre in itself as no particular musical genre shines on its own and can only be experienced in small doses packaged as choral harmony.

Religion has always found itself in various mediums of technological expressions. Indian films and their musical manifestations look toward religion and mythology for inspiration as observable in the context of South Indian cinema. Stephen Putnam Hughes[4] writes about how region, religion, and film sound shape the evolution of Tamil cinema's storylines and consumerism. He writes that earlier most of the South Indian films were produced in Bombay or Calcutta studios until Madras had its own film studio. The treatment and the texture of the films through 1931 to 1935 usually fell within the categories of the mythological (purana) or devotional (bhakti films). Even through the 1940s, films themed around Hindu religion were far more compared to other topics. At the very commencement, Indian mythological silent films were in vogue. Tamil bhakti singing poets have a connection with rich Tamil literary tradition going back to the sixth century that insists on Tamil-speaking people having a distinct national identity. Tamil cinema managed to give wings to this imagined heritage whereby audiences became complicit in a particular

---

[3] Manuel Peter, *Cassette Culture: Popular Music and Technology in North India* (Chicago: Chicago University Press, 1993).

[4] Stephen Putnam Hughes, "Tamil Mythological Cinema and the Politics of Secular Modernism," in *Aesthetic Formations: Media, Religion, and the Senses,* ed. Birgit Meyers (New York: Palgrave Macmillan, 2009), 93.

Tamil religious past. Slowly, social films emerged as a genre in Tamil cinema. The stories were usually adapted from popular novels and dramas, and plots focused on crime, romance, comedy, satire, and sometimes stunts (Hughes, 2009: 95, 98, 111). Although Shillong Chamber Choir gave a new mien to Bollywood music through choral arrangements, they also sang songs in different languages. For instance, they have a song called "Madi Madi" in Malayalam for the film *Goodbye December* in 2013. This was a debut movie project for the Shillong Chamber Choir. Let us return to the discussion about songs themed around religion in films. It is of course not a new phenomenon but finding a texture and a materiality that makes hymns and melodic romantic utterances merge in the right proportion is what makes the Shillong Chamber Choir special.

Praying does not always thrive on attaining the mystical guidance and secret wisdom possessed by the greatest saints. One can experience the hidden meaning of sacred through scriptures and the architecture of knowledge it outlines. This is how religion transforms in public. Brian Larkin[5] discussed how Islam navigates itself through new technological infrastructure and dwells in the public sphere. The nature of divine takes on a new energy as the collective experience is different from an otherwise intimate activity. Nigerian cleric Sheikh Abubakar Gumi founded Izala, one of the significant religious movements in West Africa. He was easily identifiable by both supporters and opponents through his radio and TV broadcast along with their cassette replications. Izala focused on a religion rooted in surfaces and not depth. Gumi popularized his *tafsir* through these broadcasts. He held that the holy texts of Islam, Quran, and Hadith helped build knowledge rather than the magical epiphany (*baraka*) or spiritual overflow (*fayda*) of a Sufi Sheikh. Gumi's methodology combined Arabic and Western pedagogy since he was a product of the School for Arabic Studies (SAS). He also translated his teachings into vernacular along with translating portions of Hadith and Quran into Hausa (Larkin, 2009: 117–27).[6] This shift in perspective from intimate to public becomes interesting to understand how faith organically structures and shapes the musical meanings choral music entails. The stylistic rendition is choral harmony but the intent of the collective is the wisdom and strength drawn from the Bible. Both the founders and choral conductors from Shillong discussed in this chapter dedicate their art, training, and creative process to faith.

[5] Brian Larkin, "Islamic Renewal, Radio, and the Surface of Things Brian Larkin," in *Aesthetic Formations: Media, Religion, and the Senses*, ed. Birgit Meyer (New York: Palgrave Macmillan, 2009), 117.

[6] Brian Larkin, "Islamic Renewal and Radio and the Surface of the Things," in *Aesthetic Formations: Media, Religion and the Senses*, ed. Birgit Meyer (USA: Palgrave Macmillan, 2009).

Choral Voices as Ethnographic Objects

Locating choral sounds and presenting them in a manner that extends the possibilities of the content and form of the genre and showcasing interstices of the public and personal attributes of art, faith, and the landscape are particularly telling about Shillong. Choral voices emerge as ethnographic objects scripting stories of marginalization, evangelization, and cosmopolitanism. Otherwise known for their jazz, rock, and big band scene, for the first time Shillong found itself under the global gaze because of its Christian musical tradition. Instead of the otherwise famous Graham Boys Choir in Darjeeling or the Mizo gospel voices, Shillong, one of the most cosmopolitan cities in the Northeast India, found itself being recognized for their harmonic suppleness.

> In situ approaches to installations enlarge the ethnographic object by expanding its boundaries to include more of what was left behind, even if only in replica, after the object was excised from its physical, social, and cultural settings. Because the metonymic nature of ethnographic objects invites mimetic evocations of what was left behind, in situ approaches to installation tend toward environmental and re-creative displays. . . . At their most mimetic, in situ installations include live persons, preferably actual representatives of the cultures on display.[7]

Later in the text, the author, while discussing who has the necessary qualifications to perform culture, speaks of a tacit understanding of how descent gains currency over consent in situations of cultural performances. In folklife festivals, there are clearcut instructions regarding those performing having the insider knowledge of the art form in question. Of the ones who absorb the trade of a particular community despite being an outsider may or may not have the license to perform. Those without a license are assigned to watch. Those with a license earn the title of a revivalist at best (Kirshenblatt-Gimblett, 1998: 20, 75). This becomes important in spelling out how choral formats became an ingenious mode to introduce Medley as a genre. Ever since the success of the reality TV show, as a region associated with Christianity due to the Welsh Calvinist missionary influence, Meghalaya, one of the lesser politically volatile zones of the Northeast, became prominent to the Indian subcontinent and the world at large as they were seen as natural vocalists for whom faith is fundamental to their existence. Here, the situation is twofold. On the one hand, choral harmony

---

[7] Barbara Kirshenblatt-Gimblett, *Destination Culture* (Berkley: University of California Press, 1998).

insists on the insider knowledge earned through descent while introducing Medley as a genre makes them revivalists. Further, a few questions pop up: Which ethnographic fragment is the authentic version of culture? How does one appreciate indigenous Khasi music if choral voices are seen to authenticate one integral aspect of cultural authenticity? Can culture and religion cohabit yet demonstrate degrees of differentiation and isolation? What determines the folkloric repository of colonized geography? Is the indigenous totally devoid of outside influences? How important are collaborations and reimagination of genres in crafting narratives about communities? Does the tessitura of sacrality differ as it journeys from the loft to the recording studio?

In his ethnography about the Songhay sensory world,[8] Paul Stoller gives specific ways of listening to the sounds of the musical instruments and poetry while immersing into the spirit possession ceremonies. The *godji* (violin), one of the most sacred instruments, emits a crying sound and *gasi* (drums) naturally "clacks" or "rolls" during the possession and *sorko* (the praise singer) chants the names of the spirits along with their genealogies and supernatural exploits. The medium's body undergoes transformation due to the impact of the musical instruments and praise names and slowly possession takes place (Stoller, 1989: 109, 112). This essential layering of specific sonic emotions and textures outline the coming together of the spirit possession ceremonies. In a similar manner, Aroha Choir, who also adopt Medley as a mode of presentation, puts enormous emphasis on the tonal qualities and vocalic expressivities of individual singers. To ensure a seamless choral harmonization, layered attributes of the sonic become the ethnographic fragments to render it a holistic meaning.

On the question of attaining cultural authenticity, understanding the rootedness and growth of musical categories becomes important. Janaki Bakhle makes an interesting argument about the modernization and secularization project of music in the late nineteenth and twentieth centuries. In the entire premise of rationalization, there was deprecation toward colonial rule. While Indian classical music held onto a subcontinental appeal, never shadowed by "Western classical chords, orchestration, or harmony," it showcased linkages to repertoires of classical music reliant on mysticism and spirituality. Many of these offshoots are famously known as *qawwalis*, *kirtans*, or *bhajans*. She also refers to the spatiality and the content of Indian music to be secular and religious at the same time if one is willing to break free of the definitions found in Protestant

---

[8] Paul Stoller, *The Taste of Ethnographic Things* (Philadelphia: University of Pennsylvania Press, 1989).

Christianity and the Colonial empire building. She also finds Paluskar's use of bhakti as a state-sponsored Brahminized culture industry in the same league as Hindu extremism in India. Even though he welcomed women as a part of this schema, Paluskar aimed at shaping a specific Indian female subjectivity dwelling on the notions of chastity, spirituality, docility, and a Hindu religiosity. Bhatkande also demonstrated ample prejudices against music performers but he ensured that the texts in Sanskrit, Bengali, Tamil, Persian, and Urdu, which were part of his curriculum, sparked off critical debates rather than being treated as sacred texts. At the same time, he also opposed the idea that Indian music particularly required a sacred descent. Taking the two figures associated with modernizing Indian classical music, Bakhle puts forth a plea not to abandon music's association with secularism in totality and rather explore its conflicted but constant evolution (Bakhle, 2008: 262, 271, 278, 282, 284). Thus, gospel music and choral music with its clearcut lineage in Protestant Christianity and Colonial empire building also shows capacity for stylistic transformation and differential meanings in unfamiliar spatial settings. This also indicates how culture and religion coexist and cocreate newer communitarian expressions.

Regional music steeped into devotional tropes has the capacity to make a mark on politics of the state. Stefan Fiol writes about "Nauchami Narayana," which became the chart-topping song in the history of Garhwali-language popular music within a couple of months of its release and was partially responsible for the loss of the Congress Party in the state assembly elections of 2007. The Gramophone Company of India (HMV) and All India Radio had monopoly over the airwaves and music recordings under sale till the 1970s, which censored any content critical of the state. This continued even after the media industries were decentralized. Popular music making commentary on regional politics was also not understood in a larger scale by the companies that produced music as they did not feel confident about the depth of support and the commercial potential as they were not aware of the intricacies of the politics in the mountains. For instance, Rama Cassette company, a Delhi-based private music company was skeptical to produce Narendra Singh Negi's album *Uttarakhandyu Jago* ("Rise Up, Uttarakhandis!") in the early 1990s, which was a protest song album backing the Uttarakhand movement. They had eventually released the album but Negi himself had to organize his finances. The same artist released "Nauchami Narayana" only after retiring from his government post at the Samachar Vibhag (News and Information Division). The name of the Narayana evokes the mischievous and charming Hindu deity Krishna as well as the then-serving minister of Congress. The composition incorporates features of the *jagar* ritual which is allied to spiritual possession and awakening of powerful gods and deities (*dhunyal*) through control over the human medium's body (*lehn/raunsi*) and dance (*mannan*). Later, as a response to the clamor caused due to the song, Negi had released another song election called "Negi Da Yana Git Na Laga" ("Brother Negi, Don't Sing This Kind of Song"), where he explicitly talks about the precarious position of a government employee prohibited to compose and sing politically charged regional language songs (Fiol, 2012: 447, 462, 468). This discussion about Uttarakhandi popular music and its role in determining the political issues and aberrations of the state bring to light how regional language songs are capable of shedding light on specific problems as well as popularize songs and ethnic communities that do not otherwise enjoy national limelight. On the one hand, regional language songs may act as vehicles of protest and question state power and, on the other hand, regional language songs or ethnic community representations may also emerge as cultural envoys. Shillong Chamber Choir also became one of the renowned representatives from India after their popularity post their win in the reality TV show India's Got Talent. The Medley as a genre helps communicate novelty, ethnicity, sacrality, and popular culture industry-Bollywood.

Short Historical Snippets about Christianity and Musicality in Khasi and Lushai Hills

Wales and Meghalaya go back a long way. Celtic Christianity in Wales was a fourth-century phenomenon. During the eighteenth century, Evangelic Awakening impacted both Wales and England. The Presbyterian Church formed in 1811 was closely linked to the organization and assistance of the London Missionary Society (LMS). Jacob Tomlin during his return from China to Wales via India felt that Khasi hills was a promising site to share the preaching of the gospel and added that they will be keener to discover it than the Hindus. He fondly remembered his brief stay in the Sohra region. Thus, Thomas Jones, the first missionary of the newly formed Welsh Calvinist Methodist Foreign Mission Society (WCMFM) left for the journey. He departed from Wales in November 1840 and arrived in Kolkata in April 1841. He stayed in Kolkata briefly till he moved to Sohra on June 22, 1841. Jones founded the Roman script in place of the Bengali script. He formed Khasi alphabets drawing from the

Sohra dialect. He also got the first Khasi literatures in Roman script published (Nongbri, 2017).

Meghalaya experiences a continued strife to make sense of the tribal situations, archival silences, locally conducive traditions (*ka riti*) and custom (*ka dustur*), and Christianity shaped by cross-cultural meetings. Christianity gained popularity due to the efforts of the missionaries during the early colonial era alongside the missionary print culture (May 2016).

K. Mark Swer wrote about Khasi musical history and mentioned that according to W. R. Laitphlang, a deacon of the Khasi Jaintia Presbyterian Church and one of the older music chroniclers, folding organs became a church feature in the 1900s and in the 1930s, it was joined by the piano. Acoustic guitar became a church instrument rather reluctantly during the 1960s. Shillong had a Jaiaw Orchestra led by Webster Davis that was founded in the year 1948 (Swer, 2017).[9]

Evan Roberts had reached Cherrapunji during the beginning of January 1874 and set up a tonic sol-fa class for the youth in Shillong. Hugh Roberts, another missionary, was responsible for teaching the old notation but the guidelines were laid down by Evan Roberts. He faced opposition but did equivalent work in Shangpung in the Jaintia hills and also made an elementary textbook in Khasi language. The book elaborated on the principles of tonic sol-fa. This was based on the work of Eleazor Roberts of Liverpool (Rees, 2002: 44, 45).

A few letter exchanges between Welsh missionaries working at the Welsh Missionary Hospital in India gave insight into the musical milieu in one of the chapel services at Jaiaw. On a letter addressed to her sister dated September 23, 1945, Ms, Marian Pritchard mentioned the following hymns—"For his mercy aye endures," "Ever faithful," "Yr. Arghwyddywfy mugail" (The Lord is my Shepherd) and "Diolch iti yr Hollalu—og Ddew" (Thanks to you my almighty God). She also mentions where to locate them in the Hymnbook: (a) Harts 290, (b) Morgannwg 112, (c) Bethel 222, (d) Diolch Iti 38. She mentions that the Khasis always liked to end with "Diolch Iti" after a special meeting. In the 1980s, one of Khasi choirs had traveled to Wales. They sang the Hallelujah Chorus; a copy of which is available in the Calvinist Methodist Archive at the National Library of Wales.[10]

---

[9] Mark K Swer, "Khasi Foxtrot Tango," *RAIOT: Challenging the Consensus*, February 25, 2017, www .raiot.in/khasi-foxtrot-tango/ (accessed Februrary 25, 2017).

[10] "Hallelujah Chorus" Calvinist Methodist Archive, *National Library of Wales, Aberystwyth*, https://archive.org/details/78_hallelujah-chorus_oratorio-chorus-handel_gbia0300716a (accessed November 15, 2016).

The Lushais were musical and got along well with the Welsh. Choirs had become an important feature of Mizo society. By the 1920s, the touring choir was formed. In 1929, the first Mizo choir gave concerts at Sylhet, Kolkata, Calcutta Radio, Patna, Varanasi, Allahabad, Lucknow, Delhi, Ludhiana, and Agra. The influence of colonialism had quite an effect on the Mizos. Even though the outer forms were Western, the inward meaning and expressivity was "Mizo-ized." Music continued to be important even after they took on a new religion. The churches and chapels in the hill villages had a large drum, which they called the Gong. This was used to summon people to the service. Apart from the Gong, other popular instruments were violins, trumpets, organs, and flutes (Pachuau and Schendel, 2015).[11]

Khasis have had and continue to have indigenous organizations upholding cultural specificities. Seng Khasi, an organization that celebrates Khasi religion, culture, and identity was founded in the year 1899 by U. Jeebon Roy and remains till today. Among its many activities, every year, Seng Khasi organizes Ka Shad Suk *Mynsiem* (thanksgiving dance) and archery competitions. The Pnars had set up Seinraj after 1947 to showcase the cultural and religious rights of the Jaintias. U. Pati Laloo, U. Pati Ryngad, U. Sahan Lanong, U. Harison Kyndiah, U. Wikin Shullai, U. Kistobin Rymbai and a few others provided the leadership. Seinraj organizes Ka Beh Dein Khlam festival, an important cultural and religious festival for the Pnars (Jyrwa, 2011: 153, 154, 158).[12]

La Riti set up by Helen Giri in 2006, makes cultural miniatures and weaves traditional shawls and dance costumes of the Khasis. It has provided employment to many who undergo financial instability and the ones who are specially challenged. There is also a La Riti printing press. It is an organization that seeks to preserve traditional artifacts. It does not merge culture and religion (Personal Interview, January 14, 2015).

Discussing Genre, Intertextuality, and Territorialization

Genres inform us what to expect from a particular musical act. In a way, it guides us to ways of listening. In the introduction to the book *Genre in Popular Music*,

---

[11] The choir was led by Reverend Lalla Ram and was accompanied by Katie Hughes. The repertoire comprised pieces from Handel's Messiah, Alfred Gaul's "The Holy City" and hymns and songs by Mizo composers. A Mizo translation of "Messiah" was included in the choral repertoire. Open-air singing of Christmas carols by youngsters in the neighborhood, which was less formal in nature, also emerged (Pachuau and Schendel, 2015).

[12] Jyrwa J. Fortis, *Christianity in Khasi Culture* (Shillong: Mrs. M. B. Jyrwa, 2011).

Fabian Holt[13] (2007) discusses how genre is useful in navigating American popular music. The idea of genre emerged in the mid-nineteenth century coinciding with the evolution of popular cultures and modernism. Genres consist of particular repetitive gestures and conventions, permanently, organized around a collective. Genre boundaries are framed around cultural and musical practices belonging to a specific social space. He insists that whereas films and photography follow standardized protocols which give rise to specific categories, types of music do not fit a permanent record label. The latter have underlying ideological assumptions and often times, hybridity is seen to be a break-off from genres. The author is mindful about genre crossovers gaining emphasis in certain cultural contexts. He looks at choir societies and celebrity fan cultures as examples. European and American Art Music maintains a standardized position in the field of education, timeless compositions, and in the enjoyment of patronage from social elites. Nineteenth-century American Art music included nationalism as a part of its discourse to be aligned with the European bourgeois model. This not only set them apart as art music but also put a constraint on their ability of innovation. Hybrid musical exchanges that run in the opposite direction of comfort zone are usually associated with popular-music genres. On the one hand, they exceed the possibilities of the genre format and, on the other hand, represent chaos. Early-twentieth-century American folk music impacted popular-music to a large extent. This shows how folk music gets written into popular-music imagination while nationalism discourse locates itself within the art music or classical music. Shillong shows that such neat compartmentalized influences do not exist. Holding on to the spirit of revivalism, one sees various motifs finding voices in a Medley format. Thus, one sees indigenous, folk, national, and classical tropes all rolled into one.

I am looking at the "process of intermediation" as a genre in itself. As I have mentioned at the outset, the chapter looks at how "Medley" allows the reimagination of the choral in the regional context. Medley embraces the nation-building project at large when the choristers act as cultural ambassadors or as producers of alternative art palatable to a global audience, when they create crossovers that incorporate Bollywood, Broadway, Opera, and sacred hymns. While Holt directs us to analyzing the issues between the mainstream and the genre where there is an existing gap between the dominant culture and the marginal culture, in the case of the choirs in Shillong, Medley unites the aspects

---

[13] Fabian Holt, *Genre in Popular Music* (Chicago: University of Chicago Press, 2017).

of standardization and performativity. It becomes an extension of the "genre culture" and the mainstream responds favorably to the novelty in the realm of exploring the different epitomes of classical of specific genres coming together as a Medley. Thus, the Medley becomes "classical-across-genres."

Holt speaks about poetics that is shaped by a decentered notion of genre. The in-between poetics is in flow and works toward breaking the statis or the core—boundary models. This in-betweenness posits the music and, at the same time, it gauges how the borders respond to the transformations and pluralities. This in-betweenness is what Deleuze (1987)[14] calls "chaosmos" or the move from intra-assemblage to inter-assemblage.

Holt looked at a few case studies from South America to assess this poetics. He looked at the notions of authenticity and purity to understand the in-betweenness. Looking at one of his case studies, that of Ricky Martin's "Cup of Life," Holt begins with the song's first public performance at a stadium of Paris during the 1998 World Cup final. Latin Pop recognized as "the signifier of colourful festivity" featured prominently as the favored sound of the White Atlantic audience. The following year, he won the Grammy and performed the song at the same event and with that Ricky Martin moved across boundaries. There was a transformation from an ethnic "Latino" identity to an "Anglo" mainstream one that he adopted. The song's meaning acquired a totally different form when, in the year 2001, it was being performed at the inaugural festivities at Washington DC for President George W. Bush. On the one hand, it sanctioned the unspoken reception of poverty and racism on the part of the government and, on the other hand, it saw a Puerto Rican supporting a president whose value system was structured around those ideas (Holt, 2007).

Why is this case study important for my ethnography? The repertoires of both the choirs incorporate an in-between poetics. Medley is the signifier of the choral music in Shillong. For the Shillong Chamber Choir, the reality TV show win at the national level shaped their Bollywood Broadway approach in the Medleys. For the Aroha Choir, music education tied together the members. The ethos and musical styles of the choir conductor led to the formation of their repertoire. Both the choirs essentialize classical-across-genres. What does classical-across-genres mean? It refers to all those songs that come to represent the high points of diverse musicalities forming a genre. It directs one toward

---

14 Gilles Deleuze and Guattari Felix, *A Thousand Plateaus: Capitalism and Schizophrenia,* trans. Brian Massumi (London: University of Minnesota Press, 1987).

the composers/bands whose music has been canonized as per a specific genre. For instance, the music of Salil Chowdhury, Shankar-Jaikishen, A. R. Rahman, the Beatles, Queen, Gershwin, Mozart, Handel, and so forth are combined and arranged for a choir.

This classical-across-genres situates their in-between poetics. While discussing repertoires, genre naturally emerges as an important element. Crossovers/Medleys are motifs that undergird the choirs from Shillong. Choirs are usually seen as an integral component of Christianity. It lends support to the worship. As a music genre too, hymns and gospel traditions dominate its imaginations. This is not to rule out the various choral groups that exist independent of the church. There are experimental choral groups associated with educational institutes like the Yale Whiffenpoofs, Penn Masala, or vocal ensembles of the University of Berkley, and so on. Shillong Chamber Choir and Aroha Choir have a strong idea of faith as their organizing principle. They also build on the ideas of nation-building. Finally, while widening the possibilities of notating Western classical music, they also contest the musicological elitism of Western classical music.

In the article, "Repetition, Improvisation and Tradition," Roma Chatterji (2016)[15] adopts a Deleuzian framework of repetition and time to explore how the embodied artisan becomes a machine or automation, an open vehicle; and at the same time responds to the permanence and evolution of events in the environment. My exchanges with the choir members introduced me to their performance code, which has an ingrained idea of discipline and consistency. Their idea of expression is geared toward the production of a sound that travels from modes of a singularity. Here, Medley is seen as a singularity to that of an anticipated aurality (Deleuze, 1994).[16] Deleuze's notion of "refrain" and "territorialisation of sound" helps grasp as to how Bollywood sounds are the primary qualifiers to ascertain Medley as a genre. The inward and exterior particles work toward a collective articulation; in this case, it is vocalization. The motif that returns, acts as a qualifier. Nonetheless, its inclination toward change and further exchanges influences the idea that it symbolizes. "Schizophonic mimesis" (Steven Feld, 2000) becomes part of the choral[17] repertoire. He points

---

[15] Roma Chatterji, "Repetition, Improvisation and Tradition: Deleuzian Themes in the Folk Art of Bengal," *Cultural Analysis* 15, no. 1 (2016): 99–127.

[16] Gilles Deleuze, *Difference and Repetition* (New York: Columbia University Press, 1994).

[17] Following Barnwell, whose ideas coincide with Thomas Turino's features of participatory music throughout the world; "Choral singing is rehearsed, performances are often conducted, the sound and the use of voice tends to be more European, and the arrangements tend to be more 'classical,'

toward a host of interactive and extractive practices generating traffic in the absorption and circulation of sound recordings. The latter forges an indexical relationship to the place and the people that they hold and circulate. New possibilities surface due to material and commodity conditions, leading to a new context and a reimagined materiality. I look at this "schizophonic mimesis" adding to the idea of intertextuality.

To capture the phenomenon of intertextuality and synchronicity, I look at how Veena Das (1995)[18] approaches the notion of soap opera. Taking Hum Log as an example (1994), she says that the intertextual element of the soap opera was retained due to the presence of Ashok Kumar as a discussant toward the end of the episode, a famous actor of the Hindi films, through whom, characters of the film world were accessible to the audience, in a fresh role. Further, naming of the characters,*Badki* (the eldest), *Majhli* (the middle), and *Chutki* (the little one), established intertextuality with folk tales.[19] The Bollywood Industry of the 1990s has a different story to tell.[20]

Bollywood as a culture industry penetrates websites, cassettes, television shows, radio, and so forth both outside and within India. Ashish Rajadhyaksha (2003) discusses the impact of cultural insiderism on a diasporic citizen and the focus of the new corporate economy concentrates on the supplementary aspects of Indian cinema.

The Shillong Chamber Choir searches for a cultural insiderism in the realm of the national mainstream. Medley of the film song from the movie *Jhankar Beats* "Tu Ashiqui hain" (You are the object of my adoration); sung by KK, set amid a church background (2003) and the classical song "Lord of Hope" from Handel's "Messiah" (1741) comprise a Medley in the reality TV show,[21] give insight as to how Bollywood as a culture industry is circulated in current times. The Shillong

---

although in the case of gospel music there is still space for improvisation and movement in performance" (Barnwell, 1987 quoted in Bithell, 2014: 125).

[18] Veena Das, "On Soap Opera: What Kind of Anthropological Object Is It?" in *Worlds Apart: Modernity Through the Prism of the Local*, ed. Daniel Miller (New York and London: Routledge, 1995), 169–89.

[19] The prime-time screening of the show indicated that the representation of the social values was in sync with the bureaucratic apparatus. The letters sent out by the viewers, probably coming from lower middle-class background, were at times using the tele-screen as a space to vent out the discomfort, threat, and aspirations induced by family as an institution (Veena Das, 1995).

[20] The term "Bollywood" was in all probability invented in a self-critical manner by the journal "Screen" in Bombay to bring out the regional essence of the Indian Film industry. Presently, its usage maybe linked to Britain's Channel 4's ethnic programming (Rajadhyaksha, 2003).

[21] Reality TV shows like "Sa Re Ga Ma Pa," "Voice of India," "Fame Gurukul," "Indian Idol," "Coke Studio," and "India's Got Talent" have been crucial in introducing distinct talent, appeal, and physical appearance of the artist; altering ideas of intimacy and distance with an omnipresent mass media in a globalized environment (Kvetko, 2008 in Kvetko, 2014).

Chamber Choir Medley example shows how songs from two different centuries, the eighteenth and the twenty-first centuries; and two motley musical genres show synchronicity[22] in the spiritual realm.

Satellite Television for the Asian Region (STAR) in May 1991 provided international programs like CNN, HBO, and MTV. Indipop featured in 1993. There were personalities like Baba Sehgal and Alisha Chinai, but it became popular after its association with Bollywood (Kvetko, 2004; 2014). The hybridized sounds featured in the sound films of the 1930s was produced from local, regional, and international sources (Getter, 2014). Bhangra, an expression of sacrality during harvest festivals, merged with Western hip hop and reggae. It later grounded itself in the film-dominated popular culture scene. Digitized small studio recordings and a distinct vocality interjected by global genres was produced (Getter, 2014[23]; Greene, 2014[24]; Roy, 2010[25]; Sarrazin, 2014).[26]

For the Shillong Chamber, it is the Bollywood motif that defines their performativity. The Aroha Choir used the Christmas song motif as my interaction with them coincided with their preparation toward the Christmas concert. The Medleys draw on intertextuality in the realm of different musical genres and the synchronicity of time interjected by repetition adds to this framework, albeit differently. Repetition, in this case, acquires legitimacy when the Bollywood motif or the Christmas motif presents itself.[27] In another circumstance, to understand the vocalizing of Songak in Korea, a feature of the church sociality, Nicholas Harkness (2015)[28] draws on the Bakhtinian notion of "chronotope" (1981)[29] to qualify the vocalic sounds as either moral or immoral, clean or

[22] The temporal registers speak about a diachronic register: time as sequence; and synchronic one: events take place simultaneously (Levi-Strauss, 1977 in Chatterji, 2016: 116).
[23] Joseph Getter, "Kollywood Goes Global: New Sounds and Contexts for Tamil Film Music in the 21st Century," in *More than Bollywood: Studies in Indian Popular Music*, ed. Gregory D. Booth and Bradley Shope (New York: Oxford University Press, 2014), 60–74.
[24] Paul Greene, "Bollywood in the Era of Film Song Avatars: DJing, Remixing, and Change in the Film Music Industry of North India," in *More Than Bollywood: Studies in Indian Popular Music*, ed. Gregory D. Booth and Bradley Shope (New York: Oxford University Press, 2014).
[25] Anjali Gera Roy, *Bhangra Moves: From Ludhiana to London and Beyond* (Farnham: Ashgate Publishing, 2010).
[26] Rahman's compositions in the film "Roja (1992)," put forth the idea of immediacy, produced aurally as well as visually. In the Post-Fusion era, the processes of creation, rather than the film song in itself becomes interesting (Sarrazin, 2014).
[27] Drawing examples about the synchronicity of time, observable in folk theater or sacred myth, she explains that the logic of repetition does not work with soap opera. This is because the flow of time in the order of narrative and the order of life run parallel. Also, the popularity that Hum Log enjoyed during its initial days of screening was never revived again (Das, 1995).
[28] Nicholas Harkness. "Voicing Christian Aspiration: The Semiotic Anthropology of Voice in Seoul". *Ethnography* 16, no 3 (2015): 313–330. Copy at https://tinyurl.com/y8kqo5or.
[29] MM Bakhtin, *The Dialogic Imagination: Four Essays.* (Austin: University of Texas Press, 1981).

unclean and traditional or modern. He discusses "ethno-national aspiration" shaped by spirituality. Shillong Chamber Choir, by adopting Bollywoodized aspirations within the format of the choral rendition, they are speaking with the cosmopolitan, mainstream, social, and the musical world. Apart from Bollywood, the other mainstream relevant for Shillong Chamber Choir is the Broadway. The latter practices its own intertextuality. Scott Warfield (2008) draws out the life of Broadway vis-à-vis rock musicals. Examples like "Hair" (1968), "Your Thing" (1968), "Jesus Christ Superstar" (1973), "Godspell" (1971), "Grease" (1971), "Smokey Joe's Café" (1995), "Wiz" (1975), and "Dreamgirls" (1981) bring out not just the vocabulary of rock but gospel, soul, pop, and mowtown, all incorporating the elements of a Broadway format. (Short Story), *Promises Promises* (film). Terry TeachOut (2014) 12 explains how Broadway looks toward classics in literature and more recently classics in films for themes. He mentions works like *King and I* (novel/film) and *Guys and Dolls.*

Aroha Choir, through their Christmas spirit, is communicating festivity, oneness across denominations and specific vocalizations. Now that the phenomenon of intertextuality has been explained through various mediums, I will engage with both the choirs in the following sections.

Shillong Chamber Choir

The popularity of the Shillong Chamber Choir has brought Meghalaya at the center stage where faith and voice mingle. My ethnographic encounters with the choir have largely been in the "green rooms" of the concert spaces across different cities—Guwahati, Shillong, Kolkata, and New Delhi, over a span of two years throughout 2014 and 2015. With its win in the reality TV show, India's Got Talent on Colours Television network founded by Sakib Zakir Ahmed, part of Global British Got Talent franchise in 2006, the Shillong Chamber Choir demonstrated two important features: how Bollywood sounds can be embodied within a choral framework and reintroduced Medley as a genre.

Choral music was discovered in Western civilization and Christianity. As a starting point, it had the Gregorian reforms of the sixth century. Choir primarily refers to a vocal ensemble practicing sacred music inside church settings as opposed to chorus which indicates vocal ensembles performing in secular environments. From 1430 onwards, sacred polyphony was rendered by multiple singers. By the end of the century, a standardized four-part range of three octaves or more became a feature. The vocal parts were called superius (later soprano), altus, tenor (due to its role of holding the cantus-firmus), and bassus (Unger, 2010: 23).[30]

Bollywood has always had harmony, and there have also been instances of a choir singing at the backdrop, to add to the fullness of the songs.[31] Genres broke away from their atomistic arrangements as early as the 1930s, when among many other forms, Western harmony and swing jazz came to be incorporated into Bollywood by the Goan arrangers and musicians. Then what sets Shillong Chamber Choir live-act apart? Is it the vocal ensemble? Is it the promise of a kind of "Bollywood Broadway"? Or is it simply a rendition of a professional sound enmeshed in nostalgia and experimentation? I would like to explore the idea of "Bollywood music as refrain" in marking new musical identities. Through various video illustrations, live-acts, and personal interviews, which fall within my larger ethnography (I made two trips to Shillong, the capital of Meghalaya, once during the month of April 2014 and later in September 2014. I stayed for about five months, the next time I visited the place), in this chapter, I try to chart out the sounds of the Shillong Chamber Choir and the Aroha Choir. Neil Nongkynrih is the conductor-composer-principal educator for the Shillong Chamber Choir. A concert pianist from London subjected to the rigors of "practicing 10 hours a day, 3 times a week, playing Mozart, Beethoven and Chopin," Neil recounts with certain solemnity, the tremendous stress ordered around stage presence, performance skills, and audience perception. After his return to India which was not planned, he was simply looking for another medium to express his idea of art. Human voice had always fascinated him and even while he was in London, he used to frequent the opera houses.

In India, he saw great potential talent. It was a "virgin territory" waiting to be discovered. He chose to work on voice, not only because he loved it but also due to the limited choice of instruments he had. "There were not enough violinists or cellists and one couldn't think of forming an orchestra with 20 pianists." Piano seems to be the preferred instrument to learn in Shillong.[32] The members of the choral group reside in the same apartment. It initially started as home-school education center. It was only in 2001 that the Shillong Chamber Choir as a multi-genre choir, performing everything from jazz to folk to Bollywood to classical to church music was born. Initially, that is in 2001, it started out as

---

[30] Melvin P. Unger, *Historical Dictionary of Choral Music* (UK: The Scarecrow Press Inc, 2010).
[31] Bollywood refers to the South Asian film industry situated in Mumbai. The term also includes its film music and scores.
[32] Piano was introduced to Shillong in the 1930s.

an institution where music was used as therapy, the shift to performance came about much later. Over the years, few members have left, while new members have been inducted. The languages that they sing in are not only the dominant languages that one gets to hear in an opera like French, Italian, and German but rather unconventional languages which do not conform to the linguistic paradigm of opera or choral repertoire, at least in the West.[33] They sing in Hindi, Bengali, Assamese, Nagamese, Manipuri, Punjabi, Khasi, Tamil, Malayalam, and Chinese. There is also a drive to reinstate the importance of one's own language strategically positing it in the aesthetic plane.

> NN: And I don't know if my opera or my writings in Khasi will contribute to any role in preserving signs but I will at least make an attempt. It is a beautiful language to sing in. You know when you hear of Operas you will always hear them singing in Italian, German or French but what about singing in Khasi? (Personal Interview, April 2014)

In Shillong, the ones who are involved in the arts and cultural activities, especially the institutions that I encountered, during fieldwork (La Riti Foundation, Jeebon Roy Institute, Martin Luther Christian University, Department of Music) seem to be quite taken with the idea of preserving the Khasi language and various other cultural symbols of importance. Thus, it came as no surprise when one of the celebrated choirs in India, spoke of endorsing the same principle, while designing their repertoire. Shillong Chamber Choir appropriates some sections of popular Bollywood songs and arranges them with other genres of music like jazz, folk, classical, hymns, or rock as per their compositional ruse. It is mediation of musical ideas. I refer to them as Medleys, which are more or less ordered around Bollywood.

> NN: and you think of this whole arena of Bollywood music, why we did it is because, by accident actually we ended up on this TV show, which I was never keen on in the beginning, because I never thought choral music and mainstream TV would go together.! That was my perception. But it just shows that life doesn't go the way you think. We are going to harmonize; we are going to give every song we sing, even a popular Hindi song a treatment of the choral style. And somehow or the other this has struck a chord with the nation, this has struck a chord with the people.

[33] There are vernacular repertoires in other parts of the Indian subcontinent. One interesting development: national anthems of the various Northeast states sung by the Shillong Chamber Choir are available on YouTube. There is an aspiration toward the mainstream but the "localised nationalisms" refer to subcultural lineages.

Before I move into the section where I elaborate on some of their repertoire, his interview with host Aled Jones, of BBC 3 program, the Choir, (2012) returns to similar ideas. Neil Nongkynrih said that based out of Northeast India, the Shillong Chamber Choir wanted to serve a multi-cuisine buffet. It was aimed to be a family act, directed toward different sections of people in India. He told that before 2010, choir music formed a limited part of the music industry in India. When Aled Jones, the host of program titled: "The Choir: Myths and Legends," asked if they saw themselves as trailblazers when it came to choir music, Neil agreed. Although he added that they are a small section, with just eighteen people forming the choir. In the show, Aled Jones talked about how certain works of Wagner, Martinu, and Sibelius were influenced by myths and legends alongside the interview segment with the founder of the Shillong Chamber Choir. Apart from playing some of the music of the composers he discussed, he also played "Dil Hain Chota Sa" and Handel's "Lift up your Hands" sung by the choir and Neil Nongkynrih and Resul Pookutty's song "Madi Madi" from the Malayalam film, *Goodbye December*.

When Neil was asked about some of Shillong Chamber Choir's memorable moments, he said that "performing for the Sikkim Earthquake Relief Programme was an ethereal Experience." Another memorable moment was performing for President Obama where there were only 200 guests." About the choir festival in Shanghai, he felt that it was too stressful for the kids. The choir prefers the laidback style compared to running the rat race. Shillong Chamber Choir's win in the reality TV show and the conscious stylistic choices that they introduce to the choral repertoire make Medleys an integral component of understanding their artistic process.

Repertoire: Medleys/Crossovers

For Shillong Chamber Choir, it is significant to unpack what I mean by Bollywoodization. The vocal ensemble refers to the number of choir singers, who actually go up to the stage during the different live-acts. I would like to talk about Bollywood Broadway elaborately through illustrations, as I go on. To begin with, the performativity centered on production of the distinct Shillong Chamber Choir sound is something akin to Bollywood Broadway. Finally, what would a professional sound entail? It is true that widely popular artists who have a huge fan following and various corporate, social, and cultural obligations need to maintain a consistent output. In certain cases, pre-recorded tracks are inserted during the live-acts to portray a conspicuous, professional sound associated with the artists. For, Shillong Chamber Choir, that is an indelible feature.[34]

Here professional sound can also be referred to as a digitally processed sound. To simply take their 2015 live recorded video version of the song directed by Salil Chowdhury, "Dil Tadap Tadap" (Longings of the heart) from the film *Madhumati* (1958), which was inspired by the Polish folk song "Szladzieweczka do gajeczka" and sung by Lata Mangeshkar and Mukesh, as an illustration, "Bollywood Broadway" can be viewed as an expansion of what was popularly known as the "Star Programs in India" during the late 1950s, and in the United Kingdom, the United States, Canada, and so on in the 1960s. Gregory Booth in his book *Behind the Curtain: Making Music in Mumbai's Film Studios*, talks about these "Star Programs," which involved the film stars, the playback singers, dancers, and an orchestra. Despite the lure of foreign travels, most musicians during those times would not want to be part of the shows for two reasons. First, the shows were irregular and sustainability for the most part of the travel turned out to be difficult. Second, when they returned, studio recordings would already be in process and this divorced the musicians from the booming work scene in the film studios. What is of course different in the case of the Shillong Chamber Choir is that they themselves make up the whole team, the protagonist actors/playback singers, the vocal ensemble, dancers-choristers, and the orchestral support provided by the Viennese Chamber Orchestra.

One noticeable aspect about the Shillong Chamber Choir performances is that mainly three singers (one male-tenor/baritone and two female, one soprano and one alto) alternate between the leading roles. Nowadays, a fourth male singer (bass) is also taking the center stage in certain cases. The live-act pays careful attention to the costume, small hand, leg, and hip and shoulder movements that complement not only the rhythmic and melodic component of the composition but also weaves in a certain kind of play acting to formulate a story line to go along with the performance. Staying on this particular song, in the video that I am referring to, one sees the women in choir dressed in beautiful white gowns and the men in the choir and the orchestra dressed in black. The setting is the beautiful Udaipur Palace with esteemed personalities as the audience. Shillong Chamber Choir specializes in Medleys, unless it is a cover version of a certain song. The other half of this song sees the lead voices

---

[34] They performed in September 2011; They performed on November 8, 2010, at the Rashtrapati Bhavan.

sing (the song)—"Somewhere My love"/Larah's theme, in keeping with the waltz tempo. The storyline quite easily emerges as one where the talks of love, desire, and light flirtations come to be expressed.

As a part of the same series, they also did a live recording of the Medley songs that guaranteed Shillong Chamber Choir's win in the reality TV show, back in the year 2006. I also find the fragments of the chosen song lyrics for this set, hinting at the way the choir functions. The Medley that I am talking about comprises Shankar-Jaikishan's 1960 song "Ajeeb Dastaan Hain Yeh" (This is quite an absurd chronicle) and RD Burman's 1975 song "Yeh Dosti Hum Nahi Torenge" (We will never end this friendship). The song "Yeh Dosti" talks about friendship's promise of being able to do the basic things like eating, drinking together, and eventually the formation of a lifestyle shaped by the association, which will break only if death comes to one of them. The choir too functions as a unit, whereby training, teaching, performing, and traveling affect the unit as a whole. Here, one interesting anecdote about the way Old Bollywood functioned needs to be mentioned. The musicians had an informal manner of playing for, and belonging to a group of a particular composer and his associated circle. Ernest Menezes clearly talks about his involvement with the Burman family in terms of consistent work but attributes his actual allegiance to Shankar-Jaikishan. The latter, Booth figures, comes more from a lineage and cultural affiliation of the Goans (Booth, 2008). This often makes one wonder how lineages work in the world of Western music in India, that too, in different areas. Now, looking at the choral soundscape in Shillong, Shillong Chamber Choir works as a reference point for anyone dabbling with the idea of choral music. Anything from traditional, experimental, adult, to even a children choir, the Shillong Chamber Choir is a source of inspiration, alongside the skepticism and the grandeur it encompasses. The idea of lineages and affiliations require a separate space for argument. For the moment, in the discussion on "Bollywood Broadway" and "Bollywood as refrain," it is sufficient to look at the way the choir functions in shaping discourses about sounds and socialities.

I would like to talk about the Medley "Baar Baar Dekho—Hazaar Baar Dekho" (Look, again and again. Look, a thousand times) and "Wonderful" by the Shillong Chamber Choir to highlight some more particularities of their sound and visualization. The group has uploaded a video version of this Medley on YouTube, shot in black and white. The way they dress and emote, it definitely transports the viewers to a 1950s or a jazz studio resembling a similar temporality, except for the sound. This is not to say that the sound does not embrace the elements of the jazz "style." It does, but the interpolation ushered in by the protocols of Bollywood and Hollywood attribute to it a certain degree of newness. The Bollywood baggage is portrayed by the male-tenor, William, loosely framed around the enactment and tonalities of the filmi persona of Shammi Kapoor.

The Hollywood shadows are internalized into the performance ethic of the female alto, Donna, when she traverses the imaginations foregrounded by Ella Fitzgerald, on the one hand, and Audrey Hepburn, on the other hand. The song featured in 1927 Broadway Musical "Funny Face" by Adele Astaire and Allen Kearns. It later featured in the movie by the same name in the year 1957 that starred Fred Astaire and Audrey Hepburn. This for one is not a live-act but an official video, available on YouTube delineating one of the "many sounds" brought forth in the Shillong Chamber Choir Medleys. Written by Ira Gershwin and composed by George Gershwin, this song was recorded by Ella Fitzgerald in the year 1959. Earlier, the new theaters in Calcutta and the presence of both foreign and amateur musicians performing Western classical music during the 1930s made many Mumbaikars trace the Bengali influence and contribution to the development of a Western sound in the film industry. However, Salil Chowdhury, who himself left Kolkata for Mumbai in the 1950s credits the Goans, for introducing harmonized arrangements, obligatos, and counterpoint essential to the characterization of Old Bollywood. During the 1980s and 1990s with the advent of keyboard and samplers, live, acoustic recordings took a back seat, only to be revived for certain specific requirements. For instance, in the year 2007, a large string orchestra (large by today's standards) had been assembled to record a background score for Shankar Ehsaan Loy. These speak of those one-off requirements that stem from meeting the demands of a theme of a particular film or certain sensibilities that undergird it. Medleys clearly emerge as genre and in the case of Shillong Chamber Choir, it is ordered around the Bollywood motif primarily. I now proceed to discuss the life and afterlife of performance.

Beyond Performance

What makes this choir interesting is their emphasis on production that goes beyond just the immediacy of performance. The latter is beyond their performance ethics. The following illustration is one of their production shows that were held at the North Eastern Hill University in October 2014. As a researcher, I found my way in through the green-room area, especially because it was a private event. The event was named Shillong Voices. The program started with a video introduction about each performer and how they passed through the audition rounds just like the video introductions of the reality TV shows. The first half saw all these Meghalaya talents, whom they were trying to promote, perform and the second phase was an act put together by the Shillong Chamber Choir. The repertoire reflected the versatility of the Shillong Chamber Choir.

They sang everything from Western classical music (Mozart), Classic Bollywood, India's Got Talent repertoire, an original Khasi Opera loosely based on Romeo and Juliet and their delightful Train Journey Song. The latter incorporates the typical imageries noticeable in an Indian train. What makes it interesting is the way some industrial sounds have been expressed through the voice and how the moment of quarreling between the passenger and the "beggar" or "Hijra" derives from one of the moments of Handel's "Messiah." Even though the lyrics are in Hindi, the compositional trope in terms of melody and harmonization for only that little phrase mirrors the particular moment from Handel's "Messiah." They also had Medleys of songs like "Kaise Paheli" from Parineeta and "Stand by Me" by the Beatles and few others, where they sang songs by Queen, Abba, and others. They had ended the program by a rendition of a composition by Neil Nongkynrih and Zakir Hussain where "Tabla bols" were beautifully blended into a choral harmony. Apart from the piano, some of the songs had tracks as accompaniment. For few of their songs, the band also accompanied the choir.

Here, there is an overlap between the style: genre structuring, making the notion of intermediation relevant. The track accompaniments perhaps explain why the choir manages to accomplish so many tours in a span of just one month. Most of the songs were lip-synced and all that shimmered on the stage were their beautiful costumes and light body movements and occasional singing.

Stanley Cavell's (2005) claim that the opera entered the Western culture as a moment of crisis of expression and his attempts at fleshing out the possibilities of incorporating opera within the structure of a film through his discussion of certain film narratives in his article "Opera in and as a Film" is helpful while trying to posit "Bollywood sounds" within a supposed Chamber music, in this case, choral structure. I find his illustration of the allusions to the Opera La Boheme in the Norman Jewison directed 1989 film, *Moonstruck*, particularly telling. There are indirect references. Unlike the opera, which begins with whimsical celebrations and burial of unconventional thoughts, and a death, the movie, begins with a morbid portrayal but the ending depicts a celebratory moment.

It does return to the concept of death, through old photographs and different individuals, in the very end. "The Train" song, composed by the Shillong Chamber Choir, which they have performed live on many occasions, choose to draw from an opera (orchestral score in this case), an aesthetic framing of arguments. The crisis that the choir tries to project here is a daily one, whereby different vendors and poverty-stricken individuals go about their pleas in a general compartment of an Indian railway express. Instead of film, the opera (orchestral score in this case), enters one of the daily doldrums of Indian travel scenes [35](Cavell, 2005).

In "Film Song and Its Other: Tracing the Boundaries of Indian Music Genres," Jayson Beaster Jones (2014)[36] distinguishes between style and genre, it becomes telling in trying to understand the phenomenon that I refer to as the "Bollywood Broadway." He asserts that the genres classify the musical elements and the discourses built around it whereas the style simply refers to the musical sound and the performativity necessary to highlight it. The author goes on to talk about the possibilities of the so-called film songs being used in absolutely different settings later, digging out the malleability of the style and genre category in contemporary India. The "stylistic mediation" as an extension of C. S Peirce's notion of "semiotic mediation" has been used by the author to complicate the life of stylistic categories like Indipop, Sufi, or return of melody, once it is part of a film song. These stylistic mediations belong to what Fabian Holt refers to as the "poetics of in-between" and Gilles Deleuze calls "chaosmos." What becomes interesting in charting out the sound of the Shillong Chamber Choir is how Bollywood motifs and popular songs, reminiscent of the other genres are wedded to create a Medley (Jones, 2014).

"Everett Holly in Marketing Classical Music to Popular Audiences in Austin, Texas," a case study of KMFA-FM (2000) talks about crossover recordings that merge various genres are not a new phenomenon. Author Stephen Godfrey gives instances of Stevie Wonder and Gladys Knight's use of parts of Handel's "Messiah," Bobby McFerrin singing "Ave Maria," and Elvis Costello's album

[35] Stanley Cavell, "Opera in and as Film 2000," in *Cavell on Films*, ed. William Rothman (New York: SUNY Press, 2005), 305–18.

[36] Jayson Beaster, "Film Song and its other: Tracing the Boundaries of Indian Music Genres," in *More Than Bollywood: Studies in Indian Popular Music*, ed. Gregory D. Booth and Bradley Shope (Oxford: Oxford University Press, 2014).

which has the Brodsky quartet, the Juliet letters. Then there are other examples whereby the shift is from classical to pop. In 1985, Kiri Te Kanawa and Tenor Jose Carreras sang Leonard Bernstein's "West Side Story." Further, Vanessa Mae's 1998 album, Storm and Nigel Kennedy's 1996 release, Kafka are a few examples. The "populist" branding that such artists acquire, sometimes, embracing what Symes refers to as the "Madonna Strategy," involve artists such as Lara St John, Ofra Harnoy, and Sylvia McNair putting up compilation projects such as the Baltimore Symphony Orchestra's dance mix, which features the music of Leonard Bernstein, John Adams, and Michael Torke. This maneuver of the artists and the record companies to make "classical music" or "classically derived music" attuned to the ears of the popular-music connoisseurs with traditionally popular images and music, is what Pollard calls the "crossover" boom, which emerged in the 1980s. It was orchestrated by the record labels such as the Deutsche Grammophon. This "crossover boom" caught on as a part of a scheme of certain radio channels such as Austin's KMFA, Classical 89.5 FM. Music by Reich, Glass, Bryars, Torke, Adams alongside Broadway show tunes, traditional fare by ensembles like Chieftains and even orchestral arrangement of songs by groups like the Beatles were introduced. Old shows dedicated to movie soundtracks were restored too. It was an all-inclusive trial to initiate classical music to novice ears.

The champions of the classical music at the station also learned of newer tropes that formed the part and parcel of the local classical performers at the Austin Symphony Orchestra, the Austin Lyric Opera, and Ballet Austin (Holly, 2000).[37] Steven Feld (2000), in his discussion about the presence of anxiety and celebration in labeling world music as a category, points out the popular music's contribution toward the emphasis on early recording of the twentieth century. Thereafter, from the middle to the late 1980s, ethnomusicology expanded its explorations beyond the charted-out, discrete musical worlds. Musical worlds born out of contact histories and colonial legacies, relegated to the realms of diaspora, migration, hybridity, urbanization, and mass media, became topical concerns. Recordings came to be recognized as legitimate sources of musical and cultural history. Built around the phenomena of "Afro-Pop," the celebratory approach tried to string together the liberating and inspiring musical exchanges

---

[37] Steven Feld, "Anxiety and Celebration: Mapping the Discourses of World Music," in *Changing Sounds: New Directions and Configurations in Popular Music*, ed. Tony Mitchell and Peter Doyle (IASMP 1999 International Conference Proceedings, Faculty of Humanities and Social Sciences, University of Technology, 9–14, Sydney, Faculty of Humanities and Social Sciences, 2000).

whereby the anxious side reflected on the form of artistic humiliation at the crossroads of indigeneity and globalization, as a commentary on the cultural homogeneity and cultural imperialism. Today recordings have come to be replaced by reality TV shows and social media (Feld, 2000).

How does the notion Bollywood as refrain play out? Refrain talks about the territorial assemblages and the expressiveness that it entails. The task at hand remains to break away from the ritualistic notions and negotiate with the internal emotions and the external circumstances. One has to mark specific motifs and counterpoints that determine the development of a style. Then there is also the catalytic function of the refrain which allows it bring together elements that do not harness a natural affinity. In a general sense, refrain comprises collective expressions which form a territory. That leads to the formation of territorial motifs and landscapes. With time, after the intensities have been adjusted, a sense of consistency gets written into the functions, motifs, and the placards of territoriality. Territorial assemblages make way for interassemblages. This is governed by de-territorialization/re-territorialization. One also has to take the fragments or black holes into consideration, which roots itself in the process of a becoming. Then there are the "machinic statements" which interrupt the consistency in the process of becoming, and adds to it certain degrees of variations. A consistent and habitual mode of being in the form of preparing one's vocalizations, planning the production layout of the specific event, and organizing the Medley comprise a few "machinic statements." The Chaffinch (bird) is rooted to its internal expressions even when it is exposed to the influences of the synthetic sounds. The initial framing imagined by the Shillong Chamber Choir was to render the vocal attributes of Western classical music. Reality TV show demanded a different framing: that of Bollywood.

However, as Neil mentions in his interview, true to their art, the Shillong Chamber Choir decided to adjust their musical framing to that of harmonization. They treat every classic song belonging to different genres within a choral music format, definitely using more than two voices, if not all four. In the case of formulating the sound of the Shillong Chamber Choir, I argue that Bollywood sounds are being territorialized to attract a certain kind of mass appeal. I am using the plural "sounds" to refer to final product of the "stylized mediations," without decoding the musical structures of the chosen illustrations per se. What they have managed to establish visually is a Western classical genre setting, with a vocal ensemble performing the "Bollywood Broadway," an orchestra playing at the backdrop and the presence of a concert pianist with a page turner. In terms of sound, which too follows the protocols of a professional, digital sound, they are trying to experiment with Bollywood, even though the latter itself is an amalgamation of various other sounds.

When I say Bollywood, I try to harp on the sounds incorporated in the Medley, easily recognizable by the Indian subcontinent. Bollywood music ("Bombay produced film music") enjoyed an undaunted popular status in India 1940s onwards till the cassettes became popular, as already explained to us by Peter Manuel in his book *Cassette Culture in India*. The Medleys by the choir, the ones discussed so far, are "classics" belonging to particular genres. Therefore, not just the style of representation, what emerges here is a pattern of the shifting ideas of the classical component across multiple genres. Shillong Chamber Choir quite fits the description of a multi-genre choir. It anchors itself to Bollywood sounds to cater to the general audience of the Indian subcontinent. In the next section, I will discuss another popular choir of Shillong.

Aroha Choir

Pauline Warjiri is a freelance musician who teaches piano and voice. She works with a lot of soloists and choirs and has a choir of her own, the Aroha Choir, which is further bifurcated into a junior and a senior choir. She started this music studio cum choir, which she refers to as a music school for practical reason in the year 2008.

In the year 1999, she went to teach at Kodaikanal International School so that her son could have free education, and that was where she rediscovered her musical zest. She and one of her colleagues from the school, a saxophone player from Germany, formed a musical alliance. Pauline also recorded an album with him in 2001. From 2002 onward, she traveled to Switzerland both for attending and later conducting workshops. In 2005 she formed the Bangalore Chamber Choir. She had participants from Mangalore, Kerala, Chennai, Delhi, Manipur, Nagaland, Mizoram, and Meghalaya, and the challenge really was how to transform into a closely knit choir, singing in multiple languages, accepting the different cultural protocols.

> PW: you know the bonding, the search for meaning, existence—why are we
> here? Life with a purpose. . . . So the main reason why I wanted to do it is
> because from the NE point of view, we have not really integrated with the
> rest of India and I thought music should be able to do that for them and you

know while I was, you know, organizing the choir, in Manipur (Paites), tribes were fighting against each other but in my choir the music brought them together. And you know, I relize how powerful it was when my brother won the India's Got Talent. Suddenly Hindi music is no longer a taboo and people are all singing Hindi music and they love Bollywood. . . . So that has bridged the gap and it is no wonder that he was awarded the Indian of the year for the kind of work he has done. For even in his group there are a lot of mixtures: tribes and traditions and languages, and they have sung in virtually all major Indian languages. I think that is a very important step. Because once you begin to appreciate another culture, language, it's a step. [April 2014] Pauline had also trained her brother Neil's choir when he had just come back from London. She focused on her school, post India's Got Talent success of Shillong Chamber Choir. In fact, Pauline had given up her musical pursuits once she got married at the age of 19. Music resurfaced into her life as a process of personal healing after a miscarriage. When doctors were unable to medicate her she resorted to music and each year set a milestone for herself. After 4 years she took a diploma exam which gave her the license to go and teach as a supply teacher in England for a while. This was in the year 1996 before she went to Kodaikanal. Also, she connected more deeply with her art, her music after she was exposed to the Initiatives of Change, Arts squad in Switzerland. There she realized that music is a derivative of a deep source and it fulfills several obligations at different times. Although the primary focus of the squad was Christianity, there were people from other faiths-Bahai faith, people from the Muslim community, from the Hindu. Atheists were there as well. So, it was mainly directed at connecting to their faith through the arts. Pauline feels that this program allowed her to think through how she could engage with art being a socially responsible musician. In fact, her repertoire largely speaks of this social responsibility. Be it in terms of integrating singers from various communities or in terms of amalgamating various cultural, social and intellectual attributes.

My frequent visits to the Aroha Music School during the months of September to November 2014 allowed me to look at their practice methods closely, helped me get to know the members personally and understand what captures the choir's aspiration. Pauline Warjri follows an orderly routine of activities, effectively dividing time between the senior choir, the junior choir, and the piano lessons at the school. I recall the first day I visited the school; she was having her rehearsals with three members of the junior choir. Seeing them sing I was overenthusiastic and due to my prior singing experience with the Goa University Choir at my other field-site, I requested her to allow me to join in the vocal exercises. She gladly entertained the idea.

The members of the Junior Choir were practicing the song "Sweet Little Jesus Boy." What made the practice stand out was that she was making them learn the parts and lyrics of the song right then. It was more of an aural learning experience. She was confident of their sight-reading abilities and thus approached a different method to introduce the song. She insisted them to support their voices with their diaphragm, especially when reaching toward higher notes. Toward the end, she playfully remarked, "I didn't even have to tell you what notes to sing."

Upon my repeated visits, I picked up their regular vocal exercises which involved lip twirling "do-re-mi-fa-so-la-ti" from lower to higher octaves and vice-versa. The other exercise involved singing all the seven notes using the support of the diaphragm, again from lower to higher octave (and vice-versa). Sometimes the octave progressions were made further interesting by using different vowel sounds each time, a-e-i-o-u. The most complicated exercise I found was the one that required the singer to hold in his/her breath, after singing each note for a fixed number of seconds and then releasing it after sometime. The latter helped in sustaining "hums" which the choir director on many accounts, regards to be best way to attack a note.

All this ultimately enabled the voice to lapse into using the throat voice, the abdomen voice, the head voice, and even falsetto, as per the requirement of the song in question. Taking out an instance from the rehearsals, I recall one of the days when the choir was practicing "For unto Us a Child Is Born" from Handel's "Messiah," the choir director emphasized how each part and each voice acquired importance. This she pointed out to be a significant feature of polyphony, whereby each singer acquires the role of a soloist.

Also, imitation becomes prominent here, allowing the Tenors to follow the sopranos and basses to follow the altos. While talking of Handel's work, she referred to Bach's symbolism of cross, due to the similarity of ideas. She insisted on vowel stressed singing to help with the precision of notes and their sound. She advised the singers to use their tongues instead of jaws to handle the sustained long notes. In other cases as well as this one, diction is central to the choir's performativity. The stress on the use of measured British accents in this case, and working on each part separately ensured a more holistic sound.

On another day while rehearsing the song "Hope Is Born" by Mark Hayes and John Parker, the choir director called attention to the possibility of playing with one's palette while singing. Again, each part was being addressed separately. One problem that the choir faces is not having enough people to cover each part. In such cases, the choir director uses the protocol of shuffling of voices, especially the ones who are comfortable moving along different ranges.

Each member of the choir maintains their individual tonal qualities which makes certain voices favorable toward portraying the rock resonance, while others have the tendency to bring out the pop, jazz, operatic, and ballad impressions. Few others belt out a deep well-rounded sound or a controlled-high-pitched timbre. These variations color each song with multiple shades yet reflecting one common hue in the form of a universal sound quite isolated from the congregational sound, which the choir director steers clear from. This time of the year, the concerts lined up for the choir is themed around Christmas which is why experimentation in terms of genres weren't too noticeable yet the repertoire was replete with jazz, calypso, pop, country, gospel, and opera idioms.

"Stylistic mediations" comes across through intonations expressed by the soloists in different songs. For example, in the song, "All Is Well with My Soul," the two soloists portray two different tonal qualities, the tenor brings out the operatic trills whereas the soprano adds to it a country tinge without altering the basic tenets of the feel of soul, which is the genre to which the song belongs to. Whatever be the final representation, the sound that is emitted depends on the control of breath and the correct use of diction. The choir uses only digital piano as an accompaniment and sometimes the choir director uses the harmonica to lay out the melody lines and its supporting parts distinctly. She takes into consideration the opinions of all the members about their attitude toward the song they are performing and pushes them to do better by providing them encouraging feedback whenever possible. Before the songs are taken up, she records each of the parts separately for them alongside providing them handwritten score sheets for each section. Even though the Christmas repertoire did not comprise original compositions, except one Bengali song by an anonymous composer "Bhuvan Bhawra" (The Earth is filled with . . .), which she likes to call the Bengali carol. The latter was composed for the Delhi concert at the president's house. Some of the songs in the repertoire were also arranged by her. One of the popularly known hymns among the arranged ones was "Silent Night."

Members of the junior choir also project different syles. Venetia Warshong has a divine voice with a doleful ring to it. Narnetta, another member, has an innocent, melodious voice. Both of them sang the slightly galloping overtone of the Khasi National Anthem, "Ri-Khasi," the melody of which the Khasis share with the Welsh National Anthem, "HenWladfyNhadau." The latter was written by Evan James ("Ieuanab Iago") and set to tune by his son, James ("Iago abIeuan"), both composed in 1856. The song unfolds pleasant imageries in front of the spectators without taking away the component of lamentation inbuilt into the structure. It was interesting to see the choir sing "Ae Mere Watanki Logon" a widely acknowledged patriotic song by Lata Mangeshkar, that has been used in Hindi films along with "Ri-Khasi" for the concert at Rashtrapati Bhavan in December 2014.

The choice of song on the one hand weaves the themes into a common narrative of Nationalistic pride, holding on to nostalgia despite embracing new possibilities. And on the other hand, the vocal timbre suggests an Indian classical idiom which is also what the melody line dictates. The slightly galloping rhythms encountered at the beginning of the song "Ri-Khasi," in a way, enhances the element of hope amid an unwritten code of suffering. The choir decides to use Bollywood here for the Hindi-speaking audience and uses a patriotic number perhaps in order to address the divided loyalties owing to a complex personal history that the members live with. There is an ongoing dialog between the cultural practices among the followers of NiamKhasi and Christianity without reordering the basic tenets of the lifestyle of the religious groups.

> PW: Yes! We do everything. We are a Masala choir. Well . . . sometimes the corporate might call us for functions or the government might call us to entertain dignitaries. So, they would tell us that they want a particular kind of music. In fact, we turn down a lot of their offers because they only wanted Bollywood music even if we are not ready to do that kind of thing. I mean we do a lot of Bollywood as well but . . . it's not our main focus.
>
> The Seng Khasi people have not traditionally invited us, although they have expressed an interest to help me. And they said that if you need any materials for research. I mean there are few books and all. They are ready to help me. I don't think they have the tradition of inviting somebody yet. Because there it is not entertainment per se, it is ritual. Well, they will at cultural functions but I don't think they organized anything of that nature to be able to incorporate what we do. It's still a journey. (April 2014)
>
> PW: Well . . . jazz has not really taken off in this country but we start with jazz standards. We are not avant garde or anything like that. So, we started first with the very popular things, the Gershwin numbers, you know, I've got rhythm, summertime, bluemoon: very popular jazz standards. And we are looking to fuse it with Hindusthani or Carnatic music. So, the first fusion that

we did was based on this Bharatnatyam, we did one of the first exercises of Bharatnatyam, the ala-ripu. So, I did a jazz on the top of the syllables that the choir was singing and then we have this Bharatnatyam dancer. And I have not gone into the pre-Christian traditions which I am very interested in but I have gone into a few folk songs which are post-Christian. I have done arrangements on them but they are contemporary/ modern but nothing which is truly indigenous, you know what I mean . . . but most of what I have done is based on the pentatonic scale which is you know, what most indigenous music is based on. . . . Also . . . we sing in different traditions you know, we do a lot of rabindrasangeet and we do Asamese folk songs. We are yet to do Garo and you know, I have written songs in Angami. (April 2014)

We come across "Medley" or crossovers once again. Only, this time, the genres move across classic jazz and classical dance.[38] Walter Benjamin's idea of translatability (1969) as a product in transition helps to capture this idea. Where there is a rupture of the original text, the translation strives to retain the resonance emitted by the original. Fidelity and freedom work together to produce a translation. It is never only about specific words but also the meanings that they connote. The original remains crucial to the translation. It associates the latter alongside the translator with a given set of expressions and themes, which are further idealized, transcending all its foreignness.

Translations immortalize the originals by rendering to the spectators its much awaited afterlife.

PW: I wrote an oratorio in 2009 with a jazz idiom in mind . . . based on the Khasi pentatonic scale and fused against operatic elements because there are songs that I have written that only opera singers can sing. I did try to use the Tangmuri. . . it is un-tuned according to the Western scale. . . . We did use the Mieng. It is a little kind of a bamboo with a sort of a hole. It's a very . . . very . . . basic instrument. It's got several parts to it . . . one instrument is going to give you one note . . . I used the Duitara. They say its duitara but it has four strings. Now Oratario has no drama but the text is religious text and everything is sung. I have just written one so far which is not even complete yet. It is called Ukten which means the word. So, the word is centered on the person of Jesus. He is called the word. He is referred to by many names and it says that when God created the world, he created it through the word. And the word was with God. He was there right from the very beginning and the gospel

[38] Walter Benjamin, "The Task of the Translator: An Introduction to the Translation of Baudelaire's Tableaux Parisiens," in *Illuminations: Essays and Reflections*, ed. Walter Benjamin (New York: Schocken Books, 1969), 69–82.

of John examines that right from the first narrative. So, that almost fascinated me, the word. (April 2014)

In the case of Aroha Choir we find that there seems to be use of indigenous musical instruments that would complement the jazz idiom that the choir director has on her mind. A typical jazz gig would have piano, double bass, saxophone, and drums proclaiming the musical language. Since the choir only uses piano accompaniment, the use of wind instruments like Tangmuri and Mieng seems only natural. Ka Duitara ka deika jing temiing (The duitara is a home instrument) fills the absence of the sound of the string. Duitara being a home instrument and a symbol of Khasi folk and Tangmuri reiterating the triumph of the cock in Khasi legends makes one wonder if there may be a strategic subtext.

In the case of Aroha, it appears that each member of the choir maintains their individual tonal qualities which makes certain voices favorable toward portraying the rock resonance, while others have the tendency to bring out the pop, jazz, operatic, and ballad impressions. Few others belt out a deep well-rounded sound or a controlled high-pitched timbre. These variations color each song with multiple shades yet reflecting one common hue in the form of a universal sound quite isolated from the congregational sound, which the choir director steers clear from. This time of the year, the concerts lined up for the choir are themed around Christmas which is why experimentation in terms of genres weren't too noticeable yet the repertoire was replete with jazz, calypso, pop, country, gospel, and opera idioms. The approach used by the Aroha Choir is best understood in the context of Cavell's idea of chance and improvisation.

In "Discomposed Music," Stanley Cavell (1976) philosophizes the object of art. Fraudulence, he says, comes across as a rampant occurrence in contemporary music. The experience of fraudulence and truth in art in turn questions the very concept of art. To understand the notion of fraudulence, one needs to understand what comprises genuine, following a critical register. Representing fraudulence is merely showing "something is imitation—not an imitation" (Cavell, 1976: 89). It retains the effects of the genuine. To understand false art, one has to understand more than what the language, the sensory organs, the logical apparatus discloses. Modern art puts both the object and the viewer on trial. The critic wants to make the art experience known because the artworld can be shared. The skill to convey should be such that it doesn't falsify the position of the critic and helps him affirm to (himself as well) the others that he sees the object. The burden of describing art is sometimes similar to the burden of producing it. Cavell equates art work to human beings. Both move us. Artwork, he says, involves people in the process, with a freedom of choice, with a set of coherent and useful actions in an indifferent atmosphere. Two virtues of composition are chance and improvisation. One takes one's own chances alongside all the dangers, imbalances, anxiety, and surprises. The chances are attractive and promising to others who choose to join the composer. Improvisation returns some area of freedom to the performer in new music.

As Cavell says, "convention as a whole is now looked upon not as a firm inheritance from the past, but as a continuing improvisation in the face of problems we no longer understand. Nothing we now have to say, no personal utterance, has its meaning conveyed in the conventions and formulas we now share" (Cavell, 1976: 201). In an artworld where conventions are eventually forced to take the garb of nihilism, what kind of improvisation finds its expression in the sound of the Shillong Chamber Choir and the Aroha Choir? Amid the process of the exchange of social and intellectual elements of two or more different musical genres, does Hindi film music, traditional music, or Indian classical guarantee access to a value of shared meanings? Also, shared meanings among whom? India's Got Talent established the creation of a value of shared meanings. The Aroha Music School also worked on an eclectic repertoire. If such is the consequence, "Bollywood music" or other "stylistic mediations" within the structure of choral music and harmony can work toward designing a new convention whereby, incorporating shared meanings via classics that have acquired popularity, across genres, ensure comprehensibility of music. This comprehensibility of music extends to a particular spectrum of spectators; those spectators who are always questioning fraudulence and genuineness in a composition; those who look forward to experimentations. There are others who are conventional, who do not fathom the marriage of two musical genres.

Further, pious among the spectators remain skeptical about the performance; especially in the choice of songs while intermediation is in process. Also, there are spectators who believe that there is no newness in the composition.

Conclusion

The choirs are defined by the novelty that they bring by positing Medley as a genre that is underlined by the premise—classical-across-genres Led by Padma Shri Neil Nongkynrieh, the Bollywood motif comes across strongly in the case of the Shillong Chamber Choir, who are best known to perform the Bollywood

Broadway. However, in their motley repertoire, there is also a Khasi Opera, Sohlyngngem. The theme is that of a Khasi girl's grief for her lost lover amid contemporary sociopolitical circumstances. The composition won the group a silver medal at the 2009 World Choir Championships in South Korea. The choir performs this particular composition, in parts or whole, during certain occasions. I had seen them perform it for a show at the North Eastern Hill University in October 2014. The Aroha Choir had a Christmas motif during my fieldwork days, but overall, they like to work with jazz idiom, overall. It is not always executed through the song selection but rather through vocalizations. I particularly remember one of the renditions by the Aroha Junior Choir where they sing "Forget Your Worries" by David Clydesdale in this context. Recently, the Aroha Junior Choir won the first prize in the acapella category at the Llangollen International music festival Eisteddfod at Wales in 2018. They performed "Disney Fly Medley" by James Ray and "One Day I'll Fly Away" by Randy Crawford. The 2006 reality TV show win in a way "territorialized" the sounds for the Shillong Chamber Choir but the classical flavor remains due to the choice of songs and compositions that are classics in their respective genres. The vocalization technique adopted by the Aroha Choir has helped them

Figure 3.1 A few members of the Shillong Chamber Choir after their performance at a school in Guwahati on November 15, 2014.

Figure 3.2 Aroha Choir at Raj Bhavan Pre-Christmas Concert. Photo Credit Ken Warjri.

Figure 3.3 Aroha Senior Choir at Caux Cultural Exchange. Photo credit Ken Warjri.

territorialize their sounds. The genre comprising crossover, kitschy elements, has something new to offer. This novelty presented to the audience is made possible by intertextuality and synchronicity. The following is illustrated by Aroha Choir's Medley comprising "Ri Khasi" and "Ae Mere Watan Ki Logon."

Synchronicity is reflected through the common theme of love for one's place and ancestry; yet it speaks of divided loyalties. Intertextuality is demonstrated by bringing together a classic from the indigenous repertoire: the Khasi national anthem and a patriotic song from the film repertoire, immortalized by Bollywood's nightingale, Lata Mangeshkar. The vocalization or stylistic idiom used by the choir is the Indian classical motif. Therefore, here, the latter is the territorialized sound. In the case of Shillong Chamber, one can discover intertextuality amid two classical music traditions: the harmonizing attribute of the choral interpretation by Neil Nongkynrieh and the instrumental attribute of the Indian classical tradition in the form of tabla bols/beats by Zakir Hussain. The synchronicity is that of adapting an existing rhythmic pattern to a contemporary vocal interpretation. Here, the rhythmic motif emerges as the territorialized sound. Thus, Bollywood motif may be the primary territorialized sound for the Shillong Chamber Choir or stylistic idiom is perhaps the same for the Aroha Choir, but the other possibilities point toward re-territorialization. Overall, Medley as a genre inscribes classical-across-genres. In the next chapter, we will see how sacrality emerges as the dominating theme in the context of Goa's choral repertoire (Figures 3.1–3.3).

4

The Language of Music

Notes from a Goan Seminary

Nostalgia (from nostos return home, and algia longing) is a longing for a home that no longer exists or has never existed. Nostalgia is a sentiment of loss and displacement, but it is also a romance with one's own fantasy. Nostalgic love can only survive in a long-distance relationship.

Svetlana Boym, *The Future of Nostalgia*

Inhabiting the Seminary

Goa became an union terrirory in 1961. The Portuguese sociocultural world played a major role in structuring the sensorium of Goa since the sixteenth century. In a major way, church organization had an eminent presence and complexity only when Goa was made the headquarters of the Portuguese activities in the East. It acquired the status of the suffragan diocese in 1533 and earned the rank of a metropolitan archdiocese in 1557 (De Souza, Teotonio R. 1994). Rachol Seminary, one of the foremost seminaries in Asia, was set up around 1610 (Albuquerque, Teresa, 1997). Sacred music emerges as a principal motif in understanding the life world of a Catholic Goan. In this connection, it becomes pertinent to ask where does one acquire a foundational training in voice. Is voicing an important attribute to learn alongside the ritualistic and scriptural training at the seminary? How does the Seminary inculcate training to be an ideal sacred subject?

Writings on music and sound from South Asia discuss nation-building projects that standardize certain genres through particular modalities. These outline specific pedagogic, performative, and embodied mannerisms. The sociohistorical trajectories and politics inform the cultural conversations that shape canonical genres such as Indian classical music. In postcolonial India, cultural performances focus on the shifting character of middle-class patronage, creation of public spaces along the sacred-secular binary. There is also the formulation of a definite kind of listening public "musicophiliacs" in the Girgaum district of Mumbai (Subramanian, 2011; Bakhle, 2005; Weidman, 2006; Kapuria, 2018; Niranjana, 2020; Sá Mario Cabral e., 1997). There are works that look at laboring bodies in diaspora, Indians in Caribbean Trinidad and London, being part of the production and circulation of crossover music (Ramnarine, 2001; Niranjana, 2006) and involvement of the laboring bodies, the mridangam makers, who majorly contribute to the aesthetic realm, yet continue to be erased from it (Krishna, 2020). In the realm of dance, performance as heuristic device may be seen as a documentation of a complicated history as well as a medium of "dramatizing the subaltern," devadasi art (Soneji, 2012). We also encounter how the aesthetic aspirations and Bollywood dancing are shaped by the neo-liberal moral-ideological sentiments of the Indian middle class (Morcom, 2013). Musical writings on Goa have presented biographical sketches of famous musicians from Goa and mapped how different genres like Indian classical, Western classical, and Bollywood film industry have forged different trajectories within and outside Goa. Few works are concerned with structure and manifestation of musical styles, others are invested in studying traditions of mando festivals or locating syncretic symbols in their modality of scripting and performing music (Sardo, 2011; Fernandes, 2012; and Pereira, Martins, 2012). Situated within a postcolonial framework of engaging with faith, institution, and music, I am interested in underlining the intent and expression of Goan sacred music.

I have studied the form and materiality of music. I chose to explore Rachol Seminary as a predominant site to look at the phenomenon of Goan sacred music because after the parish school, Rachol Seminary continues to preserve a nostalgic Portuguese past of inculcating and transmitting a Catholic-Goan sound world. This borrows from colonial, popular, and indigenous flavors, consciously merging certain historical temporalities with the ethnographic present. Given my socio-ethnic location (I have spoken about this elaborately in the prologue section of the book), I wasn't entirely sure how to inhabit the seminary space as a part of my ethnography. I was living close to the archbishop's palace at Althino. My landlady assured me that the best places to learn about musical and ritualistic traditions of Christianity would be the seminaries and the archbishop's palace. It was an uphill walk that led to the archbishop's palace. The familiar sweet-earthy-bucolic smell of orangish-red mud, typical to the Goan church scape filled the air.

I felt a strange connect. When I started out, I had no idea that priests will become the interlocutors in my work to navigate Goan sacred music.

Through an institutional biography animated by personalities who have embodied the seminary way of life, I have chosen to discuss Goan sacred music as it exists today. All the seminarians talk about their exposure to music while at the seminary. Each of them mentioned how they have been effective members of the seminary choir during their studentship days. I gathered from my conversations that this membership is highly prestigious as it alludes to one's overall potential for musicality. The chapter captures the essence of developing an aural training while forming a close relationship with God. The relevance of lyrics, melodies, rhythms, and styles of music in the domain of sacred music is indicated by the rules formulated by the Diocesan Commission of Sacred Music and Diocesan Commission of Liturgy. The necessity of immersing oneself in the act of organizing choirs, choral festivals, competitions, recitals, and compositions bring out the multiple dimensions of the musical tradition that is inculcated as a part of seminary education. The forms of the choirs in Goa represent genre-specific repertoires. It can be "classical," "folk"/"indigenous," "sacred music," or "foreign language" arrangements. There is no concept of "crossover" or Medley within a song. The Goan sacred music as a category is a product of nostalgia that is punctuated by Latin, Konkani, and Portuguese pasts. The myriad influences are woven into the musical structures such as Gregorian chants (the first 800 years of Christian worship had melody only. It took the form of cantillated prayer of a simple nature or an embellished Gradual for a solemn occasion). It was, however, monody, the single line of melody without accompaniment, that united the Christians (Albuquerque Teresa, 1997: 75), mandos (product of the Romantic movement not only because of the periodicity but also because of the art forms that inspired it like the opera, novel, fado, and ballroom dancing had roots in the Romantic movement; Pereira, Martins, and Da Costa, 2006: 37) and has recently been observed as "a peninsular Indic quadrille- a creolized music-dance form that attests to a web of people, cultures, and commodities connecting the Atlantic and Indian Oceans through the long timeline of the Portuguese empire and its relationships with other global and regional powers" (Kabir, 2021:1587). and motets (polyphonic choral setting, usually unaccompanied comprising a sacred Latin text not fixed in the liturgy (Morais, 2007: 17–18). All of these along with Western classical repertoires establish a canon of Goan sacred music. The musical forms have an independent existence as well when the forms of choirs are experimented and only the four-voice arrangement or harmonization element is borrowed from the Western classical vocalic tradition. The Cotta Family Choir and one of the earlier choirs, Gavana (however, the choral activities of Gavana was quite different), demonstrate these characteristics as explored in the vignettes. Stuti Choir gives a taste of sacred choir that takes choral music outside of church premises in Goa. Here, "Classical music" and "Indigenous music" acquire prominence. A few examples of syncretic musical practices are especially prominent during Lenten season either in the form of vernacularized passion narratives, *Tiatrs* (Konkani dramas) themed around saints comprising cantos; Zagor (Hindu musical tradition of singing overnight celebrating ancestor/God, etc.) that forms a part of Goa's indigenous tradition and specifically Catholic-Goan notion of sacred music called the motets are discussed vis-à-vis the formation of Goan sacred music as an extension of Seminary music education.

Ethnography on musical traditions in Goa that largely draws from the musical forms in Christianity, folk categories like mando and dulpod, Western classical compositions, and Medieval music charted out a sacred music repertoire. Dwelling on the one hand with notions of "voice" and how it is looked upon as a separate object which conspicuously becomes the "fan's jouissance" (Poizat Michel, 1991: 198)[1] and on the other hand the role of faith in the daily lives of the worshippers made me interested in Goan sacred music as a category. I am summoning fan's jouissance to chart out a sacral vocality that informs the sacred music repertoire. The erotic aspects that make voice an object interlocking the oral and the aural also affirms that the voice of Jesus, who uttered a loud cry before lying lifeless on the cross, surpasses the voice of a diva. This chapter explores how faith and Catholic-Goan musical tradition coincide. It leaves scope to observe what effect such an interweaving has on the laity and the regional story about creating and maintaining certain elements of a form of a Western classical tradition.

Furthermore, seminary is where the priests receive their foundational training to sharpen their ideas about the religious vocation. Liturgical services emerge as a significant activity in this process. Creating, vocalizing, and permitting sacred music informed by a Catholic-Goan ethic helps structure Catholic Church repertoires. I argue here that the "imperial affect"[2] inhabits the seminary and shapes sacred subjects. There are indigenous claim-making to contest this imperial affect in curating a Goan sacred music genre. However, a nostalgia for Latin, Konkani, and Portuguese pasts that reside at the core of the seminary

---

[1] Michel Poizat, "'The Blue Note' and 'The Objectified Voice and the Vocal Object,'" *Cambridge Opera Journal* 3, no. 3 (1991): 195–211. http://www.jstor.org/stable/823616.

[2] My coinage.

soundscape, works to fade out indigenous claim-making and conversely buttress the imperial affect.

Rachol Seminary has been the pioneer institute for inculcating the tradition of engaging with Western classical music in the process of learning theology and philosophy, the essentials in the center for the formation of priests. It was due to the foundation of music schools, music ensembles, and church music competitions by the priests and music lovers that the public life of Western classical music became an integral part of the Goan-Catholic community once again. Earlier it was a seamless part of the community because of the parish schools that primarily emphasized music education. Also, each of the priests mentioned in this chapter had a different manner of connecting to faith. One is from a family that focuses on piety as an essential element in life. One discovered his calling much later in life. There is also the story of one who experienced faith due to his own ideas, which were far more important to him beyond the worldly things. Then, there is one who did not eventually become a priest. Finally, there is one for whom literature and music almost became an extension of faith. Music was brought to each one in the course of learning to be closer to God. Perhaps faith implored them to use their talents for the greater good. Sacred Goan music as a category needs to be explored in depth. The constant return to one's indigenous melodies and rhythms inscribe a cultural reference deeply rooted in the community. In future, the older approach of competitions among parishes might facilitate the creation of interesting repertoires and involvement of the laity in the process of making music. At the moment, there are quite a few choirs in Goa like the Stuti Choir, Goa Institute of Management Choir, Goa University Choir, Namah Chorale, Aradhon Choir, Cotta Family Choir, and so on who are working toward making different forms of choir music, ordered around a sacred music tradition, not just as a way of life, but a bridge to retain some of the lost traditions.

The contribution of the Jesuits in encouraging the use of Konkani language alongside the set of instructions being delivered in Portuguese helped retain a typical "Goan-ness." It was well ingrained in the structure of the Rachol Seminary too. In a way, traces of adopting Christianity with sufficient indigenous vignettes existed in Goa much before the council of Vatican II announced the church to allow the vernacular way of life to be embraced within the larger framework of Catholic Church worship rituals. Of course, after the announcement in the 1960s, there was a spurt of compositions in Konkani and the need to find a way to adopt indigenous rhythm or melody as per the regulations of Diocesan Commission of Sacred Music.

Goa, through the category of Goan sacred music, is holding on to what Boyd refers to as the "Restorative Nostalgia" that derives from nostos and aims at a transhistorical recreation of a lost home. It is different from "Reflective Nostalgia"; that, which is ordered around algia: longing and loss. There is a dream about distant possibilities, pertaining to a different place and a different time. It forges a strong connection to a loss of collective outlines of memory; not reclaiming it in the absolute form. I look at how the seminary education creates an atmosphere to access the divine as well as develop a musical expertise that aids in worship-related activities and beyond. To explore this copresence of faith and music, I use Charles Hirschkind's (2006)[3] ethical listening of cassette sermon that is determined by the Quranic concept of Inshirah (opening of the heart in a manner that brings someone closer to God) and Sukanya Sarbadhikari's (2015)[4] notion of emplacing oneself in the celestial abode of Vrindavan through performing Kirtan. An emic view of Goan sacred music emerges though experiences of select seminarians.

Outlining Goan Sacred Music

A seminarian internalizes the sacred underpinnings of Catholic Christianity by critically approaching theological texts as well as by being part of everyday social rituals that inform the core principles of the faith. The institution encloses so many life stories and, in the process, embodies and reproduces a specific Goan-Catholic ethic. The teachers, staff, and students contribute to the existing curriculum and nurture other practices which shape the lifestyle of a priest.

In this regard, I use Charles Hirschkind's Cassette sermon (Hirschkind, 2006). It dates back to the 1979 Iranian revolution when Ayatollah Khomeini's speeches led to the overthrow of the Shah. It again reappeared in 1993 during the trial of Shayk Omar Abdul Rahman, who was convicted due to engagement with the Muslim fundamentalists for attacking the World Trade Centre. The effects of this movement are rampant across Egypt but it is prominent in the popular quarters of Cairo's lower and lower-middle classes. The cassette sermon has taken on the project of Islamic revival (*al-sahwa-al-Islamiya*) ever since its inception in the twentieth century, offering a critique of the religious and secular order

---

[3] C. Hirschkind, *The Ethical Soundscape: Cassette Sermons and Islamic Counterpublics* (New York: Columbia University Press, 2006).

[4] S. Sarbadhikary, *The Place of Devotion: Siting and Experiencing Divinity in Bengal Vaisnavism* (California: University of California Press, 2015).

(Hirschkind, 2006: 2, 3, 6). The act of listening to sermon tapes in Egypt focuses on receptivity based on humility (*Khushu*), pious fear (*b'il-taqwa*), and faith (*iman*). A little distraction does not interfere with the benefit (*tastafid minu*). The tape brings forth the Quranic concept of opening of the heart that brings one closer to God which is known as Inshirah. The cassette acts as a mnemonic instrument that allows and expands the contours for memory, ethical feeling, and moral judgments alongside forays into popular entertainment. Marcel Jousse (1990) says that the memory is activated by the body's sensory-motor past that delves into the "visceral, kinesthetic, aural, tactile" facets of the sensorium (Hirschkind, 2006: 70–4, 79). The Islamic practices of preaches have a tradition of Arabo-Islamic musical theory, Sufism and the scholarship of "im-al-balagha." The repetitive chanting of the names of God, manners of enlarging vowels (*madd*), and breathing techniques leave a strong impression on the listener. Common to the sensitive listeners of Tarab endowed music, like that of the singer Umm Kulthum; that not only requires musical and poetic manifestation from the performer but also a talent and sensitivity on the part of the audience and the sermon listener requires an ethical-aesthetic response on the part of the listener. This activates the moral radar in the various aspects of daily life (Hirschkind, 2006: 36–7). Similar to the cassette sermon method which has ethical listening as response, the training in terms of different areas of musicianship like efficiency in musical instruments, solfeggio training, classes in Gregorian chant, organizing choral concerts for the seminary annual day, language training apart from theology lessons create priests who demonstrate ethical-aesthetic listenership. Music education and varied presentations related to it become an everyday mode of listening to and responding to the ethics of being in the seminary. It impacts the understanding of sacral matters crucial to devising oneness with God.

When it comes to importing skills from the seminary to other set ups that require similar predispositions like formation of an entertainment choir, formulating guidelines for liturgical music repertoires, deciding on choral repertoires and compositional choices, Sukanya Sarbadhikary's study on Bengal Vaishnavites (2015) finds that singing Kirtans is a way of embodying Vrindavan, the celestial abode of the deities Radha and Krishna, gains resonance. Bengal Vaishnavism gives importance to the worship of Krishna's sweeter moods (*madhurya*) and not his kingly warrior moods (*aishwarya*) furthering the emotional relationships with him. This comes from the Bhagavata Purana tradition that celebrates the copresence of aesthetic, erotic, and the ecstatic devotional levels. Collective renditions find expressivity through the modes of Nam Kirtan (the musician groups sing Radha-Krishna's names in disparate tunes followed by a repetitive chanting cycle of sixteen names: *mahamantra* or *sholanam*) and Lila Kirtan (the musician groups discuss the deities' "divine activities and love play" in celestial Vrindavan through the compositions of medieval Vaishanava practitioners (Sarbadhikary, 2015: 13, 179, 181). Singing Kirtans enable the embodiment of the Vrindavan. Being in the seminary, which is earmarked by particular kinds of life choices, allows them to later bring about discerned choices regarding production and documentation of sacred music and aligning relevant elements of folk music and inherent musicalities for nonsacred music. Faith undergirds their decision-making both in implicit and explicit forms.

Finally, I look at Svetlana Boym's (2001) analysis of Moskow's restorative nostalgia as a megalomaniac imagination that looks at the past as a time of mythical giants. Massive fires that destroyed parts of the city contribute to the creation of this megalomaniac self-image. During the 1812 war against Napoleon, the Muscovites burned the city and escaped surrendering to the French. Moskow became famous as the Fire Bird, a city phoenix that rebuilds itself from the ashes each time becoming statelier and greater. The mythical time refers to one that talks of eternal rebirth instead of historical progression. The post-Soviet Moskow promises "a bigger and better future." It does not mourn its past. She also talks of total restorative projects during the 1980s and 1990s: Michaelangelo's Sistine Chapel and the Cathedral of Christ the Savior in Moscow (Boym, 2001: 56, 118). Goa, in constructing its sacred music repertoire, has followed the trajectory of restorative nostalgia choosing to engage with elements that either speak of past grandeur or moments that have ascribed to them particular creative and sacred emblems. The preservation of Konkani language by the church, composition of mandos, revisiting motets and Gregorian chants, and introducing classical music pieces highlight Goa's inclination toward restorative nostalgia. The seminarians have attempted to selectively retain specific cultural moments in the realm of music to make a repository of Goan sacred music.

Tracing the Significance of Music and Language

Music and language have a unique role in positing Goan sacred music and the seminarians have a major role in this endeavor. This section touches on the history of music and language in Goa.

Micael Martins (1997)[5] in his writings on sacred music in Goa gives an insight into the mid-sixteenth century. He says that during that time, musical notation was hardly known and learning was slow. Music compositions used to be learned orally by a group of singers who traveled from one village to the other to spread the repertoires composed by themselves and others. This was made possible through the process of intuition rather than an established musical culture. When these performances started becoming quite frequent and the performers imitated the "troubadours" or nomadic travelers in the Middle Ages, there arose the class of "Amateurs." The latter studied musical notation and went on to become "Professionals."

In 1542, after arriving in Goa, Fr. Francis Xavier brought in singing during catechism classes. In 1543, two Goan boys sang during the Mass at the inauguration of St. Paul's College (Britto, 2014).[6] In Goa, the parish schools were established as early as the sixteenth century (1545). Here, faith was infused among the pupils by introducing them to the sacred Latin music, since Latin was the official language of liturgy at that time and the magical qualities of the Gregorian and polyphonic music amid the grand architectural surroundings of Old Goa made it fascinating. Music used to be taught according to voices (Miranda, Eufemiano de Jesus, 2014).[7]

In the parish schools, the syllabus included alphabets, spellings, reading, writing, arithmetic, the procedure of conducting mass in Latin, Gregorian chant, prayer songs in Latin, Catechism, Bible history, Portuguese and Konkani languages, solfeggio, singing, violin, and organ. A structured music education was set in motion. After mastering the skill to sing for twelve Masses, pupils were sent for violin classes (Martins, 1997).

Education in a variety of subjects was monitored by the mestres in the supervision of the Vicar of the parish. Communidades Agricolas, Confrarias, Fabricas of the churches, and some rich individuals became patrons of parish schools. Children were exposed to religious activities like novenas, vespers, feasts, and processions so as to inculcate a deep sense of faith. However, the system could not sustain efficiently with the burgeoning of official primary schools. There were fewer mestres to coordinate the affairs. Efforts were made

---

[5] M. Martins, "Musica Sacra and Its Impact on Goa," in *Wind of Fire: The Music and Musicians of Goa* ed. Mario Cabral E. Sa (New Delhi: Promilla and Co. Publishers, 1997).

[6] N. Britto, "The Three Divas," in *Semina de Cultura Indo Portuguesa* (Goa: Singbals, 2014), 138–51.

[7] E. Miranda, "Goan Music in the Christian Faith and Tradition," in *Commemorating Christ in Goa: Some Sketches of the Life and Culture of Christians, Yesterday and Today*, ed. I. Vás (Goa: Third Millenium, 2014), 45–57.

in the 1930s to revive this system. In September 1932, the vicars had to present a report about the activities of their respective parish schools. This ancient tradition is continued in a few parishes of Goa (Pinto, Celsa, 2014).[8]

The congregation of Santa Monica built in 1606 and transformed into a monastery in 1636 was in fact the first religious congregation for women in Asia. In sync with the sacred tone of the monastery, the sisters placed a lot of importance on church songs and hymns, especially Gregorian chant and music. The statuses guaranteed that the sisters had an access to singing lessons, lessons in harp and organ by an elderly music teacher. This musical knowledge enabled them to contribute further to the religious services. This training helped the sisters of Santa Monica in their songs, hymns, quatrains, and ballads dedicated to the prioresses, a few religious inmates, and to the Augustinian Friars (brothers), both in sacred and nonsacred repertoires (Lopes Maria De Jesus Dos Martires, 2000).[9]

In a major way, church organization had an eminent presence and complexity only when Goa was made the headquarters of the Portuguese activities in the east. It acquired the status of the suffragan diocese in 1533 and earned the rank of a metropolitan archdiocese in 1557. Religious orders impacted the missionary field until they were suppressed in 1834–5. Even though different religious orders had set up their missionary headquarters in the capital city of Goa, Jesuits and the Franciscans are given priority for their intensive labor in the capital and rural areas of Goa. Jesuits handled matters related to the establishment of the church in Salcete and the Franciscans in Bardez. The Dominicans made their contributions in the island-taluka surrounding the city (De Souza Teotonio R., 1994).[10]

It is interesting to observe the changes embraced by the Jesuits in the context of music. The reform of music in relation to the contemporary religious life was an essential engagement on the part of the society. The Jesuits, including Ignatius Loyola and his companions, were ambivalent about the values of engaging in a musical activity. As early as 1539, the first draft of the Formula of the Institute endorsed by the pope officially prohibited those in holy orders from playing

---

[8] C. Pinto, "475 years of Education: The Role of Archdiocese," in *Commemorating Christ in Goa: Some Sketches of the Life and Culture of Christians, Yesterday and Today*, ed. I. Vás (Goa: Third Millenium, 2014).

[9] M. Lopes, "The Sisters of Santa Monica in the 18th Century: Details of Their Daily Life," in *Goa and Portugal: History and Development*, ed. C. Borges, O. Pereira and H. Stubbe (New Delhi: Concept Publishing Company, 2000), 238–48.

[10] T. de Souza, "The Voiceless in Goan History," in *Goa to Me*, ed. T. de Souza (New Delhi: Concept Publishing Company, 1994), 69–85.

organs, and reciting and chanting in chorus during religious ceremonies or Catholic liturgical sessions. This is because participating in choirs was equivalent to practicing monasticism according to the Jesuits. Also, music was considered a hindrance in executing the works of mercy by the Formula of the Institute. They also felt that the energy spent in maintaining a stable musical tradition would be contrary to the mobile nature of the missionary work.

Unlike the monastic vision of the church, whereby there would be two different parts for the priests on the one hand and the laities on the other hand, absence of a choir changed the church architecture. Jesuit churches like Il Gesu had no room for deep choir stalls, located to the side or behind the altar or between the altar and the nave. Ambulatory and radial chapels also started to vanish.

Meanwhile, the Jesuits began to realize the importance of music in their pedagogic vocation. Statuses for College of Coimbra which dates back to 1548 attest to the use of music. It also brought into focus the necessity on the part of inhabitants to chant daily for two hours on Sundays and holidays and also on the eve of holidays. Jesuits therefore incorporated music in their curriculum, as liturgical music in churches and colleges and in theater performances. Due to the change in architecture, the balcony at the rear of the church became common and was the new choir loft for the rising musical and choral groups of the laity (Osswald, 2013).[11]

Native languages were considered to be important, especially as a mark of self-expression. Jesuits tended to the conservation of the Konkani language. Not only did they have an ongoing practice of studying grammatical and literary Konkani, they were also the first to produce literary works and grammar printed in the Konkani language. In the eighteenth century, works written in Konkani by a Czech Jesuit named Karel Prickryl, who was in Goa from 1748 to 1761, and a Spanish Jesuit named Hervas y Pandure, who was in Goa from 1735 to 1809, have left an impression (Mascarhenas, Mira, 1989).[12]

The Confraternity of the Holy Faith, built in 1541 at Old Goa, had a college which trained young converts to take up evangelization in their own countries. Formal instructions were in Portuguese but a great emphasis was stressed on local language. Ignatius Loyola had made it clear to the members of his Society of

---

[11] C. Osswald, *Written in Stone: Jesuit Buildings in Goa and their Artistic and Architectural Features* (Goa: Goa 1556, 2013).

[12] M. Mascarhenas, "The Church in the Eighteenth Century," in *Essays in Goan History*, ed. T. Souza (New Delhi: Concept Publishing Company, 1989), 81–102.

Jesus the importance of being firmly rooted in the study of one's native language wherever they were. In March 1567, Pope Pius V made an urgent plea to the parish priests to equip themselves in the native language. Konkani was taught in Old Goa and the most effective contribution of the Jesuits in this regard was their printing press which contributed to a thriving teaching tradition and development of a Konkani literature.

Rangel printing press which was initiated in 1886, was the first notation printing press at Bastora (Bardez Goa). It led to the circulation of the musical legacy of various native composers. Pequeno solfeggio booklet in three volumes by Eduardo Baptista was introduced to the parish schools after it gained approval on September 8, 1898. It discussed the basics about melodic, theoretical, and practical references. In fact, violin manufacturing in Goa dates back to 1925 (Martins, Micael, 1997).

Inside the Seminary

Reimagining one's field requires one to immerse oneself in the given event during another time either by accessing the same social processes and institutions or by allowing oneself to revisit only certain moments of the process. It is interesting to observe the modes of its functioning, how things undergo transformation in the course of time and the inherent anticipation. Here it is relevant to look at Foucault's Archaeology of Knowledge (Foucault, Michel, 2013). Here, he talks of how archaeology illustrates an "enunciative homogeneity" marked by its own temporalities which do not include all kinds of identity and differences that are located in the language. At this level, a hierarchical order is created but it stands in stark opposition to the small discrete occurrences that they may be forgotten in the ordering of the emergent archive. For instance, Foucault says that is it difficult to confirm if it was Linnaeus or Buffon, Broussais or Bichat that spoke the truth was the most rigorous with one's postulate or which one of them had the "oeuvre" that had utmost potential in laying out the general principle of science (Foucault, 2013: 142, 166).[13] In the process of curating the sacred music of Goa, many influences are brought together, not necessarily through a chronology or by the logic of musicality or sacrality but by a series of discernment adopted by specific personalities and institutions.

[13] M. Foucault, *Archaeology of Knowledge* (New York: Pantheon Books, 1972).

Ethnography on musical traditions in Goa that largely draws from the musical forms in Christianity, folk categories like mando and dulpod, Western classical compositions, and Medieval music charted out a sacred music repertoire. Dwelling on the one hand with notions of "voice" and how it is looked upon as a separate object which conspicuously becomes the fan's jouissance (Poizat Michel, 1992)[14] and on the other hand the role of faith in the daily lives of the worshippers made me interested in Goan sacred music as a category. This chapter explores how faith and Goan musical tradition coincide. It leaves scope to observe what effect such an interweaving has on the laity and the regional story about creating and maintaining certain elements of a form of a Western classical tradition.

The Jesuit College of Salcette was founded in 1574 and two years later "Vernacular Class" "Escola Da Lingua Canarina" was introduced. "Canarin," a word of Arabic origin, refers to those living on the "kinari" or coastline. This laid the foundation stone for growing period of Konkani literature which lasted for about a century, 1585–1685. Jesuit students were exposed to an intensive Konkani course in the first semester. Here they were even encouraged to talk to the local people in Konkani so that they were well equipped to preach in Konkani by the end of the semester. In the second semester, they studied moral theology. The progress was noteworthy as one could gauge from the rendition of a song and verse composed in Konkani. Also, the author mentions an instance about a Konkani verse composed and sung by a Goan, praising preaching in Konkani by the Jesuits in church.

Young students at the parish schools learned the doctrine, which by now was translated to Konkani and they were happy to sing it on their way to the church or school. In this manner, religion entered their houses, making it accessible to the family members and slaves. Also, there were inter-parish recitation contests conducted by the Jesuits for the children.

Rachol was considered to be the best defended fort in the entire province in 1606. Three years later, on the vespers of the Feast of All Saints, there was a Mass at the church that was set up the previous year for the same occasion. In 1610 when both the church and the college had been built, the Jesuits moved from Margao permanently to the church and the college of All Saints at Rachol. Soon the college transformed into a seminary for priests. Jesuits were known for producing a great many secular priests during the initial phase. In 1646, the Jesuit Provincial recorded the fathers of the society teaching the Brahmins

---

[14] M. Poizat, *The Angel's Cry: Beyond the Pleasure Principle in Opera*, trans. A. Denner (New York: Cornell University Press, 1992).

singing, reading, accounts, musical instruments, Latin, theology, philosophy, and so forth till the time they were ordained as priests.

A ship arrived in Goa on September 25, 1759 that had a copy of the royal decree that ordered the arrest of all Jesuits in Portugal and its colonies and demanded acquisition of their belongings due to fabricated charges of their complicity in murdering the king Joseph I.

In Portugal, the orders for the expulsion of the Jesuits came from the Portuguese Prime Minister Sebastião Jose de Carvalho e Mello who was later made the Marquis of Pombal. Gregory Naik SJ (2019).[15]

Owing to the allegation that they amassed wealth and tampered with the village records. After them, the Oratorian Fathers were appointed. However, due to the discontinuity of the state subsidy in 1774, the work that was being furthered by the Oratorian Fathers also stopped.

In 1888, Rachol Seminary reached greater heights due to the introduction of the classes of Gregorian chant and sacred music. The seminary musical society called the "Palestrinean Choir" had St. Cecilia as its patroness. The choir comprising about a hundred students sang for the high masses at Old Goa. Also, there was an intensive study of Latin, the universal language of the church. Of course, philosophy and theology were treated at a deeper level (Albuquerque Teresa, 1997).[16]

Meeting the Seminarians

I am centering my vignettes around Rachol Seminary, which makes it relevant to start with my discussion with the then choir master of the St. Cecilia Choir of the Rachol Seminary, Fr. Simon D'Cunha in December 2013. I found out that the brothers who are studying for priesthood have some seminary activities which involve singing. Once a year, on the 31st of July, they have a Latin mass celebrating the feast of the Jesuit Father, St. Ignatius Loyola.

It is a tradition for them to sing in Latin and the music that is sung during the mass usually belongs to the classical period. Also, in the month of December, for the seminary day, an Opera is organized or the seminary choir sings. In case a bigger choir and different voices are needed, people are called from the outside.

---

[15] Naik SJ Gregory, Jesuits of the Goa Province: A Historical Overview. (Goa: Xavier Centre of Historical Research, 2019), (1542–2000).
[16] T. Albuquerque, *The Rachol Legacy* (Bombay: Wenden Offset Private Limited, 1997).

See, in priesthood we are studying three years of philosophy, that is academic, plus four years of theology and in that we have lectures of music also. We are teaching classical music as well as Gregorian chants—we teach them for one year and there is Indian music too.

In Seminary, we give much importance to the music. With much importance, we teach solfeggio to them and violin. They can pick up any instrument which they want to learn. So, we teach them these instruments—violin, clarinet and flute, cello, double bass. In this Saint Cecilia Choir, we have 16–18 members who are known as effective members[17] so if any function is there, these members are singing.

In the Seminary, we have a choir and a choir president. Our Rector who is the head of the seminary is our choir president. Then the Conductor is the vice president and among the students, there is one more—who is known as the choir master. He is also helping in the activity. It depends on the skill. As a seminarian, I was a choir master for two years. During my years at Rachol (7 years), I was a member of the choir, an effective member. On 23rd October, 2008, I became a priest.

The seminarians are also encouraged to go for Trinity College examinations for music theory or any instruments of their choice. The above conversation shows how various aspects of music education are incorporated as a daily feature in the formation house of the priests. The Rachol Seminary choir is TTBB,[18] which is why, during bigger celebrations, singers are invited from outside to include all the four voices. One of the most memorable concerts given by the Santa Cecilia Choir in recent times was in 2007, when a 130-member choir was directed by Fr. Romeo, the previous choir conductor in the big concert hall of the seminary. The conversation also talks about the importance of Gregorian music and classical music and the prestige associated with being a part of Rachol Seminary and its daily activities. In the Monte Festival held in February 2019, the Santa Cecilia Choir performed again under the baton of Fr. Romeo. The following history of the Rachol Seminary gives an idea of the significance of the institution in the lives of the Goans.

I always wanted to be a priest. My family is not into priesthood at all. . . . In fact I think that the last priest in my family died in 1904 or 1902. More than 100 years ago, the last priest in my family died. And before that priest, another priest who died in my family was in 1765. And I am the third priest in the family . . . I am a very happy priest. I can tell you. I am so happy that I have chosen this line which fulfills my life.

[17] Members who are principal singers and are also assigned specialized responsibilities.
[18] Tenor and bass voice only.

Father Loiola, secretary to the archbishop, one of the founder members of the Goa Guitar Guild and a composer gave me an overview of the thriving choral scene in Goa, twentieth century onward. He mentioned about Antonio Figuerido's Goa Symphony Orchestra and a choir that was founded in the late 1940s or early 1950s. Camille Xavier's 1965 choir called Goin Xo Nad, which means melody of Goa, had an eminent contribution. Camille Xavier was also the choir conductor of the Rachol Seminary during that time and opened a school of music in Margao, which continues till today. Goin Xo Nad clearly brings out the syncretic musical experimentation as it was mainly formed to encourage the folk songs of Goa which used to be sung in four voices. It was not a religious choir but they did include some sacred music in the choir. The folk music was mainly mandos and dulpods that were sung in South Goa. They had a lot of shows in Goa during those days. He mentioned about another choir that was founded by Fr. Thomas Sequiera called the *Gavana* which in Konkani has an interesting meaning as Fr. Loiola explained to me. *Ga* means *gaubi* (singers), *ba* means *vaxopi* (musicians-instrumentalists), and *na* means *naxbi* (dancers) so it was a group which had voices, instruments, and dance. The group which was formed sometime in the 1980s made quite a name in Goa. They were invited for shows in various places in Europe, in Rome, Portugal, Canada, and so on.

Fr. Loiola also spoke about the choir competitions conducted by different agencies or institutions or agencies that emerged in the 1980s whereby many churches prepared for Christmas carol or church hymn competitions. In this context, he also mentioned about a choir that he had formed while he was a parish priest at the Loutolim Church between the years 1987 and 1992. They were called the "Saviorites of Loutolim."

Why savior? because the church or the village is dedicated to the savior of the world so, Saviourites. It was a very good four voice because I used to have arrangements; I used to make arrangements for the choir. It varied from 4 to 6 voices and I love to play with the voices. Every year they used to come back mostly with the first prize—very seldom the second prize and hardly the third price . . . it was always in the prize list. It was mostly acapella with a little bit of keyboard, lead guitar and a base guitar. That was then but today the choir that is there in the same church—they have violins, two keyboards . . . they have quite an orchestral/ensemble there that accompanies the choir, which is in 4 voices. They sing very well and they also have instruments that I did not have then. The Loutolim Church Choir is one of the best church choirs in Goa today.

It is interesting how he sheds light on the essential contribution that these inter-church competitions did in terms of music. It helped many church choirs to develop themselves and the spirit of competition kept the enthusiasm of making music alive. The other choirs that he mentioned about clearly talk about the importance of folk or indigenous music in the lives of the Goans. Fr. Loiola's own relationship with music has also been quite remarkable. As a twelve-year-old boy, while taking piano lessons at the minor seminary he realized that he could play the same tune from different scales but learning by book was never his forte. He always had an ear for music and loved the sound of classical guitar. Perhaps he was even the first Indian student to appear for classical guitar examinations under the Trinity College in 1972. Fr. Camille Xavier had quietly supported his musical experiences by encouraging him to take up classical guitar seriously and singing in his choir Goin Xo Nad. Compositions, however, always came easy to him because of the overall musicianship skills. His other duties related to managing the matters of the archbishop keep him away from it though. Fr. Loiola is also a member of the Diocesan Commission of Sacred Music, which has a regular publication every two years in Konkani called Devachea Mogachim Gitam translated as the songs/sounds of God's children. He explained how new compositions get approval. The church, he said, has the diocesan commission of liturgy to approve the lyrics and the diocesan commission for sacred music which approves the music. These songs are choral songs, some simple melodies and a few that are in one or two voices but most of them are in four voices. There are also orchestral works. He explained how melodies are approved. He demonstrated how melodies need to be sung and according to the letter of the song. He gave an example of the offertory during mass. The lyrics of the song, he said, have to be "I offer myself to you." The commission looks at the words that have already been approved by the Diocesan Commission for Liturgy and the composition that has come. They have to ensure that the composition manages to translate the feelings of the song. The song must aid people to pray.

Another composer I met was Fr. Bernard Cotta, who began his music education with his father who was a choir master at the Santa Cruz Parish.

My father was a choirmaster in Santa Cruz (my place). He started with the parochial school where everybody used to go for music school—there I studied with him. He used to teach me. He was the only one. The choirmaster was the heart and soul of the whole village—he taught music plus reading and writing also. During my childhood, that school was mainly a music school. But maybe in nineteenth century, the parochial schools were given the opportunity to read other textbooks along with music.

He later went to study at the Rachol Seminary. During his years as a parish priest, he first had a choir in Mapusa between 1971 and 1975, and 1976 onward he had a choir in Salcette. In 1983, he was chosen to teach at the Rachol Seminary, where he taught for twenty-four years. In Rachol Seminary he taught music for the seminarians and during this time he was in many places around the seminary. There he had his choirs in Fatorda, Ambora, Ilha de Rachol, Mongul, Margao, and now he is the parish priest of Manora Chapel. He also goes to the music school at Margao mainly to monitor the activities there. He takes the classes for Gregorian chants at Rachol Seminary. He plays many instruments such as the violin, keyboard, guitar, and more.

I quote some excerpts related to the subject of composition which says a lot about the context within which he started composing and also how he employs instruments in terms of arranging different types of sacred songs.

> I started to compose one song at the age of 12 and it was in Konkani. . . . Lyrics were given by someone and I was asked to write the music. I said I will write the music. Then, at that particular age, nobody taught me how to write in notations.

> Then afterwards, I composed many other songs, especially devotional songs, liturgical songs. Then I do the mandos, dulpods. Then I got Konkani plays— Operattas. I had written one on the life of or saint, Father Joseph Vaz. There I gave 120 melodies, which were non-stop.

> I see the lyrics first then I put in the music. For that particular music what instrument is suitable, then I think. Suppose the Trumpet: it is like triumphant, then I put a trumpet. If it is like a simple one, I put it a clarinet tone or saxophone tone and for the violins: suppose something elevating to the spiritual life— violins are there to accompany. It is like that . . . violin is a real joy to playing. The sound is like a celestial sound, a good sound. So I like that and now because of the children I play guitar, Keyboard-organ and I like the sound of bells or a bell like tone for a children's song.

He goes on to explain how the choir masters used to be the soul of the entire village earlier. They taught music, basic arithmetic, and reading but soon everything changed. He even spoke about his efforts to foster Goan music. He tries to take his students to the Mando festivals which are held as per certain age groups like seven to twelve, thirteen to nineteen, and a senior group that includes people who are fifteen years old and above.

As a part of my fieldwork, I attended one of the Gregorian chants classes that he took on February 17, 2016. The book that he was referring to was titled *An Introduction to Gregorian Chants* by Romeo Monteiro. The class involved a small group of boys singing in turns and discussing about flats, dynamics, and dotted notes.[19] All the students were asked to sing in parts. It involved reading and singing. The latter resembled recitation. For instance, while singing "Adoro te devote," a theme in adoration, first they read the solfeggio; this was followed by reading of the words. Only then, they started singing it, like a chant. When they moved on to do "Ave Regina" (Hail Queen), the theoretical part was explained where the part about special neums-pressus was explained. An announcement was made as to how each note had to be sounded in gentle repercussion. The training toward Gregorian chant at the seminary is quite meticulous and requires serious engagement on the part of the pupils, whether they are musically gifted or not.

The previous life stories remind one how the mode of expressing oneself linguistically and a continuity of indigenous references in the form of folk melodies and rhythms were largely shaped by the series of events in the past. Compositions and use of specific instruments depended not only on one's skills but an overall feel of musicality. What emerges quite prominently is a sense of nostalgia toward sacred music, both in Latin and Konkani annotated by Goa's own indigenous pool of music.

I also spoke to Fr. Eufemio Miranda, founder of the Stuti Choir, a choir which began in 2008 while he was the parish priest of St. Inez Church. The purpose of the choir was to take music beyond Panjim and Kala Academy. For their first program, which had music of Bach, Beethoven, Schubert, and Goan folk and religious music, they performed at Aldona, Calangute, Shishini, Margao, and Savorde. Over the years, they had a couple of conductors who conducted the choir for specific periods. There was Nauzet Daruwala, Nigel Dickinson, Miguel Cotta, and finally Antonio Vaz. In recent years, between the years 2016 and 2017, they had guest conductors from Bombay and Portugal too, for intermittent periods.

I was born in a family, where my father was a teacher of Portuguese. He loved language, poetry and music. My mother also loved music. She learnt the piano. They used to sing to us some of the melody lines by Chopin and Mozart. So, in our family, there was always some kind of poetry, music and an atmosphere of

[19] Graphic symbol for notes which are explained in Chapter 1.

great joy. I went to the Seminary to become a priest. And in those times, it was compulsory to learn Latin. And because of my Portuguese background, I was an extremely good student of Latin. I got over distinction in Latin and that gave me, I would say, a great enthusiasm to pursue all my academic studies in languages. In seminary, we had to study many languages, first was Portuguese and Latin. Then next year, it was Portuguese, French and Latin. Then we had to learn Latin, Konkani, Marathi and things like that. All these languages but I excelled in the studies of languages, always. I loved poetry also. Because poetry has got music also. In the seminary, music was also a part of the curriculum, music was a compulsory subject. Everybody had to learn music. Even those people, who did not have an ear for music. Those who were out of tune in singing—even those people had to learn music. And in the seminary of Saligaon, where I spent my secondary education, there were many opportunities to perform music. I also learnt the Violin. Later on, when I went to the major seminary, in the Rachol Seminary, there were studies on Philosophy and later theology. Again, music was very much part of the curriculum. And I did it very well I tell you. I learnt Solfeggio. I could read with great ease. Then I could perform also. I could sing in the choir. Rachol Seminary had a choir and I was an effective member of that choir. So I was a member and in my last year, I became the assistant to the director of the choir. The choir was always directed by the teacher of music. He was always a priest and he took me as his assistant. In his absence, I had to coordinate all the work of the choir. So, music was very much a part of my priestly formation. I was in Rachol Seminary between the years 1960–67. I became a priest in 1967.

He spoke about his days at the seminary when he sang as a soprano till the age of twelve. He then went on to talk about various kinds of folk music like Dekini, Kunbi, and Dhalo music. In 1964, Victor Paranjoti's performance of the "Konkan Ballad" moved him greatly. There was also a musical collaboration between Victor Paranjoti[20] and Camille Xavier. He talked about the different musical traditions among the Hindu and Christian communities when it came to folk music; he maintained that the mandos[21] and dulpods were exclusive to the Christian communities. He said that rhythmically, Dekini and Kunbi music stand out and when it is adapted for choral singing, the harmonization gives it another dimension. He mentioned the subtle existence of caste, which comes

---

[20] Composer from Bombay.
[21] Mando: a folk music form in two voices associated with the upper caste converts initially as explained by Maria Aurora Couto, 2004. Goa: a daughter's story.

up only during the context of marriage. The church, however, is strict about performing folk music. Lyrics determine whether the music is sacred or not.

> Yes. That's why, sometimes, I am in dilemma. When you are in a dilemma, I like to speak with a certain freedom. I allow my freedom to speak. You understand what I mean. One piece of folk music can be sung there. I put that way and I go forward. It would not take such a big offence in performing such a beautiful Goan music inside the church. And even when we perform in the church, we remove the Blessed Sacrament from the Sanctum Santorium and the church is made a place, just for performance; like a venue.

He recalls one Monte Festival, when some of his colleagues took great offense when he performed Goan folk music, inside the church premises. In his defense, he did not really know whether the Stuti Choral Ensemble would be performing at the courtyard or inside, till the very last moment. While talking about it, he still says that he should perhaps be understood and pardoned for it. He further expresses his concern about pinning down the idea of sacred music by referring to the works of the Western classical composers.

> In the churches, the music that should be performed should be religious or in any manner sacred. Okay, you know, sacred music, religious music, liturgical music is chant but western classical music of let me say, during the time of Bach or later on, Mozart. Bach was a deeply religious man. Handel was a deeply religious man. And they composed so many operas or oratorios on Biblical themes. Now, can an oratorio be performed in the church? They say, yes, can be performed because after all it was, it has got Biblical themes; somewhat sacred music. Then I put out the question. Can Brandenburg Concerto by Bach be performed in the church? My colleague who sets rules and is an expert says that he feels that it could not be performed and I would say that it could be performed. Why? Because a Brandenburg Concerto by Johann Sebastian Bach is of such a high quality, it will elevate your soul, which is much superior I would say to some of the modern rhythms that we sing in the Church. We don't have much elevation. You would say that this modern piece can be sung, because, after all it is sacred but when you perform that music in the church, you feel like dancing! Whereas, if you perform Bach's concerto—you say it cannot be performed; but it is music that elevates you. Concertos of Bach, Concertos of Handel are spiritual music. I listen to their music and then I pray. So, the line dividing this sacred, religious and the former times music is so thin. Some people are very particular. But I am more liberal when it comes to the music of the Baroque's time, music of the time of Mozart. Mozart for example composed a sonata; a church sonata also. Sonata

is not to be performed in the church. But church sonata means that his intention was that the sonata could be performed in the church.[22]

I also spoke to a family choir in Goa, one of the few remaining ones in contemporary times. Their story takes us on a journey as to how musical impression nurtured at Rachol embraced many forms and took on the form of an entertainment. They were definitely one of the highlights of the tourism industry in Goa, at least when they started out in the hotels, with their range of pop and folksy numbers from Goa, Portugal, Spain, and so on.

Miguel Cotta went to the Saligao Seminary at the age of eleven. After six years, he went to the Rachol Seminary. There, among other things, he discovered the Gregorian chants. He was initially preparing for priesthood, but after his mother's death in 1963, Miguel immersed himself into music. In 1965, he joined the folk band Goencho Nad. The first performance was held in Bangalore at the All-India Congress meeting. The group sung mandos and dulpods. Mostly, Catholics (Brahmin converts) from the villages of Loutolim, Benaulim, and Curtorim held the expertise of the mandos. One of the renowned composers, Agapito De Miranda (father in law of Miguel) composed a mando for their wedding and engagement. He got married in 1975. For their parents' wedding, Torcato de Figuerido from Loutolim had composed a mando. Lisette de Miranda y Cotta taught piano and voice at the School of Music in Margao as well as in Vasco. Earlier, she was a student of Maestro Camille Xavier, director of the School of Music. He had LTCL in the year 1970. She was also a primary school teacher at the Fatima Convent in Margao. Shantale Cotta learned music at the School of Music and the Kala Academy and taught music in Maina Church at Curtolim, Grace Church at Margao, and Navolim Church. Franz Schubert Cotta taught violin and guitar in various church schools.

---

[22] M. Poizat, *The Angel's Cry: Beyond the Pleasure Principle in Opera*, trans. A. Denner (New York: Cornell University Press, 1992). The dilemma can be explained by what Poizant explains: it is perhaps interesting to touch upon the notion of the fan's jouissance which I had talked about at the beginning of the chapter. Songs during the liturgy of the Catholic Church were always plainsongs without vocal excesses, as the focus had been the intelligibility of the sacred text. The latter continued to enjoy a superior position compared to the musical meter. There was a high surveillance around the notion of jouissance. Pure singing was welcomed only after the Word and always in that order. This was also one of the reasons as to why musical instruments were earlier banned and mostly associated with pagan and popular celebrations. The origin of the plainsong which was a creation of Pope Gregory actually came to be practiced two centuries after his death. A thousand years later, when polyphonic singing became part of Catholic liturgy in the sixteenth century, the combination of voices and text made intelligibility of words no longer a primary concern. This brings to the fore how jouissance alters the domain of regulation. In the context of this chapter, not just regulation of singing but also the regulation of who sings underwent a transformation once jouissance was at its pinnacle (93–107).

"They don't have the taste of the old Mandos. They no longer sing that well." In the year 1965, when the Mando festival was revived, we participated. For the choral concerts, we used to sing in four voices. There are violins, cello and double bass. In the second year, Victor Paranjoti came to judge. Gradually we got invitations and opportunities to participate in higher places. In 1967, we were invited to perform at the Bulabhai Desai Auditorium, in Bombay. Our founder died a few days before the performance. It was a big blow for Goencho Nad. He was our inspiration. Internal politics surfaced among the members of the Goencho Nad. I was part of the Saligaon Choir during the academic year 1960–61. Afterwards, I was chosen to be an effective member of the Rachol Seminary Choir between 1961 and 1964. Very few are selected as effective members. My mother died in the year 1963. After leaving the seminary, I used to work at the hospital in the morning and in the evening gave music tuitions at the school of music in Margao. I taught solfeggio and voice.

During the 1980s, Conjunto Harmonia practiced at our place. There were 25 members and it was organized along four voices. We sung Goan folk as well as Classical music in acappella. We performed for 6-7 years for the Christmas Carol festivals. Then, part of Conjunto Harmonia went to Gavana. We continued singing with them till the year 1992-1993, as a hobby. The members were irregular and eventually the group disbanded.

In 1992, we started our own family choir. At that time, my kids were teenagers. It was a permanent paid job for us during that time. We performed at Leela hotels, six days a week. The common songs were mostly from the category of Dulpods, Old Portuguese, Spanish, Italian songs and light songs like pop. We sing in three voices—Tenor, Soprano and Alto. Three notes are enough to hold the harmony. Of course, Bass gives a better effect. We used to sing for three hours, 7.30-10.30 pm, six days a week for three years. We are the only *Choral* group in Goa. In other places, we mostly have bands. During the years 1997-98, there were no performances in hotels. We used to sing common wedding and funeral songs from the song books that were available. When we perform in hotels, we use instruments like the Guitar, Violin, Percussion, Mandolin and Accordion. For Weddings and Funerals, Schubert plays the Piano. Accordion is not allowed in the church and four members cannot really do a miracle. While performing in the church, only playing with hands is allowed but outside the church, while serenading, organ with beats is allowed. The original organ has a continuous sound. It sustains the notes whereas, in case of Piano, you can play on the beats. Since 1978, we have been playing at Alfama Cafe in Cidade de Goa at Dona Paula, all around the year, on Tuesdays and Sundays from 7.30pm-10.30 pm. We also play in Alila Diwa at Betalbatim situated near Martin's corner, during November to April on Wednesdays and Fridays. The Wedding season is usually December and January. The prices vary according to the songs that they choose. Usually, we like to perform common Portuguese, Italian, French, Russian, Spanish and Konkani songs because we like to cater to all the guests who come, having different nationalities. We sometimes do classical and semi-classical songs like Hallelujah from Handel's Messiah; the short version for weddings and Caeser Franck's Panis Angelicus. When there are new songs, we need to practice. However, we are rehearsing and performing all the time. We also record our songs; all four of us sing and digitally, Franz manages all the instruments. The recordings take place at Magic Touch studio; earlier he was the only guy in Margao doing it.

He talks about how different kinds of opportunities dictate the form and mood of music. Earlier days when competitions took place, singing mandos was quite common and there were many choir groups that facilitated practicing and performing Goan folk songs. As a family choir, they perform for weddings and funerals. The church makes the choice of instruments limited and the repertoire is directed at the intended audience. For their contractual hotel gigs, the repertoire includes songs in multiple languages, Goan folk songs, pop numbers. A wide range of instruments are used. What makes them stand out is the choral treatment of the various songs that they do in contrary to bands. They arrange any given songs in different voices, harmonizing in three and sometimes four voices. They have agreements with the owners regarding the timing of their performance. The Cotta Family Choir has even recorded a few of their songs.

Franz Schubert Cotta, who is otherwise an advocate by profession is a multi-instrumentalist and looks into the aspect of recording. He can play Mouth Organ (Harmonica) and had formal school training in violin, guitar, and Portuguese guitar. The latter has twelve strings and plastic caps or turtle shells for the thumb and the index finger. He attended a two-month workshop in Portugal. He also plays the keyboard and a few wind instruments. He dabbles with the studio mix and amplification. The different equipment allow one to play parts of instruments. The skeleton is usually worked out earlier and is ready; but the inspiration comes in the studio. The process of recording involves harmonizing in one's own voice and then the first, second, and third layers, like a layered sandwich, are put together in an orderly manner. One has to ensure that the chords go well and synchronize with progression. For religious hymns, he uses violin, keyboard, and acoustic guitar. The imagination of the sound that one wants to create paves way for the choice of instruments. His favorites are guitar and mandolin; for composing and arranging, he prefers the piano or keyboard.

He also has a jazz ensemble. There is one lady and five gentlemen. They play bass guitar, drums, tenor sax, and keyboards. He plays the saxophone. They do jazz and sometimes jazz pop. They are more like hobby musicians who get together for gigs.

> As a family choir, we do only one genre of music. What I mean is that the clients are different and we change the music accordingly but we don't do fusions. We do Portuguese popular and folk songs, regional songs from North and South Goa; Goan folk music. When I am singing and performing with family, we do pop and semi-classical. We have performed in Denmark, Macau, Bangalore, Calcutta and Delhi. Initially, public performance was more relaxed and then it became part of the system. Today, the appreciation for live music is gone. While doing Wedding songs also, the couples get finicky and they are hard to satisfy. We try to oblige with the requests. Sometimes, we have no audience. There isn't much future to this family choir. It is taking another kind of course. The opportunity came along and we are a choir. The family choir stays together. We speak Portuguese at home. As a musician, I would say we are informal and flexible; we like change and experimentation. Faith is a different.

The family choir started out when there was a demand for live music and they enjoyed commercial gigs at the hotels as well as entertainment services that they rendered for weddings. He flagged the variety of musical styles that they are adept at handling for different events but how fusion is not a part of their imagination. Perhaps they are one of the few Portuguese-speaking families in recent times.

Syncretic Musical Experimentations in Goan Sacred Music

For the first generation of the newly converted Hindus who were oriented toward recitation or singing of the puranas in Marathi or Konkani in their temples, fraught with pastoral concern, the priest gurus came up with poetic compositions translating into spiritual instructions. The Adi Purana (Old Testament) and Deva Purana (New Testament), together known as Krista Purana, one of the best known by Fr. Thomas Stephens, was the appropriate literature to explore the teachings of Jesus. There were also passion narratives arranged in verses and music and at times drama. Earlier in Goa, during the Lenten season and on the Christmas Eve, recitation of the puranas and passion narratives was common. Today something along those lines can be found in

Tiracol and South Mangalore. Fr. Thomas Stephens was the first Englishman in India and also the rector of the Holy Spirit, Margao, in 1594.

During the seventeenth and the nineteenth centuries, churches in Goa saw the spurt of local choir masters (*maestre-capela* or *mistri*). They used to be well versed in playing one or more instruments like the violin, harmonium, double bass, clarinet, flute, and brass. They made their contribution by creating many hymns, responsorials, litanies, and so on, which spoke of syncretism between the East and West. A few old hymns like Diptivoni Sulokinni, Santam Tum Mata, or Santan Amchi Mai belonging to the seventeenth or eighteenth century were pure Konkani poetry put to a melody which was quintessentially Goan. In that, there was an inclination to the Western harmony and the syncopation of notes rendered it the Eastern-Indian feel. The hymn can easily be sung accompanied by the Indian drum (*tabla*), percussion (cymbal, *kansalli*), and so on. There had been instances when choir masters borrowed beautiful Western melodies and adapted them to Konkani lyrics for various occasions. Fr. Miranda discovered sometime in the year 2014 that the melody line of the hymn of the Advent season "le le Jezu Amchea Somia" was borrowed from Francois Joseph Gossec's Siciliana (second movement from the Christian Suite) and was only modified as per the lyrical requirements, possibly by the choir master himself. He goes on to give a few more examples. Adeste Fideles, an original Gregorian chant became native to not only Goa but many parts of the world owing to the support of the Catholic Church. The Santa Cecilia Choir of the Rachol Seminary would sing the Magnificat Ad Vesperas with a melody from W. A. Mozart's Don Giovanni alternating with the Gregorian and a Tantum Ergo based on L. V. Beethoven's "Creation Hymn" (Miranda, Eufemiano de Jesus, 2014: 45–57).[23]

Tiatr or Konkani drama is one of the popular forms of mass entertainment in Goa and especially for the Konkani-speaking population in the diaspora. Apart from the social and political themes, Tiatrs also have religious subjects staged mainly during the Lenten season. These plays are mostly written by the clergy and based on the lives of the saints, Jesus, biblical episodes, or themes having the undertones of Christian and human values. Tiatrs comprise songs which are called Cantaram. The songs usually contain one verse and a chorus but sometimes playwrights write longer cants. Zagor, one of the indigenous musical forms, usually more popular among the Hindus, they do play a prominent role

[23] E. Miranda, "Goan Music in the Christian Faith and Tradition," in *Commemorating Christ in Goa: Some Sketches of the Life and Culture of Christians, Yesterday and Today*, ed. I. Vás (Goa: Third Millenium, 2014), 45–57.

for the Christian communities as well. The most prominent Christian Zagor takes place at Siolim on the first Monday after Christmas. In Calangute, Zagors are organized during Easter (Fernandes, Andre Rafael, 2014).

Goan Sacred Music: Motets

Collections of the archive of Patriarchal Palace, Panaji (Collection of the convent of the Order of St. Monica), at the Cathedral of Old Goa, and at the Seminary of Rachol bring to the fore the existence of a Goan sacred polyphonic repertoire ranging from religious villancicos of the seventeenth century, polyphonic music for Holy Week of the eighteenth century and masses and other sacred works of the nineteenth century. Later Daman was also made a part of this project and a relatively significant breadth of about 100 motets comprising the sacred repertoire of Goan origin was discovered.

The rendition is mostly tonal with either Latin or Konkani texts. The themes are mainly taken from the Passion of the Christ, as they appear in the New Testament and also few books from the Old Testament. In some cases, simple Latin texts are compiled from different liturgical offices of the Holy Week. Due to the reference to a letter by the Jesuit Priest Gaspar Dias (1525–82) dated September 30, 1567, the tradition of playing and singing polyphonic motets in Goa can be traced back to the second half of the sixteenth century. A large number of choir masters that the author encountered retained the copying errors in the original material due to the exact photocopying and the lack of either revision or correction on the separate parts. Performance of religious music and particularly motets continued uninterrupted all through the seventeenth to the nineteenth century with constant encouragement from the colleges run by the Jesuits and other religious orders alongside the parish schools.

Lourdhino Barreto, who had been the choir master of the Rachol Seminary choir for a long time and also the director for the Kala Academy, has been one of the prolific composers of Goa. His writing on motets gives an idea of the structure and style of the genre. The Goan motet's structure is quite simple he says. Usually, it is in two parts at a distance of a third or sixth interval and only at times, that too either in the beginning or during the end, it incorporates four parts. Despite such a simple structure, the passion music has a beautiful sound. It has been a part of church activities since the beginning of the seventeenth century. Some of the basic characteristics of motets are that it is in Latin, based on the text of the Scripture and have played an important role during the para-liturgical celebrations, particularly the Lenten seasons.

In the Goan context, motet is a genre of sacred music, which may or may not be polyphonically set, premised on liturgical text either in Latin or Konkani or another vernacular language (Morais, 2007: 10).[24]

Another prominent feature of Goan motets is the acute religious dedication ingrained within the performances, whether it involves the priests or lay folk. The listener always has to remember that these compositions were written for various offices of Holy Week and were not to be listened to as simple concert items disassociated with the underlying liturgical purposes.

Manuel Morais (2007) in his essay on motets laid emphasis on certain other details. He says that when they are written for four voices, tiple (treble or the melody line), alto, tenor, and baixa (baixo), the instruments that are used are two violins, quite infrequently, two clarinets and a three-stringed double bass, popularized by the term "Rebecao." He writes that there are instances where pipe organ and harmonium are found as well. An "Indultum" given by the "holy see" allows Goan motets to use instruments during Holy Week celebrations which is otherwise forbidden. While conducting, the Goans never use the full score. They either use one of the parts (e.g., treble) or conduct the pieces from memory. Musicians who are part of the ensembles have mostly learned orally even though they use their separate written parts; the latter actually helps in memorization.

The Lenten motets are part of the handwritten collections of the choir masters and have easily crossed more than a hundred. Goan composers have not only restricted themselves to the passion motet but have also explored the psalmody of the Vespers and Responsorios of Matins, particularly those concerned with Christmas Eve. The motets brought out the "melancholy, depth of feeling and Christ's sufferings" and the psalmody of the Vespers and the Responsorios of Matins reflected, "Solemnity, gaiety and vivacity" echoing somewhat the sentiments of the fireworks at the climax of the solemn Vespers (Morais, 2007: 13).

During the liturgical celebration of the Holy Week, specifically during the Triduum of Maundy Thursday, Good Friday, and Easter Saturday, this tiny and

---

[24] M. Morais, *The Polyphonic Holy Week Motets from Goa (19th and 20th Centuries)/ Motetes Polifonicos de Goa para a Semana Santa (secs. XIXXX)* (Portugal: 2007).

rare repertoire of sacred music classified as motets as per genre is continued as a singing tradition across Goa, Daman, and Diu.

Conclusion

The ethnographic vignettes discussed reaffirms that the seminary is much more than an apprenticeship into priesthood. Music dominates the Catholic-Goan sensorium. Almost as an extension of the parish school, the Rachol Seminary ensures that the lessons in solfeggio, Gregorian chant, mastering a musical instrument of one's choice and membership to the seminary choir must be practiced in tandem with learning about the ritualistic and sacral quality expected of anyone taking on the mantle of priesthood. One's ethnic cultural environment broadens the spectrum of Christianity and in the case of Goa, due to the Portuguese imperialist connections, a carefully cultivated sacred music genre becomes synonymous with the Goan-Catholic ethic.

I chose to invoke two different religious and devotional traditions that convey the notion of piety, memory, and an ethically curated aesthetic to understand how the seminary, one of the foremost features of Catholic religiosity embodies a sacred sound world alongside nurturing the seminarians to become ideal sacred subjects. Hirschkind (2006), while discussing Islamic Revival in Egypt, demonstrates the significance of a palpable materiality that enables affective listening and attuning oneself to the grain of faith. Sarbadhikary (2015) talks about how the Bengali Vaishnavas understand their relationship with Vrindavan. She explains that the intent of faith cannot be seen in a tangible form but can be experienced through dwelling in the inward sanctum of belief.

Being in the seminary, which is earmarked by particular kinds of life choices, allows them to later bring about discerned choices regarding production and documentation of sacred music and aligning relevant elements of folk music and inherent musicalities for nonsacred music. Faith undergirds their decision-making both in implicit and explicit forms.

Rachol Seminary firmly finds a footing as an omnipresent reference to Catholic rituals and sound systems. It is one of those nostalgic monuments that shapes various musical sensibilities and enlivens the peculiar Goan-Catholic ethic. The latter embodies an "imperial affect." This makes one delve into what Angela Barreto Xavier and Ines G Zupanov refer to about the native informants from the seventeenth- and eighteenth-century Goan and other Portuguese

Figure 4.1 Rachol Seminary, Goa. Photo credit Sebanti Chatterjee.

colonial spaces. The authors label these informants and writers as "Orientalists from Within." They mostly interspersed their Asiatic selves with what they held as a more prestigious biblical narrative (Xavier and Zupanov, 2015: 246).[25] Again, the selective curation and representation of Goan sacred music driven by the lifeforce of the Rachol Seminary resonates with Boym's "restorative nostalgia."

The seminary derives its character from the personalities that inhabit it and yet these personalities who become stalwarts of creative processes in the domain of sacred music acquire the ethics of performativity and affect from the seminary. Thus, imperial affect nurtures an Iberian-tinged Goan sacred music, whereby what gets branded as indigenously Goan also carries a Catholic Christian past (see Figures 4.1–4.5).

---

[25] Angela Barreto Xavier and Ines G. Zupanov, *Catholic Orientalism: Portuguese Empire, Indian Knowledge (16th-18th Centuries)* (New Delhi: Oxford University Press, 2015).

Figure 4.2 Stuti Choir performing at the Holy Cross Church, Margao, in December 2013. Photo credit Sebanti Chatterjee.

Figure 4.3 Manora Chapel, Goa. Photo credit Sebanti Chatterjee.

Figure 4.4 St. Francis Xavier's Church, Chicalim. Photo credit Sebanti Chatterjee.

Figure 4.5 Archbishop's palace. Photo credit Sebanti Chatterjee.

5

Mapping Choral Voices

The Role of People and Places

Many musicians—whether players in orchestras or freelancers—consider quartet players to be odd, obsessed, introspective separatist breed, perpetually travelling to exotic destinations and garnering adulation as if by right. If they knew the costs of that too-uncertain adulation, they would not resent us quite so much. Quite apart from our shaky finances and our continual anxiety about getting bookings, it is our proximity to each other and only to each other which, more often than we recognise, constricts our spirits and makes us stranger than we are. Perhaps even our states of exaltation are akin to dizziness that comes from lacking air.

Vikram Seth, *An Equal Music*

When considering the voices of communities in Goa and Shillong, the first thing that comes to my mind is the sound of a church bell on a Sunday afternoon. The sound signals events that are ordered around the mass or service, everyday rituals, hymns, and community participation. Faith—Christianity, to be precise—is a connecting motif in my exploration of these voices. However, the voices pitched at different registers belt out songs that extend beyond hymns, Medleys, and intonations; they articulate both artistic and everyday melodies that are rooted in a particular place. Voice in itself emerges as one of the central imageries evoked by the sound of the church bell.

Voice is an implicit signpost for my interest in choral traditions across two distinct sites. I would like to talk about voices—not just the ones belonging to various registers but also voice as a collective. I asked the musicians I met about the voices that they sing in. What is the voice of a soloist? What is the voice of the congregation? Is there a community voice? How does one cue into a performance voice? The aforementioned questions did not elicit any definitive responses but eventually I started to explore the ideas of voice through the lens of registers, musical, and extramusical. I also examined the relationship between processes of vocalization, performativity, and associated places.

During my travels, I was identified as a mezzo-soprano. I had the opportunity to sing soprano (the melody line), watch rigorous rehearsals, and experience performances as a researcher, participant, and audience. Did geographical location impact these experiences? There is no one way to address this issue. What, then, is the role of the voice/s? I try to provide a tangible explanation that puts all these concepts in one place. Naturally, the notes that translate into the "grain of voice" (Barthes, 1977) are not tangible objects per se. I aim to move beyond the musical elements specific to a particular voice and focus more on the timbres and tonalities that merge and stand out to depict specific meanings and sentiments. Grant Olwage writes about the Black voice as a 'timbral entity'. He interrogates if the black choral voice was a demonstration of resistance or rather assimilationist in nature. He speaks of a hybrid voices impacted by the 'timbral habitus' (210–14).[1] Through conversations with various musicians, I assembled an idea of voice that I gleaned while understanding their choral traditions. As Saskia Kersenboom suggests, the faculty of voice requires a thorough engagement with heterogeneity in the constantly shifting world of culture, structuring conversations, and confrontations "in a committed presence." Rather than participant observation, "Participant participation"—or exposing oneself to the actual creation, praxes, and sensibilities of human cultures—becomes relevant. Participant participation enables an exercise of one's own faculty of voice (Kersenboom, 2007: 203–4).

In Goa, I learned to sing, participated in three concerts with the Goa University Choir, and organized a symposium as part of a religious music festival. I also attended the rehearsals and Christmas concerts of another choir group. In Shillong, I actively participated in rehearsals and attended the programs of three choir groups. At both the sites, I visited music schools and met other institutional and entertainment choirs and solo artists. The narratives that I use in this chapter talk about the importance of voice and its representations.

Deleuze's (1987) notion of assemblage and Klee's (1953) concept of lines become helpful in understanding the process of hierarchization of voices. Then, I discuss how musical sensibilities constitute an idea of a place. I draw from Fiona Magowan's work on Yolognu mourning songs and linkages with music ecology, largely in tandem with the ideas of Tim Ingold (2011) and Steven Feld (1996). I also explore how indigenous strands of Christianity impact a vocalic tradition. The final section looks at how the idea of "mirroring" (Chatterji, 2016) helps frame novelty and nostalgia in the choral music repertoires of Shillong and Goa, respectively.

---

[1]   Grant Olwage, "The Class and Colour of Tone: An Essay on the Social History of Vocal Timbre," *Ethnomusicology Forum* 13, no. 2 (2004): 203–26. http://www.jstor.org/stable/20184481.

Hierarchization of Voices

Each choir has certain essential features and voices that constitute it. Choir music is linked to Christianity and the Western classical form of opera. A hierarchy emerges due to the soprano-diva imagination, and the vocalization techniques ordered around the two female voices—soprano and alto—highlight the hierarchization at play. Later, we will see the "esthetic formation" posited along the Aristotelian concept of "aisthesis," which focuses on sensory immersion in the world, incorporating certain peculiarities that acquire relevance as we focus on the timbre, color, and mood of the voices. These elements of voices move along the terrains that constitute a place and performativity. Birgit Meyer expands the notion of Benedict Anderson's "community" and makes it a "formation." Instead of freezing the possibilities of the term "community" to a bounded social group, a social formation is seen as undergoing processes that are embodied in aesthetic forms; this highlights the performativity of the community. Religious transitions further complicate the "secular public realm" and the interiorized patterns of religiosity pertinent to specific groups. Thus, an "aesthetic formation" is marked by new media styles and structures and its underlying connections to religion (Meyer, 2009b: 7, 20). In the case of the choral voices, the "aesthetic formation" incorporates the signature of the vocal registers alongside the intent suited to a particular religious denomination or entertainment spectrum. Thus "aesthetic formation" is an important lens through which one can explore the voices in a choral tradition, as singing in choirs has an immediate connection to Christianity. The vocalists of the choirs with which I interacted do not belong to a particular parish or church but render their vocalizations to various forms of choirs, which may be sacred as well as secular.

The principal voices in a choir—soprano, alto, tenor, and bass—have their own grammar of singularity as well as totality. The soprano-diva association that mainly holds true in operatic setups undermines the presence and contribution of the remaining voices. The high pitch, sharpness, and controlled vibrations that a score might demand make the soprano a highly skilled and aesthetically niche voice. These very attributes limit the potential of the voice to be realized in other styles of singing. Alto, the more versatile of the female voices, requires not only a greater sense of alignment with harmony (as it gives support to the melody line) but also urges singers to explore deeper tones along with those located on another register till the point that the voice ruptures into a dissonant shrill. At this point, a mezzo-soprano voice comes to the rescue, managing the middle ranges completely. All in all, an alto voice has more flexibility depending on the quality that a singer chooses to assign to it; this could be a raspy, country, or husky hue.

A tenor is the highest male voice and makes a unique contribution to the overall composition. At the outset, loudness matters so as to contrast the sharpness of the soprano. Usually, this vocal range works well in other musical genres too. Opera, of course, prefers a dramatic quality, but it can render itself to emotive, bluesy, and folksy moods too. On the surface of it, the bass voice is unnoticed in the hierarchized imagination of tonal formations, yet it is essential in balancing out the entire score. However, it is not as important in choral groups as in opera. It holds together the lowest, deepest tones that highlight the attributes of the three other voices. In my discussions with many musicians, it was important for me to disengage with the hierarchization of voices. In particular, the reasons as to why hierarchical imagination of tonal formations exist put forth by the soprano and alto voices made me question the attributes pertaining to a particular voice. The qualities stand out during solo renditions, but in a group arrangement, the totality matters more than the singularity.

> Let us start with the general stereotype of soprano—as a diva, okay—it's hilarious. The voice type depends completely on the fact that you are born a certain way, with certain physical structures, and that's the voice that you have. You can extend your range, but the main aspect or the quality remains. It's not about singing high or low; it's about singing well and singing with good technique. For the soprano voice, you have to keep letting people know that it's not about singing high; it's about maintaining the evenness of the tone throughout. So, even if I do have all the top notes, but I would say that I would want to, and I would want that for my students too, to have an even tone throughout. That is absolutely important, as that's when the top notes get good. You can't play the viola the way you play the violin. You can play the viola notes, but you can't hold the same body—it won't hold the same tone. This is because the range of each instrument is different. (F, Goa, February 2014)

An evenness of tone shapes a particular vocal register. One cannot choose to ignore the nexus of body and tonality. Voice type depends on one's anatomy. This initial acceptance is what garners a professional label for a voice. The quality of the voice of a particular range improves as it acquires firmness and versatility with adequate training and practice. Thus, a soprano voice entails more than just singing high but rather the ability to balance out the notes within the high register so that shape of the tone is supple and pristine. F explains this further with the analogy of the viola and violin notes and the tones that they produce.

In his discussion on classical music, Roland Barthes (1977) distinguishes between what Julia Kristeva refers to as the "pheno-text" and the "geno-text." A "geno song" is concerned with the interplay between melody and language, taking into account the tropes of shapeliness to spell out the sound-signifiers and letters. A "pheno song" is all about the rendition working out the perfect tone, internalizing the code of the melisma, and appropriating the genre and its underlying principles in toto.

With interest in semiology, and Western popular culture, Barthes is always curious about who is reading the text and how authorship, readership, and experiences shape social phenomena. Barthes talks about the materiality of the body—which elicits a certain "signification" encompassing the melisma or the timbre that adds to the inward experience of making music—determines the quality of the performance. Even though music pedagogy deliberately ignores this aspect, namely, the "grain of voice" (or "the body in voice as it sings") and instead focuses on emotive modes, it is ultimately the "gesture support" that renders a certain degree of intelligibility to music.

> I sing the tenor voice. It is the highest range of the male voice. My voice sounds beautiful. If you are adding colour to the main frame in the canvas, it is like—the brown tone and the red tone should blend together. I like tenor. The bass voice is the lower register of the male voice. It can't bring out emotions. Drones are difficult for me. I prefer being in a group. There is synergy as a group. It is like united we stand; divided we fall. (G, Shillong, January 2015)

G talks about the importance of the tenor voice and the joy of singing collectively.

Every singer is supposed to have "three different voices." There is one main voice, but while the singer moves from their lowest to their highest tone, the transition must be effortless and consistent (Wechesberg, 1997: 137).

> Faith has a lot to do with hard work. You can't get it all from God. There should at least be 10% from our side. If you want to be an artist, you need to have a good moral lifestyle. You are a messenger of God and should be an inspiration to others. You need to work hard [at] what you do. Music is a journey. There are ups and downs. In the beginning, I used to sing the alto voice. With practice, I developed a higher range. After three years, I could sing the soprano part, but it was difficult. If it was given to me, I could sing. The soprano is easy to sing because it is the melody. Alto adds a sort of oomph factor. You must have a

good ear. Not everyone can do it. In the beginning, I would sound raspy, like Tina Turner. With time, I learnt to develop [my] soft palette, the arch above the throat. Earlier, I could never sing softly. I would breathe out, humming on the soft palette. After humming for hours, I could really reach those high notes, because you [do] not sound squeaky if you reach those high notes. I sing classical, pop, jazz, and the blues but haven't really done the jazz stuff. Jazz is very difficult. One needs to improvise and play with it. (J, Shillong, January 2015)

J makes some pertinent observations that reiterates the implicit stereotypical assumptions related to choral singing. This ranges from one's regional affiliations, soprano-diva associations crooning in a crown of excellence metaphor, and deep-rooted ethics in tandem with a lifestyle ordered around faith. Choral singing for J developed organically. It not just led her to explore the vocal register that she enjoyed and trained for but also enabled her to develop the ability to move between registers and develop a healthy critique.

I have a husky voice. I sing alto. Sopranos are divas by default. They are the cornerstone of the building. They sing the melody line. The other voices are embellishments to the soprano. The altos are like the supporting act—they maximize impact. The alto voice accentuates the highs and marks the lows more than the other parts. Altos and sopranos are very complementary. After a certain point, your brain figures out the alto part. Maybe older people are put into the alto range as they can no longer experiment with their vocal cords. (K, Shillong, January 2015)

K has an interesting observation about voice. Unlike the distinct melody line belted out by the sopranos, the altos really manage the show from backstage. Without alto support, the sound is flat and the dynamics are lost. Alto has certain limitations too; it arrests the extension of one's range beyond a certain point. However, in terms of musicality, altos need to be more intuitive in aural mapping of the given sound structure. The altos must anticipate in advance what would make the main melody shine.

When I was auditioned by Professor Santiago, my voice was identified to be a mezzo-soprano. However, I joined the altos. I like singing this voice because it is not a strain [on] my vocal cords. When singing in the choir, I preferred the higher notes, as my voice does stand out in that range. In my opinion, the alto is as important as the other three voices, as it is the altos that act as a support to the choir. The experience of singing at the Ketevan Festival was enriching, and singing with a professional choir from Seville—Professor Santiago's choir—enhanced my vocal ability. It [is] important to study your voice prior to the rehearsal to be able to participate effectively during rehearsal. After the performance, I felt a great sense of satisfaction and pride, and gratitude to God, for giving me this opportunity. (K2, Goa, February 2016)

C recalls singing with the Seville Chamber Choir as a part of the Ketevan Festival, where they performed pieces by Bach and Morten Lauridsen's "Lux Aeternam." She asserts the importance of the alto voice not just in terms of providing support to higher voice but also due to its own sonic character and how it enhances specific moments in a performance.

The voice that I sang for the concert was soprano. I came to sing this voice since I auditioned for this voice when I first joined the choir. The challenging parts of [the soprano] are the high notes we have to take and [the moments] when we have to sing those high notes in piano (soft sound). For this concert, the semiquavers for Bach were a challenging part of our voice. To train our voices, we do scales, each time taking it one semitone higher. (C, Goa, February 2016)

C and K2 refer to experiences of comfort and discomfort that they associate with their individual voices before and after a public concert. Familiarity and practice help them cope with unanticipated challenges.

I sing Soprano. It's the only voice I know. My mother knows it because she needs to train the others. It was never so much that I wanted to learn, but because I was a strong soprano, I used to sing soprano. Like my sister—she knows both the voices but because she is not a strong soprano, she became a strong alto. Her voice was more suited to that. (M1, Goa, January 2014)

M1 does not sight read, but she has a high vocal range and so finds the soprano voice ideal. The melody line is easier to approach without music literacy.

In the beginning, I had problems. I was a soloist and an Indian classical singer. Indian classical singers sing from the chest; choirs use head voices. Earlier, I used to strain my chest. I never [knew] how K (another Soprano from the Aroha Choir) makes [that] beautiful, sharp [tone]. Then, after trying, watching, hearing, and also reading about a lot of techniques, I improved. Aunty Pauline helped too. I listened to Sarah Brightman, Jackie Evancho, etc. I had the tendency to [imitate the] Lata Mangeshkar shrill. (A, Shillong, January 2014)

Gregory Booth mentions how Hindi film playback singer Lata Mangeshkar's "high, pure Soprano voice" clearly emerged as the new vocal style, setting the trend from the 1950s onward (Booth, 2008). Sanjay Srivastava makes a compelling argument about how Lata Mangeshkar's adolescent-girl falsetto came to be recognized as the ideal Indian popular-music voice in the film culture at large. Her playback voice made Lata prototypical of the masculine ideal of "the virgin mother" and "the medieval princess-poetess Meera Bai." Lata's voice also altered the performer-audience relationship. The timbre and tonality of her voice fed into audiences' imagination a certain notion of "femininity and its sexuality." It also originated from a compositional context, resting heavily on "literariness" as opposed to "orality."[2] Lata's departure from her early-career "nausal quality"—akin to the performativity of the Pakistani Singer Noorjehan—to the "purified" idea of a Hindu voice during the peak of her popularity is largely indicative of the Sanskritizing trope that took shape post-Independence. Her falsetto is generated from the throat, unlike the head voice necessary to shape the sound required of a high-pitched soprano. Therefore, it is essential to be aware of the musical traditions that one wants to project in the process of embodiment.

> I realized that breathing exercises fill one's lungs [with] air, which helps in controlling one's voice. Two aspects that I learnt about voice were: never strain your voice; [practice singing in a] low pitch but to a limit. Also, the first and last tonic chords are very important for a singer. You can sing with ease and then you are ready for the stage. Lip twirls aid one in not going flat. It helps one to stand on a note. Swelling is another technique that helps in holding on to a note.
>
> In Indian classical singing, if one does not stand on a note for long, the voice gets flat. Runs help the voice to not get flat on a note but, [they] tend to make the voice shrill. It improves the texture. Drawing lines between the Indian classical tradition and the Western classical tradition and singing them together in a particular song is very difficult. I used to set my alarm clock for one minute and see how much I could hold and control my breath. The shift is very difficult, especially jumping from high notes to low notes. (A, Shillong, April 2014)

It is important to be aware of specific techniques relevant to each vocal tradition. Being a soloist in the Hindustani classical tradition alongside honing a soprano voice requires one to develop myriad musical sensibilities. Of immense significance are the singer's adaptability and curiosity to explore ways of engaging and negotiating with their circumstances.

---

[2] Srivastava, Sanjay (2004: 2020). The performative context of "orality" here refers to a situation where the skill of the performer is not reducible to a singular characteristic—definitely not to their voice. Literariness in this context becomes the prerogative of a particular gender (male) and class (the bourgeois worldview).

Amanda Weidman's work *Singing the Classical, Voicing the Modern* (2006) talks about the politics of ushering in certain kinds of Carnatic voices during the end of the nineteenth century in the wake of upper-caste women singing in public. On the one hand, it stood for the abolition of the Devadasi system while propagating domesticity and interiority, most commonly associated with the urban middle class; on the other hand, microphones and gramophones enabled amplification and new cultures of listening. The Tamil music movement, which stemmed from the stark distinction between classical language and music, maneuvered ways to make Tamil a compositional language for Carnatic classical music. Clearly, in the narratives mentioned earlier, the general tendency to marvel at the soprano voice and the presentation of music in vernacular languages mirrors Weidman's propositions about certain aspects of Carnatic classical music.

The hierarchy of female voices in the choral and Western classical traditions, namely the soprano (whose range is B3 to G6) and alto or contralto (whose range is E3 to F5)[3] is at play. To explain my proposition about how the hierarchization is in motion, I borrow Paul Klee's explanation of lines—active, passive, and medial. He states the following: "active line: I fell (the man fells the tree with his axe); medial line: I fall (the tree falls under the axe stroke of the man); passive line: I am being felled (the tree lies felled)" (Klee, 1953: 21). Voices too can be articulated along these lines. Looking at the hierarchy of voices in the choral music scene, I observe that the bass voice inhabits the medial line, the soprano occupies the active line, and the alto and tenor voices mediate between the active and passive lines. The soprano, being the melody line, is naturally identified as the active line; the alto and tenor, which occupy the lines below it, come into prominence depending on how the musical score pans out as a whole. Mostly, they too lie on the active line, but during certain moments, they are defined as passive lines. By virtue of filling in silences and holding the architecture of the piece together, being the lowest line, the bass voice takes the medial line.

To understand the hierarchy in detail, I use Deleuze's notion of assemblage that acquires importance.

When we talk about the nature of assemblage at a horizontal level, it has two compartments—content and expression. The assemblage is not only a "machinic assemblage" "of bodies of actions and animations" whereby there is mediation and interaction between the bodies. It is also a "collective assemblage" of the

3   https://ktvocalstudio.com/ranges-tessitura-contemporary-voice/ (accessed June 23, 2022).

enunciation of acts and statements of transition that are not of the bodies but are ascribed to the bodies. On the vertical axis, the assemblage contains territorial and re-territorialized sides that structure it and traces of de-territorialization that shift its position. Deleuze gives the example of a feudal assemblage, where he talks about the interstices between the bodies that define feudalism spanning the "body of earth and social body, the body of overlord, vassal, serf, body of the knight"—the whole machinic assemblage. Then, there are "statements, expressions, the juridical regime of heraldry," all of the noncorporeal changes, like oaths and the collective assemblage of enunciation. "On the vertical axis, there are the feudal territorialities, re-territorializations, and lines of de-territorialization that take away both the knight and his mount, statements, and acts. Then there is room to think about crusades" (Deleuze, 1987: 88, 89). In a similar vein, in a choral group assemblage, naturally, there are the sopranos, altos, tenors, and bassists; there are also factors like the timbre and range of each voice, stylistic elements, vocalization patterns, sacred music repertoires, cross-over repertoires (Medleys), sung texts, chants, pauses, and transformations that do not concern the gestures like rehearsals and improvisations by the conductor. Finally, the choral group is the collective assemblage that articulates music.

There is a pattern of activities organized around choral music. There is musical training, both individual and ordered by a particular school or conductor. The rehearsals are processes of "machinization," usually followed by performances. The vertical axis in this case entails crossovers; it emulates traditional sounds within the conditioning of territorialization, re-territorialization, and de-territorialization. The territorialization of sounds helps formulate repertoires that highlight characteristics of specific genres or introduce new modes of imagining existing genres. Here, I refer to territorialization and the subsequent stages of re-territorialization and de-territorialization to further Birgit Meyer's "aesthetic formations." Thus, I constitute a place and semantics of performativity. What happens in the realm of choral traditions, at least in the concerned sites, is that it does not follow a specific formula. It is informed by regional sensibilities that are usually visceral and has tropes of indigeneity rooted in Christianity.

Music and the Constitution of a Place

The indigenous identity which traverses Goa, Mumbai, Shillong, and Mizoram, as the narratives of several musicians reveal, is mostly a solidified version of faith pertinent to specific regions. There is a need to firmly ground oneself in the sociocultural roots of a place and communicate about one's own social and musical journey through the medium of voice that the singer chooses to inhabit. The sociocultural ambit merges with the religious ethic of both the communities that I met. Despite belonging to different denominations—and, sometimes, even faiths—particular expressions that the faith manifests involve the indigenous practices, which is crafted by local as well as cosmopolitan aspirations. For most of the musicians I met, religious affiliations consciously or unconsciously shape their worldview. Does this mean that the identities of the musicians vocalizing choral traditions primarily mirror their religious ethics? That is not entirely true, especially because, even regionally, there is no dominant category of faith that molds identity. For instance, how does one tease out the notion of being Goan or Khasi through one's vocalization? The connection to faith—as observable in Catholic, Presbyterian, Pentecostal, and Baptist worship settings, to mention a few—is inevitable, as choirs are essentially born out of worship or liturgy rituals. But the musicians here are not confined to religious choirs. In fact, a large number of them are either from entertainment choirs or work as vocal instructors. There are gospel artists as well. I observed that I have to consider the sociocultural ambit of the musicians in relation to their religious life. The lifestyle choices of these communities which involve finding work within Meghalaya, either with the government or pursuing a cultural profession informed by mainstream entertainment formats, somehow bring them closer to the factors that lie within the domain of Christianity. Following Christianity is an ingrained mode of being. Of course, some embrace it openly, while others treat it as an everyday habit. Degrees of devotion differ so does the intent. In my interactions with people from two different geographies, I have discovered the way faith inscribes itself in the lives of people. In Goa, the Catholics have retained the nostalgic Golden Goa period through their consumption of food, literature, art, and music. The lifestyles and religious ethics of Catholic Goans are aligned. When it comes to Shillong, there is a distinction between the tribal worldview, with all the cultural elements that order it, and the religious ethic of the Presbyterians, Pentecostals, and Catholics. Even though faith brings all these elements together, there is also separation.

To look at the phenomenon of music and constitution of place, I borrow from Tim Ingold's idea of making sense of "dwelling" in the environment vis-à-vis the larger sense of building or emerging as architects of certain houses. As he says,

> Building, then, is a process that is continually going on, for as long as people dwell in an environment. It does not begin here, with a pre-formed plan, and end there, with a finished artefact. The "final form" is but a fleeting moment in the life of any feature, when it is matched to a human purpose, likewise cut out from the flow of intentional activity. (Ingold, 2000: 188)

Thus, there is a construction of a certain perception of lifeworld which is contingent on the blueprint of a form. The processual emerges from a certain degree of constancy. I find this useful to understand how placemaking in terms of musical practice and creativity develops. The musical practitioners inhabit a particular geography, interacts with the cultural protocols rooted in an indigenous understanding of one's self, community, and creativity. The musical genres also take on certain stylistic leaps as per the intent of the musicians, the reception of the audience, and a global mapping of exchanges and experimentations. Dwelling in the process of building points to how music constitutes a place, taking its historical, contemporary, and anticipated anxieties.

> I will talk about Bombay because I had [the] experience of singing in three of the main choirs in Bombay. There are at least six very good choirs. I sang in Stopgaps, Paranjoti, and the Newman choir at different times, and it was all [a] superb experience, and I think it is very important. Being in choruses helps choral singing. It broadens your music because one can't just get up and be a soloist. One has to sing with other people; you mix with other people, you listen to other people, you listen to other voices. A very essential part of singing and being a musician is listening, so singing in choruses really works, and it works well. I really enjoyed singing with all the choirs that I have sung with. (F, Goa, January 2014)

Like many Goans, F too grew up in Bombay and traveled across both the regions in the quest for a career and home. Initially, she dabbled with both journalistic and musical projects in Bombay. After marriage, she moved to Goa and enjoyed a brief stint as a vocal teacher at the Kala Academy before moving back to Bombay to return to the city's thriving cultural scene.

This snippet captures F's experience as a choir singer in her growing years. The experience enabled her to nurture her career as a soloist and vocal teacher. For her, the importance of learning technique, the camaraderie around the activity of singing, and the qualities of voice that one is endowed with make the art of singing a challenging and exciting musical investment.

My father [Micky Correa] was a professional musician and there was always music in the house. I have not taken music lessons with a vocation in mind, but as a trial, I learnt to play the piano. I [began] singing with choirs quite a long [while] ago, actually. When I was in Bombay, I used to sing with the Cantata Choir, from 1974–77. My father was the resident jazz band leader [at] the Taj. So he lived over there. I was nine then. We lived there for about twenty-one years or so. My sister [Steele Correa] has professionally studied jazz. She is a professional jazz musician. She lives in New York. (P, Goa, January 2014)

In 1977, I got married and had to come to Goa. I used to belong to another type of music. I was with a group called Gavana. It was Goan cultural music. We—at least I—did five international trips with them. Perhaps there were two trips that I couldn't take. I used to half-sing and half-dance. I learnt to dance when I travelled. So, we did folk music, but it was arranged in four voices. We did many arrangements by Micael Martins. We did polyphonic music as well. I don't know if you have heard our CDs and cassettes. Gorette used to play and sometimes dance also; Teresa as well. Teresa used to play the cello. They were basically musicians. At one time, I had to sing soprano because we were short of sopranos. Basically, I am an alto. You know I learnt piano as a child. My father has his own style on the piano. The piano was not his main instrument, but he taught piano. So, I had learnt some things with my dad but again [took] a break and have not been playing. I have to get back to it. (P, Goa, January 2014)

P's story gives me an insight into the different types of choral groups that one could belong to. In her family, music as a profession continued at least across two generations. She does not talk specifically about the alto voice but categorizes soprano as a voice in demand.

The Cantata repertoire was classical. We had performed in Delhi and Poona in auditoriums, not just in the churches. In Bombay also, we performed in auditoriums. We performed Carmina Burana by Carl Orff and Mozart's Requiem. My sister was also part of the choir. In fact, there was a time when both my sister and I [sang]. My brother [sang] too and played the clarinet. So, when we went to Delhi, even my father came with us. My brother doesn't have [much] time now but he [still] plays the clarinet and sings as well. He had started singing for a while—in a church choir—just to keep up. He lives in the US.

Clearly, music has stayed with her since her youth and is an integral part of her everyday life even today. This comes from a certain history of accessibility of training and acquisition of musical heritage.

At one time, I thought that I would sing in the church choir but you know what? It becomes very difficult [to rehearse]. There is a choir close to my place that sings at the Governor's palace regularly. But it means another rehearsal, and those rehearsals [would] clash with some other commitments I had, and I completely skipped one choir rehearsal. I did not go back again. (P, Goa, January 2014)

There is also a strict demarcation between music as an occupation and music as leisure. Clearly, despite being drawn to different forms of choral groups, one cannot participate in all the activities.

I have been with the Stuti Choral Ensemble since it started. I took a little break last year for six months or so because my daughter got married and my other daughter was having a baby. My daughters enjoy music. They played as children. They learnt piano. My daughter's husband also plays the piano. He is not a professional musician, but he has a group with which he plays. Stuti Choral Ensemble has a classical and religious repertoire. There is [a] little bit of folk music. When it's church, they keep it to religious music. If they have concerts outside, then it's different. This is because churches have rules. The Goa University Choir does many things. This time, it is completely different. This is a different concert. [Music] is chosen according to themes, not because it is religious. (P, Goa, January 2014)

Her narrative also talks about the limitations and possibilities of certain repertoires. Goa as a region emphasizes folk music, sacred music, and classical music.

I had a very difficult childhood. I was sexually abused at four years [old]. Innocence and confidence were robbed of me early on. I would not be in denial but hope for an ideal world. It was my tenant. Mum made him my tutor.

I never ever chose music. Music chose me. I had the Shillong Chamber Choir auditions with two other school friends, in Class 9. I sang *Amazing Grace*. Neil Nongkynrih came and spoke to me. He said, "You do have a singing voice—just give it a try." He [asked] me if it was okay if he kept in touch. Music finally gave me space to belong. We used to practise from 2 pm to 10 pm every day. During the winter holidays, we had shows. It gave me therapy which I was not aware of. It was healing for me. Ever since my teenage years, my facial expressions indicated how I felt. I was known as the sunbeam of the choir. [The period] 2001–2006 was a liberating experience. In 2005, I [took] a break and in 2007, I joined Aroha. I started working in Red FM in 2007. I also work for 103.6 FM Jong Phi. The shows that I do are *Hits and Melodies* and *Radio on demand.* (G, Shillong. January 2015)

G did not plan on music. He was not even aware of his deep connection to God. It was only after he had joined the Shillong Chamber Choir as a teenager that he discovered his love for music, especially the soul genre. Thereafter, he began working in voice modulation professionally as a radio jockey.

> I was with the Shillong Chamber Choir during the shows held between 2001 and 2006; in Delhi, [we performed for] NDTV, Obama, Manmohan Singh (twice), the North East games, and Shillong Chamber Choir private concerts. We covered a lot of things—[like] heavy classical, which included Handel, Mozart, and Bach; in Jazz, we did Gerswin numbers; in rock, we did Queen. We also did traditional folk songs. I owe everything to God. God made me what I am. God wanted me to have a gifted voice. I wept when I sang *Suffer Little Children to Come unto Me for There's the Kingdom of Heaven, Jesus Said.* Children wanted to come to him. Music helped me find Him and glorify Him. Deep inside, I love the Lord, but music brought it out for me, the passion to do it—to emote any emotions. When Aunty Pauline writes music, she feeds my soul. I was her number one fan. In Bangalore, when she invited us, she sat on the piano and sang the song *Prayer of Pain.* We were touring with the Shillong Chamber Choir at that time. I remember that I had [a] non-stop flow of tears. (G, Shillong, January 2015)

G acknowledges his spirituality but intends to keep his involvement with the church and entertainment choirs separate. In the latter, he hopes to train his voice so as to develop a skilled sound, while in the former he wants to render his voice for prayer.

G establishes a connection between God and his gifted voice. This recalls the Songak sound from Korea. Many students and professionals singing Songak believe that through their method of sound production, they present their natural, God-given voices, and, at the same time, do away with the *han* (constant suffering and internal agitation) and *chong* (gatherings during scarcity) associated with a Korean past. In this process, they internalize a Euro-American style of high art (Harkness, 2015: 5, 33).

> I am more of a Khasi than a Mizo, as I have been in Shillong. I started singing at the age of nine. It was a school competition where I sang Dolly Parton's "Coat of Many Colours."[4] There was church music at the Mizo Presbyterian Church. No one sings in my family, and they were quite surprised to see me taking part in a school competition. They did not take it seriously. When my principal gave

---

[4] Dolly Parton composed the song in 1969 and it was recorded in April 1971; Source: "Coat of Many Colours: (song). Wikipedia page; accessed November 13, 2017.

me the parts to sing, my mom realized that I could sing. In 2010, I joined the Aroha Choir to train my voice. In 2012, I was part of a rock band for about four months. Music is spiritual and it cannot be tampered [with]. I prefer the genres R&B, pop, and the blues, and I like to improvise [within] songs. I do not play any instrument. I have a guitar but still I have no plans of taking it up. I would love to learn the piano. (J, Goa, January 2015)

This particular vignette talks about the potential to use one's singing voice according to one's predispositions, life choices, and community expectations. The everyday motif that involves picking a genre or style that blends in with daily happenings shapes one's musical pursuit and makes it a common leisure activity; and some, of course, like to assign permanence to its structure.

I intend to pray more and inspire more people with music and not get caught up with the glamour. I am an only child, so I would ideally like to help my parents after graduation. I have been teaching music at the Aroha Music Academy. I will eventually look for a government job. It has been four years with the choir but still I am very shy. I try to sing with the choir whenever I am free. Church is church. It serves only God. Personally, I have not grown so close to the church, but I go to many services. Mizos have gifted voice[s]. There must be a reason why God chose you—you need to voice out something. (J, Shillong, January 2015)

The importance of church and its related activities in the lives of the youngsters living in Shillong alongside their desire to embark on a career centered on performing music make voice, in this case, the alto voice, a category that interjects different genres. Singing provides a glimpse of the place to the singer herself/himself. While searching for a singing voice, youngsters also search for belonging and comfort. In belonging, there is always a contrast between lifestyle choices, career trajectories, and social expectations. J's dilemma in embodying a singing voice best suited to "performativity" is at odds with her other possible life choice of adopting dutifulness and stability.

Indigeneity and Christian Musical Tradition

The indigeneity in Christianity and Christian music traditions is well documented in the different regions of India. Among the Khasis, U Blei (the Supreme One or God) has recently acquired a masculine prefix before undergoing changes, like the feminine prefix "Ka" or a double gendered prefix U Blei-Ka Blei, even though Jesus is a masculine figure (Nongbri, 2016). Mizos incorporate the practice of embodying the evil spirit, "Thlarau Chan," in church rituals, although women act as the medium (Pachuau, 2016). Syrian Christians use Syriac as their language of liturgy (Costa, 2009). The Syrian Christian cult, based on the Mylapore shrine of Saint Thomas, draws influence from the South Indian cult of Murukan-Subrahmanya, and even from the cults of the Muslim *pirs* in the region (Robinson, 2009). Missionary Carey chose the Bengali word "d*o*ba" or "d*u*ba," which literally means "immersion," to explain the idea of Baptism. In many other dictionaries, one finds other synonyms, like *kristadharme diksha* (rite of passage into Christianity) or "namkara" (name-giving). Problems arose as this word was not the appropriate translation of Baptism according to both Indian and British missionaries. In 1834, BFBS withdrew support for the translation work of the Baptist Missionary Society in Bengal, as their translation did not convey a holistic meaning of the term "Baptism" (Torkel, 2006).

In Tamil Nadu, the contemporary Christian folk music project rejects both the cultural tropes typical to the colonial period and the seemingly benevolent, early indigenous modes, like Sanskritized Carnatic music. Reverend James Theophilus Appavoo has a socially relevant and spiritually uplifting liturgy for exploited groups, who form the majority in the Tamil Christian community. It borrows from Adi Samayam—a religion of many Dalits, which is markedly different from Brahminical Hinduism—alongside folk music and cultural indicators of resistance. The Tamil Protestant Christian community responds to disrespect toward the lower-caste culture in two ways—by reintroducing village folk culture and mirroring elite cultures. From the 1950s, light classical or popular (film) music has been in use (Sherinian, 2005). From the 1980s onward, Appavoo included village metaphors and languages with local intonations into the folk music repertoire used in liturgy. There were influences of the English or German hymnody and Carnatic music tradition. When considering indigeneity rooted in geography, we can look at *Krista Purana* (the renowned adaptation of the Bible in Marathi by the Jesuit priest Thomas Stephens), translated hymn books and Bibles in the vernacular, the merging of traditional belief systems with Christianity, and use of regional languages in worship or masses as resources (Henn, 2014).

How does music rooted in indigenous Christianity constitute a place? Steven Feld explores the idea of acoustemology that is interjected by a sound-ear-voice-centered sensorium as he explains Kaluli expressivity in the tropical rainforest. Places evoke reverberations as they draw from contemplation and embodied experiences and memories that project "resoundingness" and "reflectiveness." The aesthetic elements of the Kaluli songs appear through their "textual poesis" of "placename paths." The songs can be sung by guests and during work, leisure, and the everyday activities of men and women while they navigate their way around the forest. Ritual songs are about memorializing ancestors (Feld, 1996: 91–7, 114).

Fiona Magowan uses Tim Ingold's idea of "dwelling" to understand the Yolgnu music tradition. Forms built by human beings, either in imagination or on the ground, are determined by the intent with which they engage with particular contexts and the environment. This contrasts with the "building perspective," which focuses on the making and translating of ideal forms of reality (Ingold, 2011, 2000: 10).

The "musical experiencings" of the Yolognu people help them navigate modes of addressing nonindigenous audiences and congregations in traditional, popular, and Christian music scenes alongside their memorialization of people through the environment. Fiona Magowan talks about music socialization that is reflected in older children's training. Boys dance, acquire skills to play clapsticks and didjeridu, sing in traditional contexts, and independently learn to play the guitar and keyboard in the Christian and popular-music realm. Girls usually perform crying songs and dance in traditional contexts and sing or perform "arm action dances" in Christian contexts. These songs are sung during ritual events and contemporary events like graduation ceremonies, presentations of honorary doctorates, and welcome and farewell gatherings of dignitaries. Magowan uses the theological idea of *perichoresis* to address the Yolognu response to Christian and ancestral beliefs where there is "a dance of mutuality" to mediate between the divine forms of ancestors and the holy trinity of Christianity (Magowan, 2007: 10, 50, 142, 143).

Through the various vignettes that focus on the singularity earmarking the experiences of individual persons alongside the contrapuntal narratives that resonate with musical choices, accessibility to training, imagining the possibilities of shifting across vocal registers, and stylistic alterations chart out the nonhomogeneous idea of constituting a place. In the next section, I tease out the nuances of performativity and how the demarcations of musical genres are floated.

Music Performance

The audience is imagined or preempted by the producers, performers, and composers. The reality TV show audience is already a fabric woven into the imagination of the choral tradition. That is the way the performers situated themselves in the mainstream. Apart from the Bollywoodized incarnation, what captures the interests of the Shillong artists is the showbiz personality. The voice could lend itself to the mediums of jazz, classical, indie, or folk. The idea is to make a mark or leave an impression in the market. Here, the market represents the live music audience. The place in itself is caught between the identity shaped by faith—a regional interpretation of Christianity—and the cultural processes that are quintessentially Khasi.

Of course, it is not even a simple binary of embracing a religious identity vis-à-vis a cultural one, rooted in the local ethos. The in-between-ness of the sacred codes and cultural manifestations result in a unique identity, which becomes embodied in the vocalists. Through their performance of Medleys, or by making their voices malleable to a specific genre of music, they reflect this newness; that which is interjected by local traditions as well as traditions that were passed on to them by foreigners. How do faith and culture impact life? There seems to be a distinction between the two, which helps anchor the novelty in Shillong's repertoires. Shillong is also a cosmopolitan platform for people from the Northeast. Therefore, it is no surprise that singers from Mizoram, Nagaland, and Assam contribute to the choral scene with their own local typifications. What is mirrored in the renditions of the artists of Shillong is the newness in their approach to portraying a musical work. This is interspersed with the emblems of Christianity and Khasi traditions.

In the case of Goa, Christianity retains its local flavor. The musicians I met here all belong to the Catholic tradition. For them, religion is a way of life. Thus, choral life is an extension of their faith. Through vocal traditions, they bring out stylistic possibilities, but these are usually grounded in a sacred music motif. The nostalgia in music returns with their preference for Gregorian chants, Latin liturgies, traditional Goan folk melodies, and texts approved by the sacred music body. The introduction of medieval music repertoire by the Italian conductor, Professor Santiago Lusardi Girelli, exposed them to other kinds of chants and intonations. I have already discussed the details of the musical repertoire in Chapter 4, where music pedagogy in the realm of choral music tradition is highlighted.

The affinity that Goans establish with musicians from Portugal, Brazil, and Spain is instant. Being Goan, they respond well to the European traditions that largely shaped their aural terrain. The Catholic Goans especially internalize a peculiar being, which is European with local elements—quite unlike Hindu

Goans or those following other faiths, like Islam. In everyday conversations, the medium of expression is usually English; a few older generations still have conversations in Portuguese. Konkani is mostly used in church rather than in everyday negotiations. Thus, the sacred music repertoire of Goa, which invokes folk traditions, finds singers who perform in Konkani. Konkani-speaking styles differ between the Hindu and Christian Goans; it is also determined by geographical locations. The sacred music motif mirrors itself through different faces of nostalgia. Bollywood features in this framing of nostalgia too, not in terms of the genre but in terms of musical intricacies like arrangements and harmonics. There is no aspiration toward a mainstream; rather, there is a constant reorganization of self-identity through assertions carved out of local and international exchanges. Christianity and culture are coterminous when it comes to representing choral imaginations in Goa.

> With the Stuti Choir, it's been a year. I am a new member. I joined them because I liked their performance and thought that there is a classical side to music. It focuses also a lot on Konkani music; that's a part that I have never done before. Here you know, in my mother's choir, it is just Gospel singing, so this is something new. I wanted to get into that. I am not very proud of it, but I speak just a little bit of Konkani. I mean I can go to the fish market and maybe buy some fish, but I am not comfortable with complex sentences. (M1, Goa, January 2014)

M1 talks about Konkani language being a part of the Goan sacred music repertoire. Catholic Goans use English in daily communication. Konkani is rarely spoken. Masses in churches are held in Konkani. It belongs to the Indo-European group of languages and is associated with the most Indo-European tongue, Norwegian (Pereira, Da Costa, 2010: 26).

> I am an engineer by profession and sing with the Stuti Choir. I do not have a background in singing. It's just that I love singing and performing and I have picked up music [along] the way. I learnt everything by ear—[I play] a few instruments, also by ear.
>
> It all started when I joined the church choir, and there people noticed me. And then I was invited to sing in some other choirs. I was picked up for an opera; I was chosen for the Stuti Choir. And it's been going like that, step by step. I sing for a church choir, which is an exclusive **choir**. I [also] sang for the St Andrews Choir in Bombay and a few other small choirs here and there. Right now, I [sing] with another choir, besides the Stuti Choir; the choir is [run] by this person called Alfol. That would be just a one-off performance. Let me tell

you about that performance. If you have heard of *Jesus Christ Superstar*, this is an in-house version. Not *Jesus Christ Superstar*, but a similar thing. *Jesus Christ Superstar* was Judas's interpretation of the whole story. This is the perspective of the carpenter, the guy who made the cross. He was just a carpenter and he had a broken, deformed hand. And one day, he saw this person preaching and he went to him and this man cured him of his handicap and he went and became a very good carpenter. [Then] he was called to make a cross. He made the cross and did not know what it was for. And then, later on, he saw the person on the cross was the same person who had cured his hand. So, this is his story, with the life of Jesus in the background. It's a very nice story! A different viewpoint and the music are a variety of rock, blues, reggae, and all different kinds of music that suit each scene. It's like, for example, the priest [and] the high priest are caught between the people and the church—sorry, the temple—the temple in which the man cannot survive. People also want something to be done to him. So they start voicing their [views] in a blues [song]. Now blues is the language of the oppressed black people in America. So, this kind of music was apt for that scene because, in that scene, the priests were the oppressed people. Whereas, somewhere else, we use swing, somewhere else, we use reggae; somewhere else we use rock—each [type of] music suits the scene. (M, January 2014)

This shows how musical productions reinvent themselves by borrowing different voices across genres, each one pertinent to the scenes being enacted. It also communicates how a group of amateur singer-actors come together for an in-house version of a well-known rock opera, *Jesus Christ Superstar.*

The texts were mainly from the Bible, passages from the Bible. And it is done in a modern version, in an easily understandable language. It's an opera so there is no speaking. Everything is sung. The performers sing. It's not background vocals. Initially we had plans of having live instruments on stage but then we thought that it will be too much so all the music was pre-recorded and we sang it like mime songs. We used all kinds of instruments and used modern technology. Lot of mixing was done. In fact, this musician who was doing the mixing, he did all the music. You see, as the director said on stage, all our performers are professionals—professional teachers, professional students, professional . . . so it was a kind of play with words. In other words, none of the performers, very few of the performers, were real stage performers. Everybody was just people who just came and learnt how to perform and how to sing during practice. But we had a few performers who were from various groups. So, it's very difficult to get this whole group of people for performances at any time. But there was one time, when everything was at its lowest. No weddings and no other social commitments—that is the

season of Lent. That is generally during April–May. That is the only time we found
that we could really stage performances. (M, Goa, January 2014)

Faith is an essential thematic element of music performativity for different
communities. For instance, singing hymns is an essential aspect of worship in
the Korean community. Till the time the Bible was translated into Korean in
1910, Christianity was taught through hymns (Harkness, 2015: 83).

> So, last year, we staged about six performances. And by popular demand, we have
> been asked to do it again this year. So, this year, we are still planning on where we
> are going to perform. We chose the main cities. We have to accommodate a lot
> of people so these are stages constructed on big playgrounds and [involve high]
> costs. We had a lot of sponsors [last year]. So, this year, we have to search for
> sponsors again. Because this is not a profit-making thing, we charge a very basic
> entry [fees]. Because the idea is to target as many people as possible. (M, Goa,
> January 2015)

Here, M doesn't reflect so much about the voice that he sings in but the process of
musical production in its entirety. He gives us a sense of the multitude of sounds
and the narratives that unfold in bringing to life a rock opera This helps identify
a genre within the given vocal tradition that resonates well with a certain kind
of audience.

> It was so good because people saw it in Delhi, Dubai, and Bombay. There were
> people who had come down for the performance. And they liked it so much that
> this was taken to Dubai. They wanted the show to come to Dubai, but it was not
> possible to take the whole cast there. So, they took the script and the music to
> Dubai and performed it with their own people. Now Bombay is doing the same.
> Delhi is also doing the same. The person is Alfol Siveira. He took five years to
> write this. You see, the cast is not a fixed number. He said that [whether] we get
> thirty people or 300, [he would] make a role for everyone. So he made a role for
> everyone [who came to practice]. It is according to the number of people, and
> you see, every person contributes something. Someone may say, "Why don't we
> do it like this? Why don't we sing this and change that?" It is always evolving,
> always changing, because we [do] not stick to script in *Jesus Christ Superstar*,
> like we have to. Here, the writer, the producer, and the composer—everyone is
> with us. So, according to the mood, he changes things here and now. (M, Goa,
> January 2014)[5]

---

[5] This was taken to Delhi, Mumbai, and Dubai, apart from performances at Panjim, Margao, and
Vasco in Goa. In Dubai, only the music and script were taken; the producers used their own cast was
used. The producers in Mumbai will also do the same.

M talks about being part of a performance that is not contingent on the same set of singers and musicians. Rather, the improvisatory element of the production renders it tenable to various interpretations, unaffected by how many people participate in it.

> I come from a family that is oriented towards music. I sang with the school choir of St Edmunds. During high school, I wanted to sing pop. During my second year, I met N at a performance in MOT. She asked me to meet the director of Aroha Choir, Pauline Warjri. She was my first voice teacher; [I was] 18 years old. In the beginning, it was very scary, as everyone could sing. Slowly, I learnt classical music, Andre Boccelli, Placido Domingo, and so on. In 2012, Aroha Choir decided to participate in India's Got Talent, two years after Shillong Chamber Choir's magnificent win. The Aroha Choir was invited to the judge's room, but ultimately, [only] two participants sang. I was one of them. I sang *Nessun Dorma* (T, Shillong, January 2015).[6]

> In the interview, I was asked why I want to win. I replied, "I want to bring Western classical music to a platform where it has never been before. I want to make Shillong popular." However, it was too classical for India—how much TRP and entertainment would it have generated? Some of the combinations that I prepared for the show were the Bollywood song, *Meri Maa* and *Prayer* by Andre Bocelli and Celine Dion; *O Sole Miyo* and the Bollywood song, *Kahin Toh*. It was upto the production house and judges to decide what performance style would work for the show. This was shaped by questions, such as: how much money would they make? Would opera, do it? He recalls that for about 7-8 months, everything was paid for. (T, Shillong, January 2015)

He had a two-year contract. He usually performed for red carpet events for the Bollywood industry. His specialty was a Bollywood and opera mix. Later, he had Situ Singh Buehler and Patricia Rozario as mentors.

Bollywood music is known for its stylistic versatility. Bollywood music is also oriented toward an audience that expects good entertainment, showing the least signs of snobbery. Gregory Booth focuses on the influence of a few key figures like Naushad Ali, Shankar-Jaikishan, C. Ramachandra, Lata Mangeshkar, Antonio Vaz, and Sebastian D'Souza during the time period 1948–52. He calls this the "moment of historical conjuncture." He delves into multiple axes

---

[6] Apart from choral work, classical music finds its expressivity in opera productions. Opera requires a certain intellectual and emotional intelligence. It emerged in sixteenth-century Florence. It started as an art form during the late Renaissance. It expanded during the Baroque period and acquired a definitive body of works during the Romantic Age Wechesberg, 1997: 23–5).

associated with the Hindi film song and goes on to explain the collaborative, creative, and competitive world into which the figures immersed themselves in order to create a specific sonic order predisposed to the cultural roots of the entities and the stylistic incorporation of Indian classical, theater music, and Western dance band music, and among many others, the industry milieu and the cinematography built around the film song in question (Booth, 2008).

Not only did T undergo different techniques of vocal training, incorporating nuances that best contribute to his tenor voice, but he also embarked on various modes of entertainment opportunities. His range includes participation in a school choir, an entertainment choir, opera productions, reality TV shows, and sound design.

He left Shillong to study voice, classical tenor, at the Guildhall School of Music and Drama in 2015. He even participated in Asia's Got Talent before leaving India.

T's narrative brings to the fore the aspirations toward building a showman personality. It talks about acquiring skillsets and networks and accessing a variety of platforms to tease out the possibilities operating within a particular vocal tradition. Despite immersing into different modes of music performativity, he returns to a conventional pedagogical framework to further expand his aspirations.

We had formed Afflatus, an all-women's rock band, based out of Meghalaya after winning the MTV Campus Rock Idols in 2004. Our drummer, Mercy Miller was in Bombay and I was studying at that time. During the 1990s, we all went to Loretto. We had music teachers for guitar and drums. We also had singing and vocal training in school. For Piano, people wanted to go outside and learn. When we started out in 2004–2005, we did a diverse set, but they were mainly covers. We performed songs by *No Doubt, Nirvana, Beatles, RAM, Jowai Fates*, etc. When we re-banded in 2008, we did originals. Some of our songs were acoustic and a few involved the entire band. We were four different people with four different musical tastes. I have an eclectic taste. I only listen to rock or country. My mom would play *Tanya Tucker, Don Williams, Kenny Rogers*, etc. I have a deep love for country music. There was a *Doors* phase in college where it felt like the boundaries of consciousness were being pushed. More recently, I appreciate the harmonies and melody; after being in the church. Music is very personal. Church plays a big part, especially being a Mizo, and then being from the North East, it pushes you to explore more. It is difficult to define the affinity towards music. I grew up in an environment filled with music. Music helps to express so many emotions—numbness, happiness, rage. It is a major way as to how humans connect. I used to play the guitar for the band. We were offered an All-India tour, record companies approached us. We worked at it, we were pioneers as a girl band, but somehow things didn't align the way we had imagined it would. The guitar becomes an extension of yourself. There is nothing more beautiful than catharsis or the release of pent-up emotions. I do love the sound of it. The acoustic guitar has a wooden, hearty warmth. Then again, the electric "punk sound" of the guitar would bring out so many sounds. The pedal boards can even mimic a human voice. The guitar as an instrument is truly versatile. It gives you mobility on stage. It adds another level of connection with the audience. (K, Shillong, January 2015)

K's narrative brings out two things. Not all dreams last forever, but the enjoyment and dedication toward them make them worthwhile enterprises. There is a need to fully explore the body of the instrument to truly exploit its tonal possibilities. Being a guitarist, she explains how she attunes her presence to that of her instrument by responding to the materiality that the instrument's body provides. This is similar to F's earlier comment about how one cannot play viola notes on a violin as the latter won't hold the notes of the former, apart from the limitations of their differences in tonality.

Lakshmi Subramaniam, in her book *Veena Dhanammal—The Making of a Legend* (2009), talks about the uniqueness of Dhanammal's vocality. The trick in Dhanammal's style was in the way she plucked her instrument, which communicated her inner voice, which was marked by a melodic feel and deep acoustic space. She drew from a rich repertoire of songs in many languages, having the perfect intonation for each one. Veena Dhanammal skillfully blended her voice with that of her instrument. Her versatility is encapsulated by her comfort with the *padams* of *ksetrayya* that belonged to the *melam* tradition.

She also expressed *raga-bhava* characteristics belonging to the compositions of the Tanjore trinity of Carnatic music (Subramaniam, 2009: 57–8, 72). K's identification with her instrument brings out similar strands.

Voicing emotions or tonalities synonymous with particular ethnicities or nationalities tend to complicate the agency of an artist. One's identity is embodied per se, but in most cases, as per the musicians that I have been in conversation with, people do not portray a homogenous sense of identity. When it comes to matters of indigeneity, the latter too resembles a fractured entity.

Enka or *Naki-bushi* (crying songs) brings out vivid imageries of different kinds of longing[7] found in Japanese society with its typical "vibrato" and *kobushi* (vocal ornamentations). This genre also acquires the label of being the "national song" of Japan. Enka becomes a site of contention when it is performed by a non-Japanese (in this case, by a Korean). At the outset, Enka as a genre is backed by the Nihon Housou Kyokai media house and generates a small but active listenership through its various covers. It revels in its ability to always bring something new to the table. What becomes particularly interesting is Kim Yonja, a Korean Enka singer, whose portrayal of Korean-ness is slightly different from that of *Zainichi Kankokujin* (Koreans living in Japan), vis-à-vis the Japanese imagination of the song, place, and emotions. During 1910–45, Korea had a longstanding, hostile, colonial relationship with Japan. Some even question the genre's allegiance to Japan. Few patterns in Enka find similar threads in Pongchak, a popular Korean ballad form, based on sad melodies and lyrics. Unaffected by the "Korean wave," Kim seeks audience support through her hyper-sentimentality ("white-hot-heat"), often in the garb of "shyness and modesty" prototypical of a (Japanese) gendered nostalgia; mastery of the *hyoujungo* pronunciation; instances like the "Kimono debut"; and charity projects that make her a model citizen. Through her songs, Kim embodies three distinct identities: that of a Korean; straddling both her ancestral and present associations with Zainichi Kankokujin; and enacting Japanese performativity (Yano, 2013).

> I studied in a Christian school. I am Hindu and we have so many gods and goddesses. Since childhood, Durga Puja has been important for me. There was a time when I stopped believing in God. I believe in a certain kind of energy that gives me the power to deal with any kind of situation. My faith in God came back to me when I joined the choir. One of my choir members asked me to consider converting to Christianity. I told her that I will give it a thought. My relatives ask me how come I sing Christian songs! My brother doesn't talk to me because of that. My usual response is that they do Gospel music. Let them be, let me be. I have to understand them in order to respect them, so it helps. I feel that Aunty Pauline worships music and that comes through when she plays or makes us sing. (A, Shillong, January 2015)

Even though A belongs to an entertainment choir, the component of faith plays out in different realms. At an individual level, being in an arrangement where there is a collective sense of faith leads her to revisit her own connection.

---

[7] Departed lovers, rural hometowns, and memories of mother.

Coming from a Hindu, Bengali background, her cultural references differ, not just in religion but also through a linguistic lens.

> We have done Rabindrasangeet with the choir. It is true that Rabindrasangeet has its own beauty. The sound and the soulfulness are different; a Bengali understands that. The choir might demand a certain sound, but the feel may not come out so well. When I try to sing in Khasi, I realize that the language (and) the feel is very different. They stop sometimes with the epiglottis. In Khasi, one has to stop and sing the intonation differently. (A, January 2015)

Here, many strands of thought come together. Training in distinct vocal traditions gear one's voice in a particular mode but often one has to shift across different art forms. The multi-genre ethic which is central to Shillong's choral soundscape benefits from the move between generic categories and linguistic exchanges.

When V, a member of the Junior Aroha Choir, sang the Khasi national anthem "Ri-Khasi," which shares its melody with the Welsh National Anthem, I sensed a duality. The galloping rhythm was interjected by a hint of lament in the melody. It was part of a Medley and the other song used in it was "Ae Mere Watan ke Logon," a patriotic song which is well associated with Bollywood. Lata Mangeshkar's "adolescent-girl falsetto" timbre was brought to the Medley by another choir member, highlighting an atmosphere of patriotic nostalgia through the lens of a community's voice, formulated long ago alongside another voice that was produced for the mainstream popular culture. Another choir member, A, is trained in the Indian classical tradition and initially vocalized soprano parts by emulating the falsetto of Lata Mangeshkar. Her prior training makes it easier for her to belt out a falsetto specific to the chosen Medley. There is a juxtaposition of two different kinds of voices in "Ri-Khasi," one voice that brings to the fore the tinge of lament located in Khasi myth (khasis learned the art of crying from a mourning mother deer) voicing the Khasi national anthem, and the other voice "Ae Mere Watan Ke Logon," which talks of patriotism common to the mainstream imagination of freedom and nationality in the form of a crying appeal.

> I sang at the age of three at Motinagar during Durga Puja. I sang *bhajan*. I did a two-three-year course in Indian classical music, after which I learnt Bharatnatyam for four years. [From the] sixth standard onwards, I resumed vocal lessons and then took up dance once again.
>
> In 2012, when I performed for Doordarshan Kendra Shillong, I met W, as she was anchoring, and at that time, the Aroha Choir was looking for an Indian

classical singer for India's Got Talent. After hearing me sing *Seher de seher*, Aunty Pauline asked me to join the choir. (A, Shillong, January 2015)

Muriel Swinjghuisen Reigersberg (2013) locates the implications of the practice of choral singing and hymnody in a Lutheran Australian Aboriginal community of Hopevale, Northern Queensland. As a choral music facilitator curious to understand the paucity of men in the community choir alongside the changing aesthetics in terms of musical preferences, her study also reveals what it means to practice a faith which is in no way connected to one's indigenous roots. Unlike other places in Australia, the Hopevale community's notion of the "country" was bereft of spiritual references to flora, fauna, ancestors, natural elements, and kinship affiliations. Even the local church music had not embraced the strands of indigenous (Aboriginal) theology.[8] The movement of the hymnody, nonetheless, becomes particularly interesting during the evacuation era experienced by the "Cape Bedford people," as the Hopevalians referred to themselves, during the years 1942–9. Few individuals, like one of the elders, Walter Bowen, managed to negotiate with his ancestral language, natural elements, and kinship affiliations, as was discovered in his unpublished obituary. Such views, however, could never be representative of a collective expression of indigenity due to the lack of an Aboriginal theology within the Lutheran Church in Queensland. Nowadays, church services at Hopevale are not compulsory, which means that there is a decent turnout only during Easter and Christmas and at weddings and funerals. The linguistic challenge put forth by the Guugu Yimithirr, and also the restricted mobility of the youth to other regions, does not encourage them to create a specific identity ordered around a hymnody, like the earlier generation. Furthermore, during 2004–5, choral singing was associated with Gamba Gamba ("older, married, and respected women").

Men did not acquire a place in choral singing owing to limited opportunities directed toward them by the state and the church officials and ultimately the

---

[8] The 1873 Palmer River Gold Rush remembered for the brutal massacre of the local aboriginal groups by the settlers, led to the loss of oral culture, musical, and spiritual knowledge. Further, connections between indigenous spirituality and local country were jeopardized when mobility restrictions were enforced on certain indigenous groups. Also, the implementation of the Aboriginal Protection and Restriction of the Sale of the Opium Act in 1897 in Queensland empowered the government to imprison people of indigenous ancestry. Children were also not spared. This trend continued well into the 1960s and 1970s. The story about the forced evacuation of the Hopevalians to Woorabinda between 1942 and 1949 without prior knowledge marks an episode of death due to climatic hazards. This, too, speaks of loss, trauma, and the disconnectedness from one's "country" and ancestral knowledge. The nail in the coffin was put when the Australian Federation Government's integration and assimilation policies during 1960s and 1970s emphasized the need to adopt westernized lifestyle (Reigersberg, 2013: 88–90).

community itself. The youth preferred a modern sound, which included the use of instruments like drums, the keyboard, guitar, and bass. Muriel's case study of a choral performance at the Lotus Glen (All-Male) Correctional Centre, Mareeba, in April 2005, specifically urges one to engage with the emotion of crying when singing as well as listening to the songs sung in Guugu Yimithirr. This "crying" or "nostalgia," both inward and public, was a collective emotion of "loss and longing" linked to a shared history, language, ancestry, and country. In 2009, the author returned to discover that there was scope for indigenous Christianity to be embraced. Also, male elders occasionally joined the choirs to represent their country's tradition at the Biannual Queensland Music Festival. They even led church services when the pastor was not there. Over the years, things might have undergone more changes, but this particular experience leaves an impression as it locates history in the ever-changing landscape of the contemporary (Reigersberg, 2013).

Roma Chatterji uses the concept of "mirroring" "The Mise en Abyme—the mirror in text" to understand the pictorial narrations in the form of singing and displaying the scrolls among the Chitrakars of Bengal. She refers to the *Tsunami Pata* and *Manasa Scroll*. While the Manasa scroll has the deity's presence expressed through her attribute (the snake), who communicates to the audience the diegetical context of the narration, promising alternate possibilities, the Tsunami Song, composed by one of the Chitrakars, details the human tragedy, drawing inferences from the Mangala texts that frame the narratives. The goddess becomes the agent as well as a witness of the event. The events centered on the "mirror motif" bring forth human time and the cosmic time at one and the same time (Chatterji, 2015: 356–7, 370). Myth, like a musical score, is given shape by a bundle of events, although the events reveal themselves at varying moments in a story. Each page in an orchestral score is to be read vertically as well as from left to right. Every page is a totality. Levi-Strauss talks about the "motif of renunciation of love" and its appearance at different moments in the opera ring, every time returning to the central protagonist Brunhilde through symbols such as gold, sword, and even offspring (Levi-Strauss, 1978: 20). In the case of Goa and Shillong, in the realm of performance or performativity, the motifs of nostalgia and novelty motif present themselves in the events at different points. The vignettes used here talk about novelty in terms of articulating vocal gestures like falsetto while representing singing icons in mainstream popular music of India. The difference between head voice and throat voice comes alive due to the context of the performance or of the training that the musicians undergo.

Novelty also appears in the choir members' participation in reality shows and the expectation from the reality TV show creators to contribute a new aural sensation. Thinking through Medley began with Shillong Chamber Choir's win, and this is the novelty that Shillong as a region brings to the choral music scene. There is nostalgia in Shillong's repertoire when it comes to Aroha Choir's performance of the Khasi national anthem, "Ri-Khasi," or incorporating Khasi sounds—although the vocabulary that the Khasis embrace is that of creating something new and of creative eminence, as K talks about their endeavor as a girl band pursuing Western music. The rootedness is mirrored in contemporary representations. In Goa, as M's narration shows, Jesus Christ Superstar is a rock opera that has been imagined from the carpenter's point of view, but the religiosity binds it to the theme of Jesus. There are experimentations in terms of exploration of musical styles for different sections, but nostalgia and a sense of the everyday are mirrored by the choice of theme of the musical production. In the earlier section on constitution of place, the Stuti Choir members and the Goa University Choir members talk about different kinds of sacred music repertoires that they explore. Thus, the sacred motif extends to become the nostalgia motif for Goa.

Conclusion

This chapter, in three sections, has looked at voice and the many meanings it communicates. It first locates the voice as an entity that moves across registers to culminate in musical expressions. It adopts the grammar of the choral tradition specific to the chosen regions to carve out a sociality around it. Then, through individual journeys, the constitution of place comes to the fore. The social expectation, individual challenges, and musical possibilities color the idea of belonging. Finally, the mirroring of the motifs largely articulates the vocalization techniques adopted by the musicians. Performing novelty and nostalgia become the frames through which choral traditions in Shillong and Goa are located. All these musicians are part of the different choirs that I engaged with during my fieldwork in Goa and Shillong. However, each one identified with a particular vocalic stylization and navigated a cultural and geographical rootedness that shaped their musical imagination and belonging. Furthermore, since performance caters to the adulation, expectations, and possibilities of sacred music entertainment within and without sacred affiliations have also been discussed (see Figures 5.1–5.5).

Figure 5.1 Pauline Warjri at the Aroha Music Studio. Photo credit Sebanti Chatterjee.

Figure 5.2 Serenity Choir practicing outdoors before a concert in November 2014. Photo credit Sebanti Chatterjee.

Figure 5.3 Setting up before a concert at Capela de Monte. Photo credit Sebanti Chatterjee.

Figure 5.4 The walk to the festival Chapel of the Mount. Photo credit Sebanti Chatterjee.

Figure 5.5 Dorbar Shnong Institution representing Khasi grassroots governance Riatsamthiah. Photo credit Sebanti Chatterjee.

6

Tutti

Concluding Section

The Musical Clef Notating Certainty-Uncertainty

Music exists in the everyday. Thus, when novel Coronavirus infiltrated the everyday, music too got impacted. Severe Acute Respiratory Syndrome Corona Virus 2 (SARS-COV-2), a strain that causes Covid-19, was initially found in the city of Wuhan, Hubei, China. On January 30, 2020, the World Health Organization categorized the surge as a Public Health Emergency of International Concern and was labeled as a pandemic on March 11, 2020. We are in the third year of the pandemic with ongoing research about further mutations, assessing how contagious each of the strains is, efficacy, and the unpredictability of the vaccines. The pandemic evidently controls the dynamics of the different voices.

When the second wave hit India in March 2021, narratives about deaths and damages related to Covid-19 were slowly closing in to include friends and family known to each one of us personally. On May 19, 2021, Italo-Argentinian Maestro Santiago Girelli passed away at a hospital in South Goa due to Covid complications. After speaking to a few of the Goa University Choir members and Santiago's brother, it was painful to learn that he had already breathed his last by the time his wife and children reached Goa. Santiago was the visiting professor of Western Music, Antonio Gonsalves Chair of Goa University. He founded the Goa University Choir in July 2013.

The pandemic has not just introduced medical uncertainties regarding physical ailment but also added to the increased anxieties and other varieties of mental illness. Being a disease that observes social distance protocols, packaging kindness in various forms became one of the ways to show up. Since singing was only possible through virtual and digital realms, live music scenes such as choral music experienced a phase of dim public life. Shillong Chamber Choir founder Neil Nongkynrih started a new business venture called Uncle's Ark, whereby they began delivering groceries and domestic products especially to the elderly and others unable to step out due to rampant cases and phased lockdowns. They became the main distributors of Bob's Red Mill, a gluten-free company ideal for healthy food items. In the meantime, with no live shows or corporate gigs, the choir devoted their entire time working on various albums. In January 5, 2022, few friends from Aroha Choir and a journalist friend from Goa informed me about the untimely death of Neil Nongkynrih due to a complicated surgery at a hospital in Mumbai. Later, the Shillong Chamber Choir put out an official statement confirming the terrible news of their founder's demise.

Grief has been a usual motif in pandemic diaries but it becomes overwhelming when two key personalities, who shaped my doctoral thesis argumentations and ethnographic immersions and brought forth many radical and soothing ideas about cultural exchanges, become vignettes of departure instead of fellow academic and cultural commentators, at a time when I am finalizing my manuscript. I was personally close to Maestro Santiago as he taught me the methods and the etiquette of choral singing apart from having critical discussions about my research ideas on Goa. As for Uncle Neil, I remain a forever fangirl of the Shillong Chamber Choir. His music pushed me to explore choral singing and its variegated imaginations. The world really lost two musical gems and visionaries. Nonetheless, both the figures aged forty-two and fifty-one respectively, who were too young to depart, have left behind legacies that promise to make the creative world shinier. At a moment like this, choral music implores one to look at the sense of community it instills in everyone.

How do we perceive choral ensembles usually? Choral singing is a collaborative act that needs both conscious and unconscious training, ability to listen, adaptability as per the comfort of one's vocalic range, rehearsing, and learning to seize the moment in belting out an intricate aria yet being mindful about fading out inconspicuously.

At the outset, it is seen as an aid to worshiping rather than as having a public life of its own. Once the purpose and form of choral music are organized, the technical components take center stage. If the hymn or the part of a sacred classical piece is in a foreign language, one needs to master the diction and expression well. It becomes important to gesticulate moods such as solemnity, victory, hope, rage, despair, charm, tenderness, and buoyancy with ease. Its origins lie in the sacred, which naturally infuses a devotional spirit to the nature of its rendition. Even if it is a regular church choir, one observes certain basic discipline ingrained in the form. When the layer of performativity is added to the otherwise ritualistic expectation, then the attire, commands, and light movements gain currency. Nonetheless, choral voices have always been framed around a community with a focus on in-person jamming, listening, and formulating sounds based on the synergy and the camaraderie of the collective. Thus, the pandemic and notion of digital intimacy did not fit the choral music setup. With lockdown and restrictions regarding the size of the gathering, church services took on an online mode. The service and worship hours became shorter as singing was not allowed in most churches. The usual practice and community meet-ups also dwindled in the process. For the entertainment choirs, they had no shows due to the lack of a live audience. However, some of the festivals like the Monte Festival and Ketevan Festival in Goa put up a digital show. Despite social distance rules, the choir members had to meet up for rehearsals, finalizing the program and carrying on the usual aura of performance in the chapel or the courtyard, depending on the nature of the content, for an invisible audience on the other side of the screen. Thus, performativity took on a different lens whereby they sang, danced, and celebrated for an absent audience. They became accessible to internet viewers in the same manner as video games, except that there wasn't a way to overlap the real and the virtual world. In the world of the gamers, at least the players from the real world are able to access and insert themselves as characters through the digital world. Sound production has evolved whereby home studios have become a recurring phenomenon and basic technological software tools for creating, writing, and sequencing music, MIDI and Sibelius are being used by music practitioners—learners, educators, and performers for a long time now. Churches have begun live streaming worship services which resulted in many parishes and churches opening their YouTube channels. Choral music videos are being produced in abundance. Yet, the nuances and lifeforce of live choral singing are very different from the choral music renditions delivered in a digital interface.

Positing the Vocal Phrasing

The book looks at how choral voices are an extension of the voices of specific communities, a pivotal hook to grasp the creative process of an art form that incorporates sacred and nonsacred modalities, and through an ethnographic lens, it discerns musical attributes such as harmony, rhythm, dynamics, arrangement, presentation, and the sonic element that sets it apart from the other choirs. The stories from Goa and Shillong are organized in a manner so as to grasp the regional specificities and anchored in the direction of where their creative forces lie. It is definitely not a comparative study, and that is why the individual chapters dedicated to the regions are framed around different concepts. This leads to the question: How do culture and religion coexist and separate in the context of a sacred musical tradition, such as choral music?

In the introduction of the book *Western Music and Its Other*, Georgina Born points out that music is capable of constructing new identities and reflecting existing ones. Sociocultural identities are molded dynamically within the musical culture leading to the reproduction of those identities. The hybridities present in musical compositions are a result of embracing the elements of either the internal others like the Jews or the others whose music may be referred to as profane or subaltern like the "Arabesk" music of the Turks (Born and Hesmondhalgh, 2000).[1] The Christian communities belonging to different denominations in Goa and Shillong consciously or unconsciously play out their identitarian markers associated with faith when demonstrating choral voices.

Evangelical Christianity exhibits rootedness in the Bible as the singing voice reiterates the heightened incorporation of the Word of God in one's life. Singing one's own theology makes the connection to one's own faith stronger. Considering every free translation or direct quotation, most Christian hymns are based on the Bible. As a component of Christian education, hymns contribute to an enhancement of biblical knowledge as well as reiterate the respect accorded to the Bible as Scripture. The effectiveness of hymns is assessed partly on the basis of how it operates as a vehicle for scriptural truth (Eskew and McElrath, 1980; Radiancy Rgnca, 2004). This suggests that hymns whether performed under sacred music guidelines within churches and parishes or through Medley as a genre always have their foundation in the religious text, the Bible. Thus, choral music can never completely obliterate the religious label ascribed to it despite innovations pertaining to the cosmopolitan outlooks.

Digitalization and electronic media have a huge impact on various churches, identities, and the styles of music making. YouTube Contemporary congregational songs (CCS) videos allow the viewers various vantage points

---

[1]   Georgina Born and David Hesmondhalgh, *Western Music and Its Others: Difference, Representation, and Appropriation in Music* (Berkeley: University of California Press, 2000).

ranging from song lyrics and their theological intent, musical styles, and content, meanings that are deciphered personally, performativity, the artists (worship leaders/bands), as well as the producers (churches/events/industry). Also, the visualization demonstrates cultural values and identity. YouTube engagements help in mediating online Christian communities. This extends from the Christian music-based communities contingent on Benedict Anderson's "imagined communities." Such ideas are reflected in evangelical communities formed on the basis of a shared discursive framework, "Horizontal comradeship," interpreted as core evangelical values or a shared belief in the gospel or, in the case of Hillsong, emplacing themselves as a brand amid the globalized understanding of Christian imagined community. Like-minded Christian communities committed to the notions of intimate communications, care, and shared faith form one group but the need to understand large, unfamiliar, international online groups based on single song texts persists. The CCS as mediated through YouTube have definitely transformed their local church expressions, denominational signature style alongside their commercial characteristics to be enablers of imagined Christian community. Charismatic churches often build on identity politics and making of religious subjectivities. Commercial gospel music in Ghana has a huge mass appeal and often contributes to the brand image of its associated church (Anderson, 1991[2]; Ingalls, 2008[3]; Hartje-Doll, 2013[4]; Wagner, 2014[5]; Campbell, 2005[6];Hoover, 2006[7]; Meyer, 2009[8]; Collins, 2004[9]). This becomes more useful to understand the nature of choral music engagements during the pandemic either as a gospel or singing band aligned to a specific church or parish and independent artists who make choral music that may be solely sacred and at the same time include other nonsacred genres. YouTube channels or one-off videos on YouTube centered on congregational songs and faith have become a

[2] Benedict Anderson, *Imagined Communities: Reflections on the Origin and Spread of Nationalism* (New York: Verso, 1991).

[3] Monique Ingalls, *Awesome in This Place: Sound, Space, and Identity in Contemporary North American Evangelical Worship*. PhD diss., University of Pennsylvania (USA, 2008).

[4] Gesa Hartje-Doll, "'Hillsong' United through Music: Praise and Worship Music and the Evangelical 'Imagined Community,'" in *Christian Congregational Music: Performance, Identity, and Experience*, ed. Monique Ingalls, Carolyn Landau and Thomas Wagner (Farnham: Ashgate, 2013), 139–50.

[5] Thomas J. Wagner, *Hearing the Hillsong Sound: Music, Marketing, and Branded Spiritual Experience at a Transnational Megachurch*, PhD. diss., Royal Holloway University of London (UK, 2014).

[6] Heidi Campbell, *Exploring Religious Community Online: We Are One in the Network* (New York: Peter Lang, 2005).

[7] Stewart M Hoover, *Religion in the Media Age* (New York: Routledge, 2006).

[8] Birgit Meyer, *Aesthetic Formations: Media, Religion, and the Senses* (New York: Palgrave Macmillan, 2009).

[9] John Collins, "Ghanaian Christianity and Popular Entertainment: Full Circle," *History in Africa* 31 (2004): 407–23.

new mode of performing and responding to worship music and choral voices in different genres.

There is a deep-seated notion about the point of return. Choral music as a genre was discovered in the process of worship and together with the scripture shaped the ritualistic manifestations of Christian communities. At the same time, it is a vocalic practice and can be associated with authenticity, experimentations, and formulation of archetypal frameworks. This is similar to what Foucault talks about in *What Is an Author?* Within the fields of discursivity, and he takes Freud and Marx as examples, there is a foreseeable tendency for a return to the origin. It is more than a historical reflection or a mere embellishment; it includes the task of transforming the nature of the discursive process itself. He asserts that reexamination of Freud would modify psychoanalysis and reexamination of Marx would modify Marxism (Foucault, 1998: 219).[10] Thus, innovations with choral music lead to the creation of Medley as a genre, which accommodates both sacred and nonsacred mechanisms. On the other hand, revisiting choral compositions and festivities throws open the curation of a peculiar indigeneity that invites global and vernacular complexities.

The urgency to earmark an ethnic footprint that makes them who they are also comments on the cartographic imaginations of the communities in general. The manner in which their musical traditions and languages found a place, choral music became a cultural symbol for the Christians, particularly the Catholics in Goa. I have looked at Goa holistically as I have based a large part of my doctoral research on how one of the oldest seminaries in Asia, Rachol, nurtures the embodiment, pedagogy, and performativity of sacred music among the Christians in Goa. My own experience of doing participant observation in Goa was also under a choir conductor who was a seminarian turned professor. Jose Pereira, Micael Martins, and Antonio da Costa (2010)[11] write about Asia's first Western-style university, the Seminario de Santa Fe and later the Colegio de S Paulo (1541), upon which Luso-Indian culture was founded. This cultural expressivity later helped in harmonizing the Goan vocal music. Mando, one of the popular folk music forms of Goa, found a footing in this process alongside the already thriving sacred music owing to the parish schools. In 1954, the Legislative Diploma of the Overseas Ministry established the Academia de Música de Goa modeled on the Lisbon Conservatory to promote musical

---

[10] Michel Foucault, *Aesthetics, Methods, and Epistemology* (New York: The New Press, 1998).
[11] Costa Martins Pereira, *Song of Goa: Crown of Mandos* (Goa: Goa 1556, 2010).

culture in Goa. The Goa Symphony orchestra and Sociedade Choral De Goa was founded by Antonio De Figueiredo. Kala Academy, a state-run liberal arts center, was created in 1970. It incorporated the Academia within its premises in the following year. Thus, Goa always had state support when it comes to Western classical music. When it comes to preserving Konkani as a language, its social dialects become crucial, which are determined either by caste or by religion. The Christian Konkani community also has underlying caste stratification (Miranda, 1978: 84). Konkani has five scripts—Roman, Kannada, Malayalam, Perso-Arabic, and Devanagari. Perhaps, Roman script documents the oldest literary tradition circa sixteenth century. Father Thomas Stephens (1549–1619) authored the first printed book in Konkani—*Doutrina Crista* (1622), and the first printed grammar of Konkani (in Portuguese)—*Arte da Lingoa Canarim*—regarded as the earliest grammar in modern Indian languages (Sardessai, 2000: 34, 42).[12] Also, the fourth council of Goa in 1592 insisted on using the most common languages of the province during church services, and hence Thomas Stephens chose Konkani as the language of catechism (Pinto, 2007). The official Konkani script, however, is in Devanagari. Monsenhor Sebastiao Rodolpho Dalgado started advocating Devanagari for Konkani, which was first created in 1678 (Dalgado, 1893).[13] Rochelle Pinto (2007:45, 236)[14] while discussing print nationalisms centred around Konkani language also discusses the caste antagonisms unfolding amidst a desire for belonging to the Portuguese political scape. 1821 onwards, when print culture was re-introduced to Goa, a chasm grew between the powerful yet subordinate Chardos and the well positioned Brahmins in church and bureaucracy under the Portuguese rule. Pinto also demonstrates how Konkani print made it possible for migrant Goans to familiarise themselves with urban modernity in Bombay. While the Catholic Church was emblematic of the caste and class hierarchies in Goa, most of the critiques in the plays and novels dealt with the metaphors of Christian equality. Various other Konkani print forms focused on the relentless struggle stories around land distribution. Goans first and Indians later, the church further cemented the uniqueness between the Christian and the non-Christian Goans.

I have often been asked why Shillong and not Meghalaya? Also, why not any other place in the Northeast? I approached the Shillong choral music scene as an aftermath of the consequences of the Reality TV success at the outset. Later, once

---

[12] Manohar Sardessai, *A History of Konkani Literature* (New Delhi: Sahitya Akademi, 2000).
[13] Sebastiao Rudolpho Dalgado, *Diccionario Komkani—Portuguez* (Mumbai: Indo-Prakash, 1893).
[14] Rochelle Pinto, Between Empires: *Print and Politics in Goa.* (Goa: Oxford University Press, 2007).

I spent enough time during the course of my ethnography, many other aspects came to the fore. However, my central protagonists remain two popular choirs from Shillong. Meghalaya has two primary communities, the Khasi/Jaintia and the Garo, which together comprise about 80 percent of the population. The Khasi and Jaintia can be traced to the MonKhmer peoples, and the Garo to the Tibeto-Burman peoples. Both communities are considered Scheduled Tribes under the Sixth Schedule of the Indian Constitution. Meghalaya was formed out of Assam in 1970 and became a state in 1972 (Mc-Duie, 2019).[15]

> What does it mean to tell the past of Shillong rather than Meghalaya? Or Tura or Dawki? Urban areas no matter how small are repositories of the past, manifest in everything from seminaries to barracks, polluted waterways to brightly lit oil refineries, statues of tribal heroes a stone's throw from a statue of Nehru, vernacular cottages, and brutal cement blocks. They are crammed with texts and symbols that reveal the communities that have come, gone, stayed. The juxtapositions of objects and neighbourhoods, the pollution dynamics of wealth and poverty—centre and outskirts—tell stories of past and present that skirt the firm categories of tribal and non-tribal, inclusion and exclusion. (Pachuau, 2014: 59, quoted in Mc-Duie, 2019: 81)[16]

When the Nagas portray an "exotic" image in the Hornbill Festival by performing a certain kind of identity, they primarily do so to attract the tourist gaze. Furthermore, it indicates the shaping of a distinct Naga national culture that resonates well in a global atmosphere where indigenous identities are glorified. Cultural hybridity speaks about the complementary ideas that merge the local and global interaction to help make sense of the emerging Naga identity. Hybrid cultures insist upon leaning on to novel techniques to create new meanings of authenticity, history, and culture (Longkumer, 2015: 60).[17]

There is a constant need to understand the challenge that arises due to colonial empire building: continuation of creative processes that can be traced back to the cultural and religious frameworks of those historical moments. At the same time, there is an ongoing revision of a vernacular, ethnic, indigenous claim-making around these cultural and religious choices. Chen speaks of

---

[15] Mc-Duie-Ra Duncan, "Embracing or Challenging the Tribe? Dilemmas in Reproducing Obligatory Pasts in Meghalaya," in *Landscape, Culture, and Belonging: Writing the History of Northeast India*, ed. Bhattacharya and L. K. Pachuau (Cambridge: Cambridge University Press, 2019), 66–86.

[16] Ibid., 81.

[17] Arkotong Longkumer, "As Our Ancestors Once Lived: Representation, Performance, and Constructing a National Culture amongst the Nagas of India," *The Journal of Association for Nepal and Himalayan Studies* 35, no. 1 (2015): 51–64.

adopting a "critical syncretism" so as to break away from colonial identification and points toward a direction of identification that is outward and insists that one should "become others." The process of becoming others requires an immersed understanding of subjectivity in multilayered practices. It is the process through which one de-colonizes oneself from the self-reproducing neocolonial framework and formulates multiple reference points to redirect one's desires (Chen, 2010: 99, 101).[18] This intercultural referencing or building a system of multiple reference points is a central tenet of what Chen argues in his seminal work *Asia as Method*. However, it was originally coined by Takeuchi Yoshimi in one of his essays in *What Is Modernity?* He speaks about how Japanese politicians and business people have a tendency to compare Japanese political institutions and art with counterparts in Europe but never look for those parallels in Asia. Takeuchi proclaims that Japan should rephrase its modernization "trilaterally" by referencing to different types of modernization, akin to that of China or India. He also speaks of bidirectional cultural influence that respects and builds on East-West relations (Takeuchi, 2005: 156, 166, 167).[19] Choral music in Goa and Shillong thus generates spaces where religion and culture have a complicated relationship. A sacred musical form transgresses but never produces choral voices devoid of a sacred intent. The sacrality contingent on the vocalizations may even be temporary in nature. However, be it a rehearsal space, a performance auditorium, a sacrosanct parish, a reality TV show, or a recording studio, during the rendition of the sacred tonalities, the devotion to the scripture or the commitment to produce a sacred voice thrives. It successfully intertwines the possibilities of the point of return and multilayered practices.

---

[18] Chen Kuan-hsing, *Asia as Method: Toward Deimperialization* (Durham: Duke University Press, 2010).

[19] Yoshimi Takeuchi, *What Is Modernity? Writings of Takeuchi Yoshimi*, trans. Richard F. Calichman (New York: Columbia University Press, 2005).

Acknowledgments

It is a pleasure and honor to publish with the critically acclaimed Music and Sound Studies Series of Bloomsbury and to work with Leah Babb Rosenfeld, Senior Commissioning Editor, and Rachel Moore, Assistant Editor, who were generous with their comments and patient with my requests of extending deadlines. I am also thankful to Nivethitha Tamilselvan, Venkat Perla Ramesh, Sharmila and Sophie Campbell for walking me through the production process. A big thank you. I take this opportunity to thank two anonymous reviewers whose suggestions and comments have helped me to revise the manuscript.

I am thankful to Professor Joyashree Roy, Professor Dalia Chakraborty, Professor Prashanta Roy, and Professor Amlan Dasgupta for encouraging me to write a dissertation on public life of Western classical guitarists in Kolkata while pursuing my MA in Jadavpur University (2008–10). I am immensely grateful to Tokyo Foundation and Nippon Foundation for offering me the SYLFF fellowship to realize the project. This journey continued in 2010–12 in the Centre for Studies in Social Sciences Kolkata (CSSSC). I thank each and every faculty member of MPhil Program, CSSSC Kolkata, and especially my MPhil supervisor, Professor Lakshmi Subramanian. The book expands on my doctoral dissertation titled "Western Classical Music in Goa and Shillong: Exploring the Indigenous." I express my gratitude to Professor Roma Chatterji for her constant encouragement and motivation to transform my thesis into a book even when I was not convinced. She has been a guiding force. I thank my research committee, which had Professor Meenakshi Thapan and my Institute of Economic Growth-ICSSR supervisor, Professor Sanjay Srivastava, who has been extremely supportive during my post PhD career.

DSE, as we call it, remains special for many reasons. I thank Sarbani for sharing her home and helping me to settle in Delhi. Delhi School of Economics campus, especially JP Tea Stall, provided the much-needed chai conversations with Nandini, Afeeda, Nikita, Neil, Prasenjit, and Preeti. I thank my comrade-in-arms Jyoti and Saumya for their insights, comments, and breaks in between. Ratan Tata Library provided the much-needed sanctuary that any PhD student can dream of. I also thank the Research Scholars Group, or RSG, for creating an informal space for deliberating on half-baked ideas and organizing potluck lunch and dinners. I also thank other faculty members of Delhi School of Economics for their feedback at various stages of the work.

I was fortunate to receive comments from Professor Tina K Ramnarine, who has also been my mentor during (Ryoichi Sasakawa Young Leaders Fellowship Fund) SYLFF research abroad during October 2016–December 2016 at the Royal Holloway, University of London, UK, Professor Susana Sardo, Dr. Tom Wagner, Professor Sasanka Perera, Professor Urmimala Sarkar Munshi, Professor Urmila Bhirdikhar, and Professor Yasmeen Arif. I am grateful to the National Library of Wales, Aberystwyth, and the British Library, London for allowing me to conduct brief archival work during my dissertation.

I am indebted to my interlocutors, particularly Late Santiago Lusardi Girelli, Ignacio Lusardi Monteverde, Father Loiola, Father Miranda, and Pauline Warjri. This work would not be possible without the warmth and hospitality of Ashley, Elvina, Chriselle, Jeanne, Aunty Esther, Uncle Jo, Aunty Jean, Greshma, Omar, Melroy, Karen, Jovito, Nigel, Rui, and Karl, and Sujata in Goa and Ankan, Avi, Riyan, Sam, Gordon, and Karikor and Kong Esther in Shillong. A special thanks to Aroha Choir, Shillong Chamber Choir, Serenity Choir, Goa University Choir, and Stuti Chorale Ensemble, for making me part of the musical journeys that I write about. I hope I have been able to do justice to their journey(s). Lapdiang, I cannot thank you enough for being present through almost all the episodes of this work taking shape. Alver, Frederick, and Chernoll, thank you for always being a phone-call away regarding any technical or sensitive details regarding the field. I also thank Nikhil Sardana, founder of the *Serenade* magazine, for facilitating various conversations during fieldwork.

This book has seen many ups and downs. Despite the odds, intellectual exchanges about sound, academic precarity, and life kept me going. I thank Christ University, Bengaluru, Jesus and Mary College, Delhi University, Indian Institute of Technology, Jodhpur and National Law School India University, Bangalore for helping me sail through uncertain tides. Hannah, Joanna and Rupert, it has been a pleasure exchanging notes about fieldwork, research and intellectual ideas during writing our dissertations and that remains valuable for the book as well. Radha, words are not enough to thank you for being a call away and overseeing various drafts of the manuscript and egging me on to challenge my comfort zone. Piya S., thank you for agreeing to spontaneous writing sessions, impromptu edits, and cup of hot chocolate. Ishita, thank you for handholding me during stressful writing periods, editing woes, and unmanageable mood swings. We have set up countless virtual writing hours just to put a single idea on paper. Dala, thank you for being an incredible flatmate and for your constant presence and laughter. Reva, Rajni, Ritambara, Chitra, Shailza, Tanushree, Preetha, and Nian, thank you for putting up with all my tantrums and providing me with all sorts of support unasked. I am thankful to Jayshree and Suruchi for keeping my spirits high and providing me the right doses of kindness and creativity in the most trying times. I am grateful to Suhas for being an anchor of strength, warmth, and positivity during difficult times.

Barnini, aka Babudidi, remained a constant source of solace to pursue my dream. Thank you for being my personal genie during all times. I am thankful to my parents, Deepa Chatterjee and Manabendra Nath Chatterjee, for their unending support and encouragement. Patatri (Didi), thank you for showing up in your own way. I am also thankful to Sarbojit and Smitha for being the best support system in Bangalore.

I cannot imagine a life in Kolkata without my friends. Piya Chakraborty for always having my back and showing up despite the distance, Pratyay Nath for his generosity and humor, and Devaleena and Krittika for being the perfect girl-gang, Sambuddha, Sharanya, Anwesha, Santanu, and Shinjini for being amazing friends. I want to thank Adway De, my junior from school without whose help I wouldn't have been able to submit my doctoral application to Delhi School of Economics. I cannot but forget the immense influence my first school had on me in structuring my intellectual ideas around music.

Manasa deserves a special shout-out for undertaking challenging editing tasks at a short notice. I am also thankful to Chitra Manohar and Meghna for copyediting select chapters under strict timelines.

I am especially thankful to Raisa Vaz for making the hand-drawn map of Goa as I experienced it during my ethnography, which I am using as the front cover photo for the book, Louise Dugdale for the final cover design, and Soumik Mukherjee (my co-collaborator for an IFA project to document choral voices) for editing a short video documentation from my fieldsite in Shillong, which is available on Bloomsbury website.

Finally, I want to dedicate this book to my granny—Late Renu Mukherjee, who wished that I became a medical doctor. Although I managed another way to acquire the title, I know that she would have been happy about the manuscript.

Bibliography

Archival Sources

Calvinist Methodist Archive; National Library of Wales; accessed November 15, 2016.
Sound Archive, British Library, London; accessed November 24, 2016.

Books, Articles, Theses

Adorno, T. (2012), *Quasi Una Fantasia: Essays on Modern Music*, New York: Verso.
Albuquerque, T. (1997), *The Rachol Legacy*, Bombay: Wenden Offset Private Limited.
Alles, G. (2017), "Are Adivasis Indigenous?" in G. Johnson and S. Kraft (eds.), *Handbook of Indigenous Religion*, Leiden: Brill.
Anderson, B. (1991), *Imagined Communities: Reflections on the Origin and Spread of Nationalism*, New York: Verso.
Attali, J. (1985), *Noise: The Political Economy of Music*, Minneapolis: University of Minnesota Press.
Avis, R. (2020), "Higher Music Education, India and Ethnography: A Case Study of KM Music Conservatory Students," *Ethnomusicology*, 29 (2): 230–49.
Bakhle, J. (2005), *Two Men and Music: Nationalism in the Making of Indian Classical Tradition*, USA: Oxford University Press.
Bakhle, J. (2008), "Music as the Sound of the Secular," *Comparative Studies in Society and History*, 50 (1): 256–84. http://www.jstor.org/stable/27563662.
Bakhtin, M. (1981), *The Dialogic Imagination: Four Essays*, Austin: University of Austin Press.
Barber, K. (2007), *The Anthropology of Texts, Persons and Publics: Oral and Written Culture in Africa and Beyond*, Cambridge: Cambridge University Press.
Barthes, R. (1977), "'Grain of Voice' and 'Musica Practica,'" in R. Barthes (ed.), *Image, Music Text*, 179–89 and 149–54, Great Britain: Fontana Press.
Beaster-Jones, J. (2014). "Film Song and Its Other: Stylistic Mediation and the Hindi Film Song Genre," in G. Booth and B. Shope (eds.), *More than Bollywood: Studies in Indian Popular Music*, 97–113, Oxford: Oxford University Press.
Benjamin, W. (1969). "The Task of the Translator: An Introduction to the Translation of Baudelaire's Tableaux Parisiens," in W. Benjamin (ed.), *Illuminations: Essays and Reflections*, 69–82, USA: Schocken Books.

Bicker, A., R. Ellen, and P. Parkes (2000), *Indigenous Environmental Knowledge and Its Transformations: Critical Anthropological Perspectives*, Amsterdam: Harwood Academic.

Bithell, C. (2014), *A Different Voice, A Different Song: Reclaiming Community through the Natural Voice and World Song*, USA: Oxford University Press.

Booth, G. (2008), *Behind the Curtain: Making Music in Mumbai's Film Studios*, USA: Oxford University Press.

Born, G. and D. Hesmondhalgh (2000), *Western Music and Its Others: Difference, Representation, and Appropriation in Music*, Berkeley: University of California Press.

Boym, S. (2001), *The Future of Nostalgia*, New York: Basic Books.

Bradley, D. (2009), "Global Song, Global Citizens? The World Constructed in World Music Choral Publications," in E. Gould and J. Countryman (eds.), *Exploring Social Justice: How Music Education Might Matter*, 105–20, Canadian Music Educators' Association.

Brekke, T. (2006), "Baptism and the Bible in Bengal," *History of Religions*, XLV (3): 213–33.

Britto, N. (2014), "The Three Divas," in *Semina de Cultura Indo Portuguesa*, 138–51, Goa: Singbals.

Campbell, H. (2005), *Exploring Religious Community Online: We Are One in the Network*, New York: Peter Lang.

Cavell, S. (1976), "Music Discomposed," in S. Cavell (ed.), *Must We Mean What We Say?*, 180–212, Cambridge: Cambridge University Press.

Cavell, S. (2005), "Opera in and as Film 2000," in W. Rothman (ed.), *Cavell on Films*, 305–18, USA: SUNY Press.

Chatterji, R. (2015), "The Mirror as Frame: Time and Narrative in the Folk Art of Bengal," in R. Chatterji (ed.), *Wording the World: Veena Das and Scenes of Inheritance*, 347–71, New Delhi: Orient Blackswan.

Chatterji, R. (2016), "Repetition, Improvisation and Tradition: Deleuzian Themes in the Folk Art of Bengal," *Cultural Analysis*, 15 (1): 99–127.

Chatterjee, S. (2016), "Youngest Festival in Goa: Ketevan World Sacred Music Festival," *Serenade Magazine*, March 29, https://serenademagazine.com/reviews/youngest -festival-goa-ketevan-world-sacred-music-festival/ (accessed May 31, 2021).

Chen, K. (2010), *Asia as Method: Toward Deimperialization*, Durham: Duke University Press.

Collins, J. (2004), "Ghanian Christianity and Popular Entertainment: Full Circle," *History in Africa*, 31: 407–23.

Costa, Rev C. (2009), *Apostolic Christianity in Goa and in the West Coast*, Goa: Xaverian Publication Society.

Couto, M. (2004), *Goa: A Daughter's Story*, New Delhi: Penguin Books.

Csikszentmihalyi, M. (1996), *Creativity: Flow and the Psychology of Discovery and Invention*, New York: Harper Collins.

Dalgado, S. (1893), *Diccionario Komkani–Portuguez*, Mumbai: Indo-Prakash.

Das, V. (1995), "On Soap Opera: What Kind of Anthropological Object Is It?," in D. Miller (ed.), *Worlds Apart: Modernity Through the Prism of the Local*, 169–89, New York and London: Routledge.

Dasgupta, A. (2007), *Music and Modernity: North Indian Classical Music in an Age of Mechanical Reproduction*, Kolkata: Thema.

de Souza, T. (1994), "The Voiceless in Goan History," in T. de Souza (ed.), *Goa to Me*, 69–85, New Delhi: Concept Publishing Company.

Deleuze, G. and Felix, G. (1987), *A Thousand Plateaus: Capitalism and Schizophrenia*, trans. Brian Massumi, London: University of Minnesota Press.

Deleuze, G. (1994), *Difference and Repetition*, New York: Columbia University Press.

Dickson, A. (1997), *A Brief History of Christian Music: From Biblical Times to the Present*, Wales: Lion Books.

Duncan, M. (2019), "Embracing or Challenging the Tribe? Dilemmas in Reproducing Obligatory Pasts," in Bhattacharya and L.K. Pachuau (eds.), *Meghalaya in Landscape, Culture, and Belonging: Writing the History of Northeast India*, 66–86, Cambridge: Cambridge University Press.

Elias, N. (1994), *Mozart: Portrait of a Genius*, USA: Wiley.

Ellwood, R. and A.G. Gregory, eds. (2008), *The Encyclopedia of World Religions*, Chelsea: Infobase Publishing.

Eskew, H. and McElrath, Hugh T. (1980), *Sing With Understanding: An Introduction to Christian Hymnology*, Nashville: Broadman Press.

Everett, H. (2000), "Marketing Classical Music to Popular Audiences in Austen, Texas, A Case Study of KMFA-FM," in T. Mitchell and P. Doyle (eds.), *Changing Sounds: New Directions and Configurations in Popular Music; IASMP 1999 International Conference Proceedings, Faculty of Humanities and Social Sciences, University of Technology*, 267–78, Sydney: Faculty of Humanities and Social Sciences.

Feld, S. (1996), "Waterfalls of Song: An Acoustemology of Place Resounding in Bosavi, Papua New Guinea," in S. Feld and K.H. Basso (eds.), *Senses of Place*, 91–136, New Mexico: School of American Research Press.

Feld, S. (2000), "Anxiety and Celebration: Mapping the Discourses of World Music," in T. Mitchell and P. Doyle (eds.), *Changing Sounds: New Directions and Configurations in Popular Music; IASMP 1999 International Conference Proceedings, Faculty of Humanities and Social Sciences, University of Technology*, 9–14, Sydney: Faculty of Humanities and Social Sciences.

Feld, S. (2000), "The Poetics and Politics of Pygmy Pop," in D. Hesmondhalgh and G. Born (eds.), *Western Music and Its Others: Difference, Representation and Appropriation in Music*, 254–79, Berkeley: University of California Press.

Fernandes, N. (2012), *Taj Mahal Foxtrot: The Story of Bombay's Jazz Age*, New Delhi: Roli Books.

Fernandes, A. (2014), "Cultural Manifestations of the Christian Community," in I. Vás (ed.), *Commemorating Christ in Goa: Some Sketches of the Life and Culture of Christians,*

Yesterday and Today; An Initiative of the Committee for the Exposition of the Sacred Relics of St. Francis Xavier, Archdiocese of Goa and Daman, Goa: Third Millenium.

Fiol, S. (2012), "Articulating Regionalism through Popular Music: The Case of 'Nauchami Narayana' in the Uttarakhand Himalayas," *The Journal of Asian Studies*, 71 (2): 447–73. http://www.jstor.org/stable/23263429.

Foucault, M. (1972), *Archaeology of Knowledge*, New York: Pantheon Books.

Frederique, A. (2011), *Subversive Spiritualities: How Rituals Enact the World*, New York: Oxford University Press.

Geertz, C. (1973). *The Interpretation of Cultures*, New York: Basic Books.

Getter, J. (2014), "Kollywood Goes Global: New Sounds and Contexts for Tamil Film Music in the 21st Century," in G. Booth and B. Shope (eds.), *More than Bollywood: Studies in Indian Popular Music*, 60–74, New York: Oxford University Press.

Gray, L. (2013), *Fado Resounding: Affective Politics and Urban Life*, Durham: Duke University Press.

Greene, P. (2014), "Bollywood in the Era of Film Song Avatars: DJing, Remixing, and Change in the Film Music Industry of North India," in G. Booth and B. Shope (eds.), *More than Bollywood: Studies in Indian Popular Music*, 300–15, New York: Oxford University Press.

Gregory Naik SJ (2019), *Jesuits of the Goa Province: A Historical Overview*, 1542–2000, Goa: Xavier Centre of Historical Research.

Gnecco, C. and P. Ayala (2011), *Indigenous Peoples and Archaeology in Latin America*, Walnut Creek: Left Coast Press.

Griffiths, P. (2006), *A Concise History of Western Music*, Cambridge: Cambridge University Press.

Hackett, R. (2017), "Sounds Indigenous: Negotiating Identity in an Era of World Music," in G. Johnson and S. Kraft (eds.), *Handbook of Indigenous Religion*, 108–19, Leiden: Brill.

Harkness, N. (2013), *Songs of Seoul: An Ethnography of Voice and Voicing in Christian South Korea*, Berkeley: University of California Press.

Harkness, N. (2015), "Voicing Christian Aspiration: The Semiotic Anthropology of Voice in Seoul," *Ethnography*, 16 (3): 313–30.

Hartje-Doll, G. (2013), "'Hillsong' United Through Music: Praise and Worship Music and the Evangelical 'Imagined Community,'" in M. Ingalls, C. Landau, and T. Wagner (eds.), *Congregational Music: Performance, Identity, and Experience*, 139–50, Farnham: Ashgate.

Heath, J. (2013), *Lengkhawm Zai: A Singing Tradition of Mizo Christianity in North East India*, PhD diss., Durham University Press.

Hendricks, K. (2011), "The Philosophy of Shinichi Suzuki: Music Education as Love Education," *Philosophy of Music Education Review*, 19 (2): 136–54.

Henn, A. (2014), *Hindu-Catholic Encounters in Goa: Religion, Colonialism, and Modernity*, Bloomington: Indiana University Press.

Hirschkind, C. (2006), *The Ethical Soundscape: Cassette Sermons and Islamic Counterpublics*, New York: Columbia University Press.

Holt, F. (2007), *Genre in Popular Music*, Chicago: University of Chicago Press.

Hoover, S. (2006), *Religion in the Media Age*, New York: Routledge.

Ingalls, M. (2008), *Awesome in This Place: Sound, Space, and Identity in Contemporary North American Evangelical Worship*, PhD diss., University of Pennsylvania, USA.

Ingalls, M. (2011), "Singing Heaven Down to Earth: Spiritual Journeys, Eschatological Sounds, and Community Formation in Evangelical Worship," *Ethnomusicology*, 55 (2): 255–79.

Ingold, T. (2000), *The Perception of the Environment: Essays on Livelihood, Dwelling and Skill*, New York: Routledge.

Ingold, T. (2011), *Being Alive: Essays on Movement, Knowledge and Description*, New York: Routledge.

Johnson, G. and S. Kraft (2017), "Introduction in Greg Johnson and Siv Ellen Kraft," in *Handbook of Indigenous Religion*, 1–24, UK: Brill.

Jones, W. (2013), "On the Musical Modes of the Hindus," in L. Teignmouth (ed.), *The Works of Sir William Jones: With the Life of the Author by Lord Teignmouth (Cambridge Library Collection—Perspectives from Royal Asiatic Society*, 166–210), Cambridge: Cambridge University Press.

Jousse, M. (1990), *The Oral Style*, New York: Garland Publishing Inc.

Jyrwa, J. (2011), *Christianity in Khasi Culture*, Shillong: Mrs. M.B. Jyrwa.

Kabir, A. (2021), "Rapsodia Ibero-Indiana: Transoceanic creolization and the mando of Goa," *Modern Asian Studies*, 55 (5): 1581–1636. https://doi.org/10.1017/S0026749X200 00311.

Kartomi, M. (1995), "'Traditional Music Weeps' and Other Themes in the Discourse on Music, Dance and Theatre of Indonesia, Malaysia and Thailand," *Journal of Southeast Asian Studies*, 26 (2): 366–400.

Kapuria, R. (2018), "National, modern, Hindu? The post-independence trajectory of Jalandhar's Harballabh music festival," *The Indian Economic & Social History Review*, 55 (3): 389–418.

Kersenboom, S. (2007), "The Faculty of the Voice," in H. Bruckner, E. Schombucher, and P.B. Zarrilli (eds.), *The Power of Performance: Actors, Audiences and Observers of Cultural Performances in India*, 197–208, New Delhi: Manohar Publishers and Distributors.

Klee, P. (1953), *Pedagogical Sketchbook*, USA: Praeger Publishers.

Krishna, TM. (2020), *Sebastian & Sons: A Brief History of Mrdangam Makers*, India: Westland Publications Private Limited.

Ksoo, P. (2008), *Role of Indigenous Tunes in Church Music in Khasi and Jaintia Hills*, PhD diss., Centre for Cultural and Creative Studies School of Social Sciences, North Eastern Hill University.

Kvetko, P. (2004), "Can the Indian Tune Go Global?," *TDR (1988)*, 48 (4): 183–91.

Kvetko, P. (2014), "Mimesis and Authenticity: The Case of 'Thanda Thanda Pani' and Questions of Versioning in North Indian Popular Music," in G. Booth and B. Shope (eds.), *More than Bollywood: Studies in Indian Popular Music*, 160–78, USA: Oxford University Press.

Lester, R. (2005), *Jesus in Our Wombs: Embodying Modernity in a Mexican Convent*, California: University of California Press.

Lewinski, V. (2004), *Indigenous Heritage and Intellectual Property: Genetic Resources, Traditional Knowledge, and Folklore*, The Hague and New York: Kluwer Law International.

Longkumer, A. "As Our Ancestors Once Lived: Representation, Performance, and Constructing a National Culture amongst the Nagas of India," *The Journal of Association for Nepal and Himalayan Studies*, 35 (1): 51–64.

Lopes, M. (2000), "The Sisters of Santa Monica in the 18th Century: Details of Their Daily Life," in C. Borges, O. Pereira, and H. Stubbe (eds.), *Goa and Portugal: History and Development*, 238–48, New Delhi: Concept Publishing Company.

Magowan, F. (2007), *Melodies of Mourning: Music and Emotion in Northern Australia*, Australia: University of Western Australia Press.

Mahmood, S. (2005), *Politics of Piety: The Islamic Revival and the Feminist Subject*, Princeton: Princeton University Press.

Malinowski, B. (1967), *A Diary in the Strictest Sense of the Term*, Stanford: Stanford University Press.

Manuel, P. (1993), *Cassette Culture: Popular Music and Technology in North India*, Chicago: University of Chicago Press.

Margaret, B. (2014), "Indigenous Knowledge and Traditional Knowledge," in C. Smith (ed.), *Encyclopaedia of Global Archaeology*, 3814–24, New York: Springer.

Marsden, H. (2018), *Western Classical Music in Mumbai: Global Music, Local Meanings*, PhD diss., Royal Holloway University of London.

Martins, M. (1997), "Musica Sacra and Its Impact on Goa," in M.C.E. Sa (eds.), *Wind of Fire: The Music and Musicians of Goa*, New Delhi: Promilla and Co. Publishers.

Mascarhenas, M. (1989), "The Church in the Eighteenth Century," in T. Souza (ed.), *Essays in Goan History*, 81–102, New Delhi: Concept Publishing Company.

Mc Duie-Ra, D. (2007), "The Constraints on Civil Society Beyond the State: Gender Based Insecurity in Meghalaya, India," *Voluntas: International Journal of Voluntary and Non-Profit Organizations*, 18 (4): 359–84.

Mcguire, C. (2016), "Christianity, Civilization and Music: Nineteenth Century British Missionaries and the Control of the Malagasy Hymnology," in M. Clarke (ed.), *Music and Theology in Nineteenth Century Britain*, 79–96, UK: Routledge.

Meintjes, L. (2003), *Sound of Africa!: Making Music Zulu in South African Studio*, Durham: Duke University Press.

Melvin, S. (2004), *Rhapsody in Red: How Western Classical Music Became Chinese*, New York: Algora Publishing.

Meyer, B. (2009), *Aesthetic Formations: Media, Religion, and the Senses*, 1st ed., New York: Palgrave Macmillan.

Meyer, B. (2009), "Introduction: From Imagined Communities to Aesthetic Formations: Religious Mediations, Sensational Forms and Styles of Binding," in B. Meyer (ed.), *Aesthetic Formations: Media, Religion and the Senses*, 1–30, USA: Palgrave Macmillan.

Michelle, B. (2012), *Intimate Distance: Andean Music in Japan*, Durham: Duke University Press.

Middleton, R. (1990), *Studying Popular Music*, Milton Keynes: Open University Press.

Miranda, V. (1978), "Caste, Religion and Dialect Differentiation in the Konkani Area," *Int'l J. Soc. Lang.*, 16: 77–91.

Miranda, E. (2014), "Goan Music in the Christian Faith and Tradition," in I. Vás (ed.), *Commemorating Christ in Goa: Some Sketches of the Life and Culture of Christians, Yesterday and Today*, 45–57, Goa: Third Millenium.

Morais, M. (2007), *The Polyphonic Holy Week Motets from Goa (19th and 20th Centuries)/ Motetes Polifonicos de Goa Para a Semana Santa (secs. XIX–XX)*, Portugal: Publisher Unknown.

Morcom, A. (2013), *TIllicit Worlds of Indian Dance: Cultures of Exclusion*, Oxford: Oxford University Press.

Myer, B. and M. de Witte (2013), "Heritage and the Sacred: Introduction," *Material Religion*, 9 (3): 274–81.

Negus, K. (1999), *Music Genres and Corporate Cultures*, London and New York: Routledge.

Nekola, A. (2015), "Introduction: Worship Media as Media Form and Mediated Practice: Theorizing the Intersections of Media, Music and Lived Religion," in A. Nekola and T. Wagner (eds.), *Congregational Music-Making and Community in a Mediated Age*, 1–24, London: Routledge.

Neuenfeldt, K. (2005), "Nigel Pegrum, 'Didjeridu-Friendly Sections,' and What Constitutes an 'Indigenous' CD: An Australian Case Study of Producing 'World Music' Recordings," in P.D. Greene and T. Porcello (eds.), *Wired for Sound: Engineering and Technology in Sonic Cultures*, 84–102, Hanover: Wesleyan University Press and the University Press of New England.

Niranjana, T. (2006), *Mobilizing India: Women, Music, and Migration Between India and Trinidad*, Durham: Duke University Press.

Niranjana, T. (2020), *Musicophilia in Mumbai: Performing Subjects and the Metropolitan Unconscious*, New York: Duke University Press, https://doi.org/10.1515/9781478009191.

Nongbri, B. (2016), "Change and Continuity: An Analysis of the Interaction of Khasi Traditional Religion with Christianity," in P. Malekadathil, J. Pachuau, and T. Sarkar (eds.), *Christianity in Indian History: Issues of Culture, Power and Knowledge*, 58–75, New Delhi: Primus Books.

Nongbri, B. L. (2008), "Welsh Presbyterian Mission and Protest Christianity in North East India with Special Reference to Khasi-Jaintia Hills, Meghalaya (1841–1900)," *Indian Church History Review*, 51 (1): 66–86.

Olwage, G. (2004), "The Class and Colour of Tone: An Essay on the Social History of Vocal Timbre," *Ethnomusicology Forum*, 13 (2): 203–26. http://www.jstor.org/stable/20184481.

Osswald, C. (2013), *Written in Stone: Jesuit Buildings in Goa and Their Artistic and Architectural Features*, Goa: Goa 1556.

Pachuau, J. (2016), "Christianity in Mizoram: An Ethnography," in P. Malekadathil, J. Pachuau, and T. Sarkar (eds.), *Christianity in Indian History: Issues of Culture, Power and Knowledge*, 46–57, New Delhi: PrimusBooks.

Pachuau, J. and V. Willem (2015), *The Camera as Witness: A Social History of Mizoram, Northeast India*, Cambridge: Cambridge University Press.

Palackal, J. (2004), "Ochtoechos of the Syrian Orthodox Churches in South India," *Ethnomusicology*, 48 (2): 229–50.

Pereira, J., M. Micael, and D. Antonio (2010), *Song of Goa: Crown of Mando*, Goa: Broadway Publishing House.

Pinto, R. (2007), *Between Empires: Print and Politics in Goa*, Goa: Oxford University Press.

Pinto, C. (2014). "475 Years of Education: The Role of Archdiocese," in I. Vás (ed.), *Commemorating Christ in Goa: Some Sketches of the Life and Culture of Christians, Yesterday and Today*, Goa: Third Millenium.

Poizat, M. (1992), *The Angel's Cry: Beyond the Pleasure Principle in Opera*, trans. A. Denner, New York: Cornell University Press.

Porter, M. (2014), *Ecclesial Practices*, 1 (2), 149–66, Brill.

Rajadhyaksha, A. (2003), "The Bollywoodization of the Indian Cinema: Cultural Nationalism in a Global Arena," *Inter-Asia Cultural Studies*, 4 (1): 25–39.

Ramnarine, K. (2001), *Creating Their Own Space: The Development of an Indian-Caribbean Musical Tradition*, West Indies: University of West Indies Press.

Ranciere, J. (2007), "The Surface of Design," in J. Ranciere (ed.), *The Future of Image*, 91–108. UK: Verso.

Rebecca, L. (2005), "Jesus in Our Wombs: Embodying Modernity in a Mexican Convent Ethnographic Studies," in *Subjectivity*, Berkeley: University of California Press.

Rees, B. (2002), "Evans, Robert (1849–1916)," in B. Rees (ed.), *Vehicles of Grace and Home: Welsh Missionaries in India 1800–1970*, 44–5, USA: William Carey Library.

Reigersberg, S. (2013), "Christian Choral Singing in Aboriginal Australia: Gendered Absence, Emotion and Place," in F. Magowan and L. Wrazen (eds.), *Performing Gender, Place and Emotion in Music*, 85–108, UK: Boydell and Brewer.

Remme, J. (2017), "Ethnographies Returned: The Mobilisation of Ethnographies and the Politicisation of Indigeneity in Ifugao, the Philippines," in G. Johnson and S. Kraft (eds.), *Handbook of Indigenous Religion*, 294–308, Leiden: Brill.

Rgnca, R. (2004), *Significance of Khasi Hymn Book for Christian Education*, PhD diss., Serampore College.

Riches, T. and Tom, W. (2012), "The Evolution of Hillsong Music: From Australian Pentecostal Congregation into Global Brand," *Australian Journal of Communication*, 39 (1): 17–36.

Rivara, J. (1858), "A Historical Essay on the Konkani Language," trans. T. Lobo, in A.K. Priolar (ed.), *The Printing Press in India*, 141–236, Mumbai: Marathi Samshodhana Mandal.

Robinson, R. (2009), "Negotiating Traditions: Popular Christianity in India," *Asian Journal of Social Science*, XXXVII (1): 29–54.

Rodrigues, M. (1997), "Music Education in Goa," in M. Sa (ed.), *Wind of Fire: The Music and Musicians of Goa*, 317–26, New Delhi: Promilla and Co. Publishers.

Roma, C. (2009), *Writing Identities: Folklore and Performative Arts of Purulia*, Bengal, New Delhi: Indira Gandhi National Centre for the Arts and Aryan Books International.

Roy, G. (2010), *Bhangra Moves: From Ludhiana to London and Beyond*, Farnham: Ashgate Publishing.

Sahay, N. (1968), "Impact of Christianity on the Uraon of the Chainpur Belt in Chotanagpur: An Analysis of Its Cultural Processes," *American Anthropologist*, New Series LXX (5): 923–42.

Sarbadhikary, S. (2015), *The Place of Devotion: Siting and Experiencing Divinity in Bengal Vaisnavism*, California: University of California Press.

Sardessai, M. (2000), *A History of Konkani Literature*, New Delhi: Sahitya Akademi.

Sardo, S. (2010), "Proud to be a Goan: Colonial Memories, Post-Colonial Identities and Music," *MIGRAÇÕES: Journal of the Portuguese Immigration Observatory*, no. 7: 57–71. ISSN: 1646-8104

Sardo, S. (2011), *Guerras de Jasmim e Mogarim - Música Identidade e Emoções em Goa*, Alfragide: Texto - Leya.

Sardo, S. (2022), "Lusossonia: Postcolonial Cartographies of Sounds and Memories," in Robert Samuel Newman and Delfim Correia Da Silva (eds.), *Traces on the Sea: Portuguese Interaction with Asia*, 157–87, Coimbra: Coimbra University Press.

Sardo, S. and Simões, R. (1989), "O Ensino da Música no Processo de Cristianização em Goa," in *Revista da Casa de Goa*, 3–11, Lisbon: Casa de Goa.

Sarrazin, N. (2014), "Global Masala: Digital Identities and Aesthetic Trajectories in Post-Liberalized Indian Film Music," in G. Booth and B. Shope (eds.), *More than Bollywood: Studies in Indian Popular Music*, 38–59, USA: Oxford University Press.

Seth, V. (1999), *An Equal Music*, New Delhi: Penguin Books.

Sherinian, Z. (2005), "The Indigenization of Tamil Christian Music: Musical Style and Liberation Theology, The World of Music," *Musical Reverberation from the Encounter of Local and Global Belief Systems* (VWB - Verlag für Wissenschaftund Bildung), XLVII (1): 125–65.

Sherinian, Z. (2005), "The Indigenization of Tamil Christian Music: Musical Style and Liberation Theology," *The World of Music*, 47 (1): 125–65.

Shope, B. (2014), "Latin American Music in Moving Pictures and Jazzy Cabarets in Mumbai, 1930's to 1950's," in G. Booth and B. Shope (eds.), *More than Bollywood: Studies in Indian Popular Music*, 201–15, USA: Oxford University Press.

Smith, L. (2012). *Decolonizing Methodologies: Research and Indigenous People*, London: Zed Books.

Soneji, D. (2012). *Unfinished Gestures: Devadāsīs Memory and Modernity in South India*, Chicago: University of Chicago Press, http://chicago.universitypressscholarship. com/view/10.7208/chicago/9780226768113.001.0001/upso-9780226768090.

Srivastava, S. (2004), "Voice, Gender and Space in Time of Five-Year Plans," *Economic and Political Review*, 39 (20): 2019–28.

Stephanie, N. "PARACOLONIAL Networks: Some Speculations on Local Readerships in Colonial West Africa," *Interventions: International Journal of Postcolonial Studies*, 3 (3): 336–54.

Stephen, A. (1997), "Traditional Aboriginal Knowledge and Science Versus Occidental Science," Paper prepared for the Biodiversity Convention Office of Environment Canada, http://www.nativemaps.org/?q¼node/1399 (accessed April 4, 2021).

Steven, F. (1996), "Pygmy POP. A Genealogy of Schizophonic Mimesis," *Yearbook for Traditional Music*, 28: 1–35.

Strauss-Levi, C. (1978), "Myth and Music," in Claude Levi-Strauss (ed.), *Myth and Meaning*, 20–4, UK: Routledge.

Subramanian, L. (2008), *New Mansions in Music: Performance, Pedagogy and Criticism*, UK: Routledge.

Subramanian, L. (2009), *Veena Dhanammal: The Making of a Legend*, New Delhi: Routledge.

Subramanian, L. (2011), *From the Tanjore Court to the Madras Music Academy: A Social History of Music in South India*, New Delhi: Oxford University Press.

Swer, M. (2017), "Khasi Foxtrot Tango," *RAIOT: Challenging the Consensus*, February 25, 2017, www.raiot.in/khasi-foxtrot-tango/ (accessed February 25, 2017).

Swijghuisen Reigersberg, Muriel E. (2008), *Choral Singing and the Construction of Australian Aboriginal Identities: An Applied Ethnomusicological Study in Hopevale, Northern Queensland, Australia*, PhD.

Syiem, L. (2005), *The Evolution of Khasi Music: A Study of the Classical Content*, New Delhi: Regency Publications.

Tagat, A. (2020), "Hear Shillong Chamber Choir's Multilingual Holiday Album 'Come Home Christmas,'" *RollingStoneIndia*, December 18, https://rollingstoneindia.com/ shillong-chamber-choir-holiday-album-come-home- christmas/.

Tagore, S. (1963), *Universal History of Music: Compiled from Divers Sources, Together with Various Original Notes on Hindu Music*, Varanasi: Chowkhamba Sanskrit Series Office.

Teachout, T. (2014), "The Broadway Musical Crisis," *Commentary*, July/August, www .commentarymagazine.com/articles/the-broadway-musicalcrisis/ (accessed July 4, 2018).

Tsing, A. (2005), *Friction: An Ethnography of Global Connection*, Princeton: Princeton University Press.

Turino, T. (2008), *Music as Social Life: Politics of Participation*, Chicago: University of Chicago Press.

Turnbull, Colin M. (1961), *The Forest People*, 1st Touchstone ed., New York: Simon & Schuster.

Turnbull, Colin M. and American Museum of Natural History. (1965), *Wayward Servants; the Two Worlds of the African Pygmies*, Garden City: Published for the American Museum of Natural History [by] the Natural History Press.

Ulloa, J. (2016), "Indigenous Music and Identity: Musical Spaces of Urban Mapuche Communities," in J. León and H. Simonett (eds.), *A Latin American Music Reader: Views from the South*, 356–78, Urbana, Chicago, and Springfield: Illinois University Press.

Unger, M. (2010), *Historical Dictionary of Choral Music*, UK: The Scarecrow Press Inc.

Wagner, T. (2014), *Hearing the Hillsong Sound: Music, Marketing, and Branded Spiritual Experience at a Transnational Megachurch*, PhD. diss., Royal Holloway University of London, UK.

Walsh, C. and W. Mignolo (2018), *On Decoloniality*, Durham: Duke University Press.

Walter, M. and W. Catherine (2018), *On Decoloniality: Concepts, Analytics*, Praxis, Durham and London: Duke University Press.

Warfield, S. (2002), "From Hair to Rent: Is Rock a Four-Letter Word on Broadway?," in W. Everett and P. Laird (eds.), *The Cambridge Companion to the Musical*, 235–49, Cambridge: Cambridge University Press.

Weber, M. (1958), *The Rational and Social Foundations of Music*, USA: Southern Illinois University Press.

Wechsberg, J. (1997), *The Opera*, Great Britain: The Trinity Press.

Weidman, A. (2006), *Singing the Classical, Voicing the Modern*, Durham: Duke University Press.

Woodfield, I. (2000), *Music of the Raj: A Social and Economic History of Music in Late Eighteenth Century Anglo Indian Society*, USA: Oxford University Press.

Yano, C. (2013), "Singing the Contentions of Place: Korean Singers of the Heart and Soul of Japan," in F. Magowan and L Wrazen (eds.), *Performing Gender, Place and Emotion in Music*, 147–61, UK: Boydell and Brewer.

Yoshimi, T. (2005), *What Is Modernity? Writings of Takeuchi Yoshimi*, trans. R. Calichman, New York: Columbia University Press.

Website

https://serenademagazine.com/news/monte-music-festival-2018/ (accessed March 4, 2018).

Glossary

A capella   sometimes more than one singer tackles a voice part; without accompaniment.

Alto   the line that supports the melody line in a choral arrangement; more versatile and lowest female voice, their vocal range is between E3 and F5.

Aria   Most commonly, a lyrical vocal solo having an instrumental accompaniment in an operatic style (opera, oratorio, cantata).

Bass   the foundational line that holds a composition together, lowest notes are located here; the voice range is between D2 to E4.

Choral   sung by an organized band of singers, the chorus or choir. It is the plainsong of the Roman Catholic Church and the hymn tunes of the German Protestant Church.

Dekhni   folk songs that draw inspiration from the Pre-Portuguese folk songs with themes on coastal life: river crossings, flirtatious boatmen, and long wait for the ferry; dancing girls with nose-rings and anklets are part of the imagery too. It involves sexual implication and political commentaries sometimes.

Dulpod   usually sung after the Mando; has a faster beat and entertains improvisation and variation; draws inspiration from life and society.

Duitara   a plucked stringed instrument which has four strings.

Gumott   an earthenware drum shaped like a pot.

Ka Ksing Kynthei   female drum among the Khasis (*U Ksing Shynrang*: male drum).

Mando   sung in two voices (primeiro e Segundo), first and second. The compositions are passionate and draw on love and social commentary.

Mass   a vocal and instrumental adjunct of the Eucharistic service in Christianity, having five essential choral pieces: the Kyrie, the Gloria, the Credo, the Sanctus, and the Agnus Dei.

Mezzo Soprano   second highest female voice type; range is G3 to A5.

Mestre Capela   choir master.

Motet   polyphonic choral setting, usually unaccompanied, of a sacred Latin text, not fixed in liturgy.

Opera   stage drama with orchestral accompaniment, in which music is the dominant element, with the performers singing their lines.

Oratorio   dramatic musical composition, especially on a religious theme, with arias, recitative, and choruses, and with orchestral settings.

Polyphony   multiple singers singing one part.

Recitative   the rhythm is metrically regular and text is set in a manner where the character pauses to reflect on the given situation.

Soprano   the melody line, top most line where the highest notes are located; voice range from B3 to G6, a typical Soprano can vocalize B3 to C6.

Tenor   highest male voice; the vocal range is between C3 and B4.

Tiatr   has a song component within it; it is a popular stylized form of folk theatre highly influenced by Italian opera and the French revue. The song component is called Cantaram—songs as solos or duets and chorus.

Unison   all the voices in the chorus sing together, the same part or melody; or where the voices have different parts: melodies or threads of melodies with each part allotted to more than one voice.

Villancico   a Spanish song that alternates between a refrain and a stanza; sung a capella.

Documentary—Da Capo

To view the author's documentary *Da Capo*, go to [https://www.bloomsbury.com/uk/choral-voices-9781501379833/].

Index